BIG MOUTH
THE AMAZON SPEAKS

BIG MOUTH
THE AMAZON SPEAKS

Stephen Nugent

drawings by
Humphrey Ocean

FOURTH ESTATE · LONDON

Acknowledgements

Stephen Nugent would like to thank the University of London, Central Research Fund and The Leverhulme Trust, Research Awards Advisory Committee for financial support. Thanks are also due to Dutra and Zuila in Santarém, and to Charlie and Peggy for their help over the years.

First published in Great Britain in 1990 by
Fourth Estate Limited
Classic House
113 Westbourne Grove
London W2 4UP

British Library Cataloguing in Publication Data
Nugent, Stephen
Big mouth : the Amazon speaks.
1. South America. Amazon River Basin. Description & travel
I. Title II. Ocean, Humphrey
918.1'1046
ISBN 1-872180-65-5

Typeset by York House Typographic Ltd, London
Printed by Bookcraft Ltd, Midsomer Norton

To June, Zoë and Zachary

S.N.

To Miranda, Ruby and Beatrice

H.O.

MARAJO
SOURE
BELEM
AMAZON
SANTAREM
MANAUS
TAPAJOS
XINGU
RECIFE
NICARAGUA
PANAMA
N
W
E
S
VENEZUELA
GUYANA
COLOMBIA
BELEM
MANAUS
RECIFE
PERU
BRAZIL
BRASILIA
BOLIVIA
PARAGUAY
Rio de Janeiro
Sao Paulo
SOUTH PACIFIC OCEAN
URUGUAY
SOUTH ATLANTIC OCEAN
CHILE
ARGENTINA

CONTENTS

MATADOURO MUNICIPAL URUARA
SOUZA VIEIRA

PREFACE

When asked, I have admitted that *Big Mouth* is basically a travel book. I have done so reluctantly, but I have had to bend to the received wisdom (or, rather, flag in the face of prospective debate) that if it looks like a duck, walks like a duck, and so on . . .

It is not in fact a travel book at all. It is mainly concerned with Amazonia, and not being Amazonian Ocean and I had to travel to get there, but that's about as far as the travel/tourism line goes. The travel-writing label, however, has its uses: it is promiscuously applied to all sorts of writing and simply by talking about some remote place one gains – via the mysterious mechanisms of benign opportunism – a kind of unity. That's the plan, anyway.

Actually, I hope that *Big Mouth* is something of a travel dissuader, not in the sense that what I have to say about Amazonia is so repellent that tickets should be cancelled immediately, but rather because I try to draw attention to the fact that Amazonia isn't really that exotic. This is not to deny that it has genuinely exotic aspects, but they are hard work and few travellers are likely to be able to get very close to them. If you want adventure, take up dog-fighting or cigarette smoking or some other activity which gets the adrenalin going and offers life-threatening options.

Generally speaking, the modern Amazonia which is the subject of *Big Mouth* is a predictable example of what is politely (and inaptly) called 'development', a process in which Marx observed that: 'it is notorious that conquest, enslavement, robbery, murder, briefly force, play the great part'. Amazonian development differs only because it is filtered for our consumption through a series of image grids which successfully distract the eye: Amazonia comes across as a nature preserve, a tropical forest, home of the noble savage, the toucan, the howler monkey, the electric eel, the headhunter – a long list of compelling exotica. And most people would rather watch monkeys at play than pop-eyed infant beggars at work.

Modern Amazonia is riven by contradictions of a scale appropriate to its social and biological complexity: while it is primarily viewed as a vast natural haven, most Amazonians live in cities; it covers more than half the territory of Brazil, yet it functions far outside the national mainstream; it is the reference point for much nationalistic posturing, yet many of its resources are already under the control of foreign capital; it is the home of the vintage 'noble savage', yet Amazonians probably know as much about Indians through Hollywood films as they do through their own experience. This book is about some of these contradictions, especially those engendered by two different portrayals of Amazonia: the arcadian Amazonia of popular representation; and the modernizing Amazonia of 'vast resource potential'. These portrayals – big pictures which mix unbalanced portions of fact, wish-fulfilment, greed, ignorance, and a host of lesser qualities – tend to obscure another Amazonia, that occupied by the effectively invisible Amazonians who, in spite of a 400-year history of colonization, are continually cast as frontier characters still trying to climb aboard the New World good life gravy train.

Amazonia is changing rapidly and, as is the case in other areas of heightened social conflict, the character of change is matter of disagreement. What is curious about change in Amazonia is that social forces always seem to be playing second fiddle to 'natural' ones. The angle on deforestation, widely covered in the non-specialist press, is always about trees, not land-tenure. Road-building is about erosion or food chains, not about agrarian reform. 'Threatened species', a call-to-arms for many campaigning bodies, does not necessarily extend into the upper reaches of the animal kingdom.

Thirty-five years ago, in a book – obligatorily alliterative, *The Amazing Amazon* (1954) – whose dominant stylistic feature was heavy gush, Willard Price claimed that:

> Only ten years ago it would have seemed absurd to talk of a culture in this wilderness of alligators, jaguars, giant ana-

> condas and only one half-man to the square mile – and that half-man sick with malaria and sodden with despair.

This book is mainly about and for that 'half-man' and his sister.

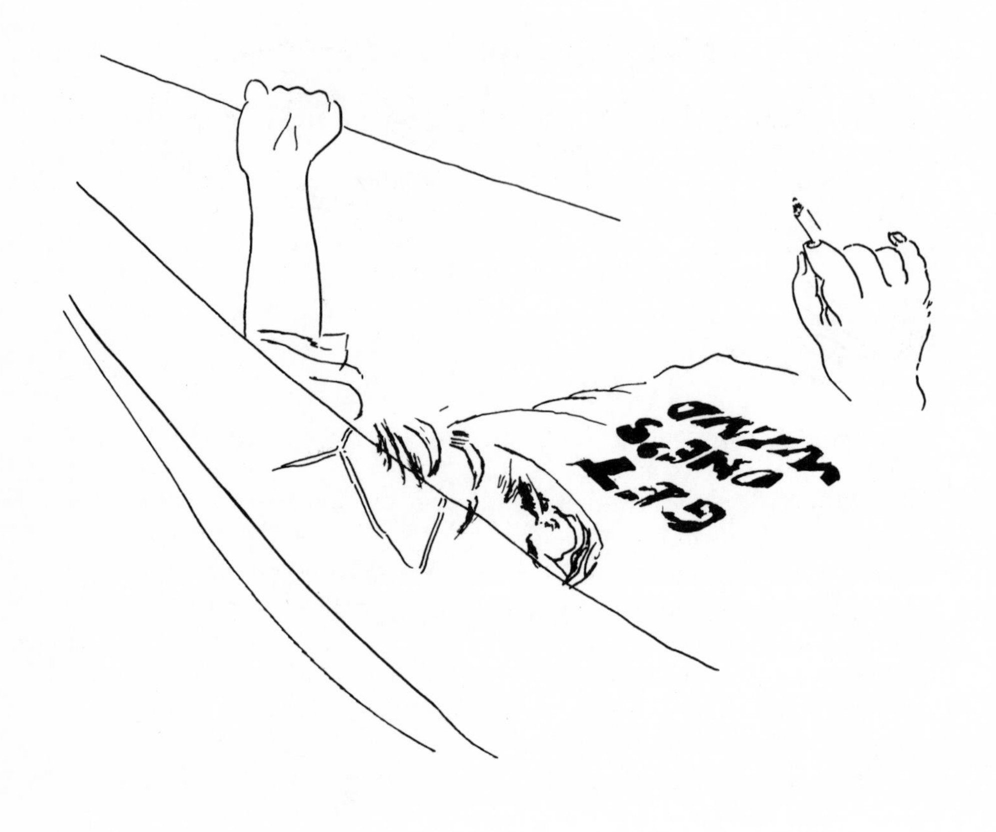
GET
ONE'S
MIND

INTRODUCTION

PANK PIECES IN YOUR TASTING

I first went to Amazonia in 1975. What then, and for a while afterwards, seemed like a continuous A to B trip has become compressed into a little chapbook of cut-down memories. The train from Nogales to Mexico City took forty-eight hours during which time I consumed a disproportionate amount of the reading material prudently set aside for dry months to come. Arriving in Mexico City, June and I discovered that the visas we'd received at the border didn't give us enough time to get out of the other end of Mexico, so we spent several days arranging for new stamps to get us back to square one. Welcome, gringo. During this time we visited the mother of a family friend. Upon hearing that we were going to Brazil, she loaded us down with onyx gifts for long-unseen Romanian relations in São Paulo. She was under the spell of a common, false syllogism: Amazonia is in Brazil; São Paulo is in Brazil; if we were going to Amazonia we would be going to São Paulo.

We broke the bus journey from Mexico City in Oaxaca, then carried on through Central America, pausing only when the bus encountered mechanical turbulence (frequently). In Guatemala I watched as a soldier walked into a tree branch which sent his helmet spinning to rest on the muzzle of his machine gun. In Tegucigalpa we spent a night in a room whose designer-brutality ambience reflected the deranged outcome of the Good Neighbour Policy. From Panama City we took a jet to Bogotá and spent the journey embraced by clouds inside the cabin because the refrigeration system had broken down. When we finally got to Amazonia and settled in Santarém, a major town on the Amazon River, I acquired a piglet which barely reached shoathood before being savaged by a mad dog. I remember a couple of other things, but they evaded capture as memories of travel because it was so easy to slot into the sedentary life of the river. While we were in Santarém (about a year and a half) we had a number of visitors and I think they were all impressed at how easy it was to fit in. The reason for this is that modern Amazonia is in many respects a foreign construction, and an appealingly flawed, uneven one with lots of spaces available to accommodate latecomers.

The vast majority of pre-colonial Amazonian societies have been expunged and the replacements are put together with string, baling wire, and a set of Rousseau-esque images of the Walt Disney/*National Geographic*/Werner Herzog/John Boorman kind. On top of that, in the past twenty years especially, the vast array of fragmented, *ad hoc* Amazonian initiatives – Indians in counterfeit Ray-Ban Wayfarers being persecuted by missionaries and goldminers alike, toothless taxi-drivers with French 'racing gloves', the apparatus of failed enterprise that looked visionary at the time but is now obviously and painfully crackpot – has been increasingly dominated by the spectre of so-called economic development. This takes the form of a large-scale extractive industry, and the somewhat decrepit but still compelling heterogeneity of post-colonial Amazonian societies is thereby threatened with summary dismissal, to be replaced by the social equivalent of a toxic open-cast mine.

This transformation has hardly gone unnoted, but the commentary, however well intentioned, just isn't up to the task. For one thing, the term 'Amazonia' simply covers too much territory, literal and metaphorical. Within this Amazonia (the physical size of which makes Britain, for example, look like a railway allotment) there is too much happening to permit adequate, unqualified generalizations. It is also the case that those students of Amazonia in the best position to comment on local developments are constrained from doing so by the apparatus of the state's planning agencies. Amazonia is big business and it's easy to stamp on the protesters.

Given these constraints, *Big Mouth* aims to deal with some topical Amazonian issues by way of a notebook and sketchpad. The book began with the working title *Big Mouth*, which remained secure until Ocean found an artefact whose name-tag could reasonably usurp *Big Mouth*'s point position. *Big Mouth* refers to the Amazon River's exit to the Atlantic, less a discrete orifice than the spectacularly dilated site of an emetic reflex which every second pushes 7 million cubic feet of water around the Switzerland-sized island of Marajo and into the ocean. *Big Mouth* sounded right, conjured up the requisite oral imagery – piranhas, vampires – and since the book is mainly about those who live within spitting distance of the *boca grande,* it looked like a pretty strong candidate.

The alternative title was hanging in an airport tourist shop in Belém, the major Amazonian city, and was one of a series of unlikely T-shirt messages attesting to the arbitrary quality of postmod existence, even in a fringe location where Baudrillard might as well be a new French perfume smuggled in from the free-trade zone of Manaus. At the time of discovery, we had compiled a showcase list of messages emblazoned on this ersatz metropolitan torso wear, minor by-products of the generic West's intervention into other national popular cultures, and worn by Brazilians of, as they say, all walks of life. The list included such wondrous verbal inventions as: 'Get One's Wind', 'Modern Concourse Nudity USA', 'Competition of Life Mascot Competition Mascot Competition', 'Ghetto Dog Quicksilver', 'On the Atomic Laboratories We Make the Nergie', 'Snon Capped Mountain Ski Jump'. It was like being at a memorial service for Philip K. Dick.

As the list grew, however, it became more trivial, an exercise in bad taste which implicitly ridiculed fashion victims in a remote site of uneven ideological development. After the brief, early period during which we felt we'd cracked the culture code, each new T-shirt message confirming our missing-link theory, such gross material evidence lost its appeal and we devoted ourselves to higher matters. Such is the substance of this book.

Ocean's eventual discovery, however, a mere four years short of the quincentenary celebration of Columbus' muleskinning the *Niña, Pinta* and *Santa Maria* into action, was a breakthrough, the final piece in the puzzle, the (semi-)millenarian logo which could not be denied: 'Pank Pieces in Your Tasting'.

It's been a source of worry because it sounds kind of plausible, in the style of 'colourless green ideas sleep furiously'. I don't know what it means, yet suspect that there is something lurking in there waiting to strike back. John Lahr, in an interview at the time of publication of *Prick Up Your Ears,* admitted that it hadn't occurred to him that ears was an anagram of arse. I think I may be missing a similar kind of connection. While waiting for the revelatory insight, however, all I can imagine is that as the Heart of Darkness conjures up the threatening

Other of imperial conquest, the Heart of Pankness sums up the current dilemmas of post-colonial mayhem.

Pank Pieces might have served well as the title of a book with various aims. Planning to take a brief trip to Amazonia, I asked Ocean if he would like to do a Parkinson to my Cook. At about the same time I had been doing fieldwork in Amazonia in the 1970s, Ocean had been playing the role of Parkinson – expedition artist – in a BBC, Captain Cook biopic, so he was the obvious candidate. But on this trip, no fieldwork, commissions or bug collections. We were to travel as tourists with ambitions no greater than acting as more or less sentient sponges, talking to people and drawing them. A purposeful pre-midlife crisis hiatus. The who-what-why-where-when brief, then, is short and sweet: anthropologist and artist at loose ends in metropolitan Amazonia.

I

AMAZONIA AND THE REAL BRAZIL

Although I have spent some years in Brazil I have never been to *official* Brazil: Rio, São Paulo, Brasilia, Salvador. The closest I've been to that Brazil is the airport in Recife. To me, Brazil is embedded in Amazonia; for most Brazilians and visitors to Brazil, I suspect, the opposite holds true. Many regard Amazonia as a distant frontier whose connections with 'real' Brazil are merely a matter of historical convention and the occasional dramatic news story. In my experience, to speak of Brazil and Amazonia as nested within one another is to promote a conceit which disguises official Brazil's relations with its margins, a conceit which has made possible the maintenance of a high level of popular ignorance about Amazonian affairs and a justification for the region's political subordination to central government. In national terms, Amazonia has become – at best – a green issue over which prospective presidential candidates can fight. The claims of President Sarney ('I am a pioneer of the ecological cause in Brazil. In 1972 I made a speech on the environment in the Senate.') and Janio Quadros as they climb aboard the green train on the backs of Amazonians are about as convincing as the Iron Lady's bin-job testifying or George Bush's eco-gland transplant.

Brazil is commonly regarded as the most First World of Third World countries (neo-Latin division), and the obvious referent is the USA. While the analogy holds in many respects – two major New World settler colonies – it collapses on (among other things) the issue of the relationship between regions and the nation. The unity attributed to the Los Angeles/New York worldview is unmatched in Brazil. When people speak of non-mainstream locales in the US – whether they be regions with their own distinctive character (Texas) or mere cipher spots (Say hi! to Show Low, Arizona) – such places are still sandwiched between the coastal escape hatches, the Big Apple and the Athens of the West. When one talks of the Brazilian interior regions, however, one is talking of points on various continua stretching from diverse centres – Brasilia, the political centre, Rio, the cultural centre, São Paulo, the industrial centre, Salvador, the Afro-American cynosure – to increasingly abstract peripheries. The irrelevance of precise definitions of these peripheries is indicated by the fact that published accounts of distances between Rio and Belém may differ by a factor of two (the sources here are guides for foreign travellers published by Varig, the national airline, and the Banco do Brasil). When, after my first trip to Brazil, I went to the Brazilian Cultural Centre in New York in search of newspapers from Belém, the staff there laughed: 'You mean they have newspapers in the Amazon?' It was as though I'd pulled into a gas station expecting to get feed for my mule. In one sense they were merely pulling my leg, which I'd foolishly laid on the counter, but they were also trying to cover up their ignorance.

The point is that the Brazilian-ness of Amazonia may be a geopolitical fact, but in practice Amazonia is another country. Until fairly recently, news of major Brazilian events (independence from Portugal, statehood) has been registered in Amazonia so long after the fact that they could qualify as dispatches from another continent. Even at the time when Amazonia's contribution to the national economy was significant – during the rubber boom of the late nineteenth century – it was quicker to get from Amazonia to Liverpool than it was to get to Rio.

The ambivalence of Amazonia's relationship with the rest of Brazil is complicated by a number of factors, not least of which is the fact that Brazilians are becoming Amazonian at an increasing rate, responding to government flag- and cheque-waving inducements and pulling up stakes elsewhere in Brazil to head for the last frontier. One consequence of this is that Amazonians of long standing find themselves with two identities: Amazonian and proud of it; and Brazilian national and embarrassed by their low social standing in the larger developmental scheme of things. In Santarém, where I was living in the mid-

1970s, this ambiguity was expressed as: Santarém is the Pearl of the Tapajós; Santarém is the asshole of a turkey.

In this light, Amazonia *is* a kind of frontier, but not in the sense that it is a social void still being brought under the control of technocratic and entrepreneurial conquistadors. It's a frontier in the sense that it's an experimental arena in which highly unregulated social forces encounter a number of, for want of a better term, traditional societies, themselves the products of highly unregulated social forces. For instance, the colonization of Amazonia which has accompanied the building of the Transamazon Highway (Transamazonica) has pretty much disregarded existing societies and settlements in Amazonia, invading Indian lands, expelling peasant smallholders, felling vast tracts of forest to create cattle pasture – in a word, exploring (in Portuguese *explorar*, usefully, means both exploit and explore). Some of the effects are generalized – such as forest-clearing – but others are specific to limited areas – gold mining for instance – and although the torture and killing of truculent peasants and Indians has risen dramatically (14 in 1964; 458 between January 1985 and June 1987, according to Amnesty International; 80 in 1988 alone[1]), there are some areas of Amazonia which are serene. The net effect, however, and in spite of intra-regional differences, is the creation of a Hobbesian playground in which, to no great surprise, the big, bad and ugly control the ball, and it requires an act of faith to distinguish the forces of law and order from the criminal fraternity.

The effects of Amazonia's distance from centres of Brazilian power have not gone unnoted in Amazonian historiography, but its remoteness is such that the basic terms of reference are largely naturalistic rather than social, and the contemporary consequences of this marginality have assumed a pernicious character. Amazonian remoteness has been institutionalized and the region is now subject to predations of a grotesque quality which, unfortunately, compare well with the horrors perpetrated in the early phases of colonization when Amerindian societies were decimated in a furore of wealth seeking from which even some of the conquerors have not recovered. What is particularly different now is that terrestrial access – mainly as a result of the Belém–Brasilia and Transamazon Highway system – has exposed the region to the possibility of accelerated penetration. The actual activities going on in Amazonia aren't that different – they're still primarily extractive – but the scale is much greater. In the intervening period, only the brief 'glory' of the rubber boom provided any cosmetic relief.

At the moment in Amazonia one is presented with a kind of split-screen view which tires the eyeballs as they adjust to rapid shifts in perspective. Against the deep rustic backdrop, the populace is as poorly provisioned as those of other nominally less advanced Latin American countries, yet surrounded by hi-tech, large-scale development projects whose benefits are accrued outside Amazonia and whose existence overshadows the already bleak prospects of an impoverished peasantry and urban mass. Encompassing both realities is the pre-sold imagery of naturalism – palms and piranhas, monkeys and mystery – which continually fictionalizes Amazonia in the name of 'natural history'.

As far as Ocean the expedition artist was concerned we were going to Brazil and there was not much I could do to disabuse him of this illusion. There was a glimmer of hope after we made a trip to Stanfords the map suppliers. As we compared different maps' versions of the locations of towns we planned to visit, he had to admit that something strange was afoot. But the food he now regards as quintessentially Brazilian is as foreign to most Brazilians as it was to him before he disembarked in Belém and met, in Gilbert Phelps' more than adequate description, a heat like 'an animal breathing in my face'. For those who don't have a particularly compelling reason to read up on Amazonian social life, it is hard not to be sucked into the idea that Amazonia is primarily a special kind of natural space in which society is a minor diversion. In fact, aside from Amerindian societies (and, to a limited but still significant degree, Amazonian peasants, *caboclos*), nature and society in Amazonia are constantly contradicting each other. Capitalist production requires certain kinds of efficiencies which are difficult to achieve in Amazonia. If you are in the timber business, say, specializing in tropical hardwoods, you are not going to find stands of the tree of your choice. In theory, you are going to have to disperse your activities over a wide range, hunt and peck rather than touch-type. What actually happens, however, is that it's easier for loggers simply to go in and fell everything, then pick out what they want, a kind of reverse triage. In Amazonia, that is a typical way of resolving the contradictions between the mechanics of capitalism and 'nature'. Not getting enough fish with nets? Use explosives.

For Europeans and North Americans the violence of the contradiction between Amazonia the nature preserve and Amazonia the metropolitan society is symbolically mollified by such accessible popular works as Jacques Cousteau's book *Amazon Journey* and John Boorman's film *The Emerald Forest*. Cousteau shows how beautiful Amazonia is in spite of modern predation. Boorman takes another tack. He shows how the people of Amazonia (in this case Indians) defeat the developers. Both of these works are typical and unfortunately skewed portrayals of contemporary developments in Amazonia.

Cousteau's account of Amazonia illustrates the interests of naturalists and ecologists in preserving the flora and fauna of the region. Such people have long warned that their subject matter is disappearing as – if not before – it is observed, but the Amazon of *Amazon Journey* is an 'expedition object': it's not a place, it's a project. Watch a French frogman cuddle a sea cow.

Boorman's film is more thoroughly disingenuous. With the fake visa, 'based on real events' (Indians steal white child, a traditional Amazonian replay of 'The Wolf Children'),[2] and the simultaneous publication of a film-maker's diary in which great play is made of the ethnographic verisimilitude to which he was committed, Boorman proceeds to misrepresent just about everything put before him. The 'good' Indians (i.e. those with the sense to steal a 'blond', value-added child) are Tonto's grandchildren, heavily afflicted with a case of deep naivety; the 'bad' Indians look like they've been salvaged from outtakes of *Hip-Hop Meets the Zulu Warriors*); the non-Indian Amazonians are pimps and whores; the salvation of Amazonia (represented in the blowing up of a hydroelectric dam) is a heroic gesture by the Lone Ranger, a gringo technician.

If it were out-and-out Jungian fantasy, we could call on charitable interpretations, but it is (convincingly) presented as an informed, albeit 'artistic', portrayal. In reality (non-artistic dimension): (1) the dam exists (Tucuruí); (2) the Indians didn't win (the Parakaná who lived in the area were 'relocated'); (3) there are more dams on the way, built by well-funded gringo technicians. Conserved in such portrayals is an image not only of guys (no gals, they're looking after the kids, or not in *Emerald Forest*'s case) in white hats waging the good fight, but also of an Amazonia floating above real events on the ground. A real story is sacrificed in the name of a comforting one.

The actual inhabitants of Amazonia tend to get lost in such accounts. They fit only uncomfortably into the two major Amazonian image routines, nature and primitives, and are thereby consigned to the margins as corrupt interlopers. Even Herzog's *Fitzcarraldo,* which seems to be heading into the Heart of Pankness, gets pulled back into more accessible Heart-of-Darkness territory. Fitzcarraldo's attempts to build a Europe within the forest could have been the starting point for a considered dismembering of colonial conceits, but Herzog gets hauled into vision-quest territory (see Les Blank's *Burden of Dreams,* a.k.a. *Portrait of the Artist as an Old Auteur*), in which Amazonians are understandably bewildered spectators.

Little though Amazonia has actually featured in the creation of Brazilian national character,[3] there is no shortage of caricatures of Amazonians peeking in at the margins. The flyleaf of a 1960s French bestseller reads, in part: 'The Amazon Basin, rich in minerals, fascinating yet forbidding in its mystery, has over the centuries attracted the dregs of civilization.' The book in question, Bodard's *Massacre on the Amazon,* is a laudable if purple account of the Vilas Boas brothers' attempts to protect Indians on the Xingu Reserve. The sentiments revealed in the term 'the dregs' are familiar in a range of Amazonian literature.

The classic nineteenth-century naturalists' accounts, such as those of Bates and Wallace, travel writing, such as Fleming's *Brazilian Adventure, Amazon Journey* and more recently O'Hanlon's *In Trouble Again,* and adventure journalism, such as that of Bodard, represent the three main genres of Amazonian writing – outside of scholarly publications – available to 'civilized' audiences, and the non-Indian Amazonian has an image problem in all of them.

Bates and Wallace between them spent fifteen years in Amazonia, and wrote a fair amount about the non-Indian Amazonians amongst whom they spent much of their time. Bates' discussion of river traders is typical:

> It is this universal love of trade which leads, I think, to three great vices very prevalent here – drinking, gambling, and lying – besides a whole host of trickeries, cheatings, and debaucheries of every description.

A century earlier such sentiments were directed towards Indians themselves and intermarriage was extolled as a possible antidote. A Portuguese official (quoted in Hemming) at the time wrote: 'Without such familiarity with white people it would be almost impossible . . . to destroy their almost congenital vices which are repeated from father to son.'

There are more moderate and more rabid views, but in the twentieth century the prevailing attitude to non-Indian Amazonians has portrayed a shabby burlesque. They are 'the dregs', those who have failed to live up to the high standards set by the generic conquistadors. It is a corollary that neo-Amazonians, the *mestiço* product of 'pure' peoples, should also have a 'society' which barely rates the name. The adjective most commonly applied to the economy and society of *caboclos* is 'stagnant', a term which usefully connotes jungle/river complex naturalism as well as moral failing. Unreliable, quixotic and malevolent, the *caboclo* lives in the cracks of a colonial mosaic in which the dominant images shift between forest-primordial and European conquest.

In its attempts to make over the world in its own image, Europe's portrayals of societies on the fringe have frequently betrayed a kind of stereo tunnel vision: in one eye is presented that which typifies the legacy of civilization; the other, meanwhile, observes the primitivism which Europe has consented to bring up to date. In Amazonia, the preferred European referent is the opera house in Manaus, while primitivism is represented by the Amazonian Indian against a backdrop of lush foliage. Out of focus if not out of view is the nether world, that vast region of social and historical marginality where the images are less than pristine and for which more explanation is required than can be summed up in a flattering archetype. Ragged urban infants selling ices are neither gratefully European nor charmingly primordial. The fact that most Amazonians are city dwellers confounds a sensibility based on images of trackless tropical forest. The canoe-paddling fisherman wearing a T-shirt emblazoned with 'Miss Nudity Concourse USA' is on the wrong set.

In contemporary writing on Amazonia, the out-of-focus Amazo-

nians are not entirely absent. They appear when needed as guides; they are present when laundry has to be done; they drive the cabs and serve up the beer, but they are almost incidental, populating the transitional zone between the airport and the Amazonian Indian theme park. Their marginality, however, has a special poignancy because, unlike poor people elsewhere who are frequently set against an extinct primordial backdrop, neo-Amazonians are overshadowed by the imagery of a lost world that is presented as having survived more or less intact. Echoing sentiments dating from the earliest period of the creation of a neo-Amazonian population, modern commentators can barely restrain themselves from complaining about how these Amazonians lower the tone and clutter up the landscape.

These comments are intended to help make one simple point: the compulsive interest in the exoticism of Amazonian naturalism and primitivism obscures the invisible armies of the region, and *Big Mouth* is mainly concerned with them – people who are Amazonian because they live there, not because they embody other people's expectations of 'real' Amazonian qualities.

Boiled down, imagery of Amazonia precipitates into Indians, caymans, piranhas, curare, electric eels, monkeys, jaguars, parrots, thick foliage, mosquitoes . . . Some of these features are assimilated into a Brazilian package, along with the Girl from Ipanema, *carnaval*, Sugarloaf, and the engorged foreign debt. But Amazonia stands on its own when it comes to the fundamentally tropical. Most Amazonians, however, would greatly resent being regarded as country bumpkins.

Because of its size and the boom/bust character of its colonial adolescence, Brazil is, as I have said, really several countries. The national capital moved from Salvador to Rio to Brasilia largely in response to (real or, as the isolation of Brasilia suggests, imagined) shifts in Brazil's export potential, and Amazonia is still a kind of thick cousin. While the other regions of Brazil, separated in terms of history, geography and economy (and within these, marked racial and class divisions providing an even greater heterogeneity), are none the less constituents of 'the nation', Amazonia is still out back somewhere.

The revulsion and indignation felt by some at the path of Amazonian development is not widely appreciated inside Brazil. A common reaction is: 'You cut down your forests and now you're telling us not to cut down ours . . . blah, blah, blah.' In the generic West, concern is mainly focussed on those aspects of Amazonian destruction (for example the 'greenhouse effect') which may alter the quality of life in nations where the standard of living is already several light-years ahead of that of the Amazonian wo/man in the street.

More interesting to Brazilians is the particularly empty argument that Amazonia is 'underutilized', on the simple grounds that the ratio of land to humans is so high. Brazil, with a population of 141 million (1987) and over 3 million square miles of territory (compared with Bangladesh, say, with 101 million people on 55,000 square miles of land), the argument goes, is 'squandering' its resources. Even worse, it has relinquished these valuable resources to mere Indians, who constitute only 0.15 per cent of the national population. Those who have defended the rights of Indians are accused – among other things – of being defenders of 'apartheid' and of using the demarcation of Indian land to disguise foreign control of Brazil's mineral resources (see Schwartzman). In fact, foreign control over a large portion of Brazil's mineral resources and much else was long ago secured. Amazonian development is no more exclusively guided by Brazilians than it is by Amazonians. It is a golden opportunity, a sound investment climate, a deal you can't pass up – as multinational firms have recognized for decades.

There is a debate about Amazonia which extends beyond specialist circles but rarely includes Amazonians. It is a debate in which it is assumed that the fundamental issue is the environment, and it appears not on the front page, but tucked away in disaster preview sections. The granting of special privilege to the eco-issue is suspi-

cious. I say that not as a tree-hater, but because the tree issue has been used as a cheap and palatable substitute for addressing political questions of a different order. The longer that Amazonia is an eco-issue, the longer a Sahel-styled reckoning can be postponed. And when Sahel-styled reckoning can no longer be ignored, there will be no shortage of rationalizations along the lines of: 'Look, there's an immediate crisis, let's send some food and think about the long-term aspects later.' By which time, of course, it will be far too late. (There may, in any case, be nothing left in the kitty. As Dust Bowl Mk II finds its legs in the States, things on the 'charity' front may start to look a bit shaky).[4]

The line of argument in which eco-focus rules supreme is still committed to the idea that Amazonia is a lost world. What much of the eco-discussion overlooks is the history of Amazonia and the fact that Amazonia is not a social void. The tree angle is certainly pertinent, but the green foliage obscures issues of social justice and the fact that solutions are likely to be political rather than environmental. But as Jimmy Lewis explained, 'that's the way things are down in Texas/Amazonia'.

For Amazonians, being out of focus is a traditional problem. They are referred to as the hopeless occupying a land without hope, the architects of stagnancy – a placing which serves only those for whom

Amazonia is little more than a pristine business environment. Indian societies, perhaps to their advantage – though I doubt it – have been assimilated into the naturalistic conception of Amazonia. Non-Indian society is simply passed over as an unfortunate experiment gone wrong. It is an Amazonia occupied by, in Eric Wolf's ironic phrase, 'people without history'.

This other Amazonia is not by any means remote or exotic. I think one of the reasons, however, why it is passed through so quickly is that it is filled with some deeply revealing examples of the big white hunter backing off with tail between legs. Much as the Edsel – Ford's spectacularly unsuccessful 'new' car of the late 1950s – left a big bump in the rug under which it was swept, Henry Ford's attempts to organize rubber plantations in Amazonia left a big entry in the debit column. A more recent case is that of Daniel Ludwig, whose Jarí project left him walking around with large amounts of egg on his face. Ludwig spent almost $1 billion on an agro-forestry/industrial complex which quickly failed its profitability exams. It included a pulp manufacturing plant built in Japan and towed to the Amazon. After the US Civil War, Confederate refugees tried to rebuild in Amazonia the good life of masters and slaves, and they too came unglued. The rubber wealth enclaves of the late nineteenth century had a similarly short half-life. All of these conquest-of-the-tropics efforts are interesting but, despite their failure, have never really dislodged the commonsense view that Amazonia is basically Mother Nature writ large, a raw materials depot. As noted earlier, in many respects the place isn't really that exotic; much of what is going on in Amazonia is perfectly normal: exploit the exploitable.

Despite some reluctance about contributing to the exoticization of Amazonia, there's little point in avoiding the fact that certain features lend themselves to hyperbole, and unfortunately no small part of Amazonia's current undoing begins with the 'underutilization' argument, the belief that there is so much of whatever there is in Amazonia that losing a little bit can't hurt too much. When Amazonia is spoken of in this context, one is likely to be presented with trivial, *Guinness Book of Records*-type information – for instance, the volume of water flowing from the mouth of the Amazon every second (17 million cubic feet) could fill Lake Ontario in about three hours. Such marvels tend to obscure the more prosaic and tragic fact that at the time of conquest Amazonia had 5 million-plus Amerindians; currently it has, generously, 200,000. No wonder it appears to be a 'natural' domain.

While the 'social' is treated as contingent in Amazonia, at the same time natural forces are of such a giant scale and unpredictable character that they don't necessarily provide a reliable frame of reference either. The flood of the Amazon River, for example, is a major annual event which marks a radical shift in the livelihoods of many Amazonians, but the height of the flood (it varies all along the course of the river, but in the middle and upper reaches the high/low levels of water can change by as much as thirteen metres), its onset and duration cannot be accurately anticipated both because the flood is largely extra-Amazonian in origin (caused by events in the Andes) and because the contributions to the flood from tributaries on the north and south banks of the river are unsynchronized. People know that the flood is going to come but, like earthquake-fault residents, all they're sure of is that it will happen eventually.

Were there more significant continuities between pre-conquest and contemporary Amazonian social formations, our understanding of Amazonia would certainly be less dominated by the imagery of a vast forest preserve. In fact, the apparent 'naturalness' of Amazonia is a relatively recent development, a side effect of European decimation of indigenous societies. It should not be surprising that what catches the eye of the European is that which s/he is largely responsible for. Much of the apparent strangeness of the juxtapositions reflects the presence of Europe lurking in the background. So it is with Belém.

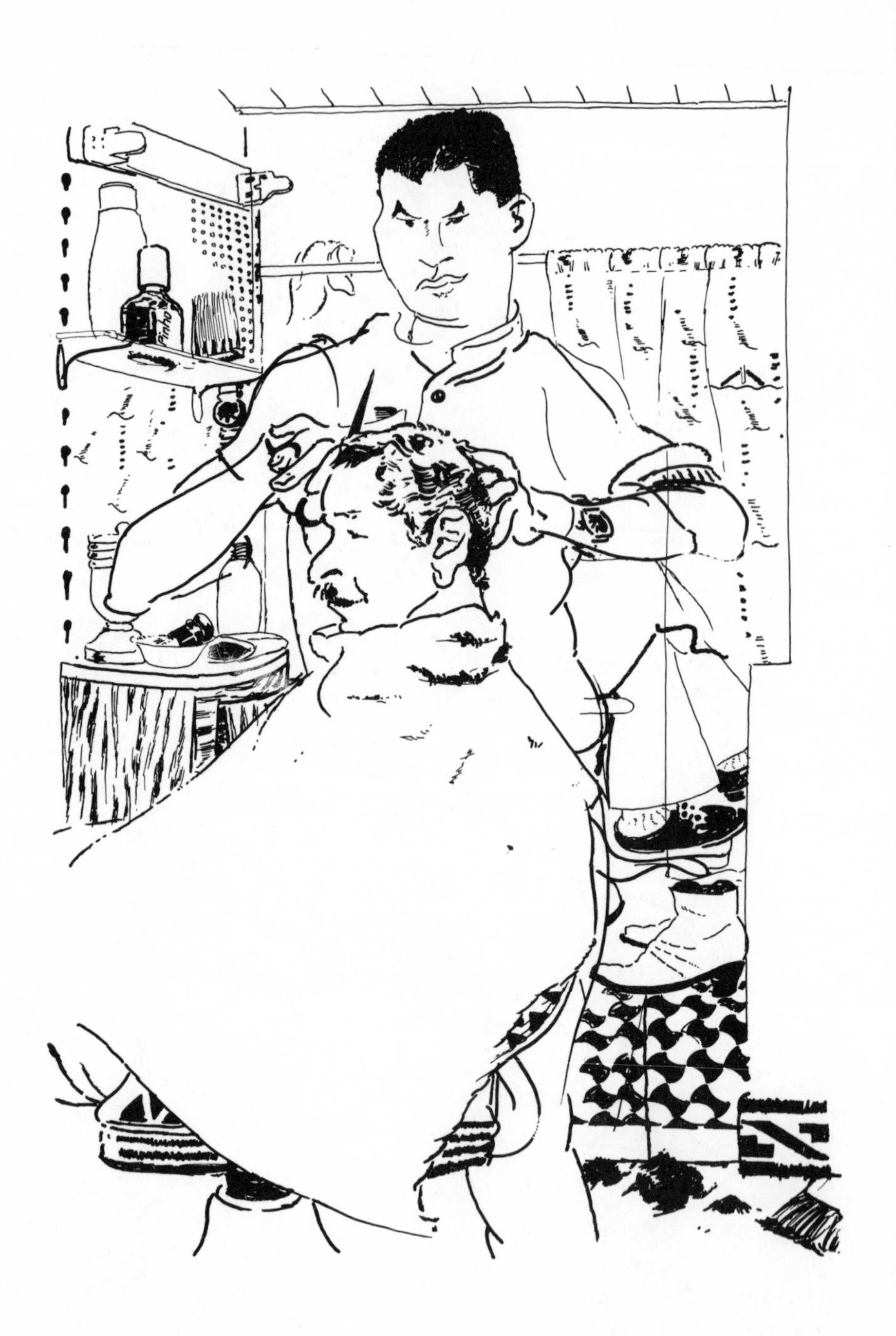
Pinho

II

CHECKING IN
THE URBAN FOREST

> I got away to Las Vegas . . . an exploit that netted me three hours of sleep and a conviction that any anthropologist who pretends he understands our dollar civilization lies in his teeth unless he has seen Las Vegas. I also discovered that I'll have to return there before I'll ever be able to write anything about it, both to assure myself that what I saw really existed and to spend a little longer looking at it. S.J. PERELMAN.

It's comforting, if not persuasive, to know that other people think that anthropologists understand things, but Perelman gets it right when he says that a return visit is both a reality check and a memory check.

Belém is not Vegas, but it prompts a similar kind of query: what's a city doing here in the midst of a landscape which looks like it should have been left unmodified? From the street, downtown Belém looks like a good-sized city, but from any river approach, it looks like it was plunked down by a crane, a mass of twenty-storey towers surrounded by a palm fringe.

This was Ocean's first real glimpse of Europe in Amazonia, but we'd had inklings of the phenomenon on first landing in Recife. Unable to procure cruzados in London ('What's 'at, mate?' queried the Barclays operative), we found ourselves currency-free at midnight and being looked after by Zenith, an airline counter clerk keen to relieve us of

dollars. After complimenting us on our choice of port of entry ('My beautiful city, you will have wonderful time. How is my English? You understand what I say?') he proceeded to facilitate unequal exchange. We ended up in a hotel run by a garrulous Jean Gabinesque entrepreneur and spent a day savouring the delights of heavy Recife rainfall before returning to the airport for the second leg. Airline schedules ensured that each leg of the journey began and ended late at night, obliterating any visual content from the passage of time, a cut-rate form of suspended animation.

By the time we arrived in Belém, Ocean had put a damper on any late-night brow-twisting vis-à-vis the New World formed in Europe's image and had seized upon the thought that perhaps we hadn't travelled that far after all. As we checked into the Hotel Aviz, instead of being impressed that we didn't have to supply our own hammocks, he was wondering how substantial the breakfast would be.

As the airport taxi approached Hotel Aviz I worried that our bankroll might be subjected to serious slimming before we had even got out amongst the quarry. A friend in Belém had recommended the hotel. Ten years before, I'd been happy with any place where some effort was made to keep the mosquito population down, but my request for advice had clearly been the subject of less mundane speculations. What loomed up on Mundurucús (a street convincingly devoid of a downtown vibe and therefore all the more dramatic as backdrop to the cosmopolitan visage of the Hotel Aviz) was what I imagined to be a Frank Sinatra kind of place. Bush-league perhaps, but with its blue neon sign, smoked-glass doors, carved-wood front desk and subfusc tiled lobby it conveyed an unexpectedly modern mood. Not our kind of place, but we checked in.

Our fears of financial damage were soon allayed. After an absence of some ten years from the world of underdevelopment (I overlook London, a special case) I had forgotten the Midas syndrome. As we stood there with pounds and dollars in our wallets we could feel them growing. In the subsequent month the official rate of inflation would rise by about one per cent a day, and dollars exchanged on the black market increased their value by more than fifty per cent. Having described to Ocean in some detail the privations he was certain to face, whatever authority I had possessed instantly dissolved.

By the time the lift had taken us to the second floor we'd been transformed from shoestring budgeteers to tropical big spenders. Never having stayed in anything other than a four-star hammock flop, I was taken aback. The bedsteads were outfitted with all manner of modern paraphernalia, including a radio and a remote control for the colour TV. There was an air conditioner and a little drinks refrigerator. The refrigerator was of particular interest. In Santarém ten years previously, a refrigerator had been a specialized and ultra-minimalist piece of furniture. Some people had them in their front rooms. If present, a refrigerator was not only the major item of furniture (preferred colour: fire-engine red; usual mode of delivery: ox-cart), it was often virtually the *only* item, as if nothing else was worthy of occupying the same consumer-durable space. It was also unlikely to have much in it, since the electricity supply was intermittent. If a refrigerator contained anything, it was a bottle of water just about cold enough to reawaken memories of the word condensation. Not that the heat was that great, but somehow drinking water from a refrigerator which was only faking it just didn't quench.

Ocean, who'd anticipated spending his first night in Amazonia fighting off, minimally, vampires and mosquitoes, threw open the refrigerator door and revealed the Brazilian economy, a chilled set of bottles containing Fanta, Coke, Cerpinha, and *agua mineral*. He stood back to admire the colour television set, AC, telephone, loudspeakers.

I'd told him that we'd be lucky to find a place with a porcelain steed, and here we were in a crib which not only had full leisure facilities, but an air-cushioned toilet seat to boot.

Aviz was the thin end of the wedge, and all my privation scare-mongering was exposed as abject and unrealistic Calvinism. Ocean kept consulting his roll, calculating and recalculating how many Cokes he could drink per hour and still not break the bank; how many bowls of *tacacá* or *vatapá* he could eat and still not approach the cost of a Big Mac. The following day, any suggestion that we walk or take a bus was countered with a trained-bird recitation to the effect that even if we spent the whole month in taxis we would still leave with plenty of portable property. A number of other cost comparisons, which he and Nigel the Bankroll cooked up with the help of a calculator recklessly thrown into a suitcase, inevitably followed. Relenting, and permitting postponement of the deflowering of the virgin soles of his Hawkins Astronauts, I realized I'd been sucker-punched by underdevelopment inflation. A modest Euro-budget was a fat wedge here. Ocean never really recovered. He became a rabid spendthrift, eating and drinking with abandon and finally boarding the return flight so laden with trinket-filled hampers that serious expedition artist could easily have been mistaken for madly acquisitive tourist.

The illness to which he had fallen victim is not uncommon, and frequently, after the initial flush has disappeared, it is accompanied by a syndrome whose symptoms are misdiagnosed as indicating recovery from the first illness. The two are rampant consumerism and post-consumptive meanness. In Ocean's case, the first stage of the illness was signalled by a rapturous desire to consume vast quantities of Amazonian cuisine as well as market-stall handicrafts (stamped leather belts, straw hats, flared trousers in primary colours, *umbanda* fetishes, the usual currency of Peckham Rye style merchants), and the second by an obsession with shifts in the rates of currency exchange.

The nadir came when, tempers frayed because we'd been ripped off in a boat-rental transaction, two superannuated adolescents could be seen arguing over a sum of money barely adequate to cover the cost of a first-class stamp.

The so-called parallel market is ubiquitous. You can go to the desk at the Hilton and get the official rate of exchange,[1] or you can brace a bellboy and get a better quote, or walk down the street to another hotel and get another ten per cent. Everyone's in the exchange business, and there is a considerable degree of one-upmanship: 'Oh, is that all you got? Try the barber around the corner, he's doing two eighty-five today.' You've really arrived when your connection is willing to take personal cheques. For Brazilians it's a nightmare. For foreigners awash with Midas currency it's an obsession. You can cash too much one day and miss out on that crucial market shift which would have put another two pence in your pocket.

Ocean's discovery that the gap between European life and the tropical enclave could be so easily bridged by money normalized everything and he was ready to get to work. I don't know what his expectations of his first day in Amazonia were, but I'm sure they didn't include the dramatic revelation that Hotel Aviz, in spite of its relative grandeur, had been plunked down in the middle of such a run-down neighbourhood. At night, the setting was tropically cosmopolitan: palm silhouettes, taxis, a light cleansing drizzle. By day, eating breakfast in the fourth-floor dining room, sunlight on full, the neighbourhood looked like the back of King's Cross station, an urban wasteland in which it was hard to tell what was going up and what was coming down.

Walking down Mundurucús towards the river, two pale gringos are hardly newsworthy, but definitely due some rubbernecking. Dirt streets, occasional patches of tarmac with a lunar complexion. Kids with kites. Butchers doing good Sunday business. And as we reach the road which follows the river bank, we have to cross a narrow wooden bridge over a vast open sewer filled with all manner of detritus. Turning towards the centre, we pass a number of warehouses, factories and colonial-period government buildings. There is a barren plaza with statues of military figures and the road shrinks to pre-modern dimensions, passing through terraces of eighteenth and nineteenth century tile-fronted residences, occasionally opening on to shaded plazas, before ending in the major market area. By late morning, the retail frenzy has ended, the beer drinkers are keeping the *tabernas* in business, and we find ourselves hiding under a thatch-

roofed bar watching the vultures stalk the waterfront as a group of derelicts build a fire to boil and launder their clothes. It's like a cruel refit of a popular postcard which shows naked Indian maids cavorting by a stream at their tropical leisure *à la Déjeuner Sur l'Herbe.*

Images of Brazil for export are generally sexy, whether this be in the hi-tech, it-can-sell mode or as portrayed in the more traditional Latina beach-bunny postcard. Even the more squalid aspects of contemporary life – kidnapping for childless Western cosmopolitans – connote fecundity and licentiousness, a south-of-the-border, easy come/easy go mentality. Behind these bowderlized projections, however, is a seriousness of purpose vis-à-vis bodies and sexuality which is more sober than European fascination with tropical mores might perceive.

A dozen years ago, sitting in a movie house in the middle of Amazonia, feet raised so as not to interfere with the passage of rats below, waiting to see the unlikely combination of Shelley Winters and Leonard Nimoy in the even less likely vehicle of Genet's *The Balcony,* I received vital information about Third World modernization. The newsreel included a featurette on the opening of a new plastic surgery clinic in Rio, an event, if the elaborate ribbon-cutting ceremony was anything to go by, comparable in importance to the opening of a major section of motorway.

More vital information came via an acquaintance of my wife. Though they were barely past the how-do-you-do stage, she told my wife in some detail of a recent trip to the state capital for a vagina-tightening operation ('My husband's after the servant girls . . . '). Of course, being a scientist, I compiled these data and realized that plastic surgeons were to Brazil what astronauts had been to America in an earlier epoch: symbols of transcendent possibility, icons of human mastery over nature, the experts of all experts in the age of scientific expertise. In short, plastic surgery was unambiguously where the action was.

On the verge of returning to the field and, for my sins, looking through the Brazilian equivalents of *Time* and *Newsweek,* I came across a quote which put it all into perspective. In a statement whose simplicity belies the magnificence of his monicker, *La Sapienza,* the appropriately baptized Massimo Monti, Professor of Plastic and Reconstructive Surgery at the University of Rome, says: 'Big tits are in'. Massimo (who looks as though a little physician heal thyself wouldn't go amiss in the baggy-eye department) is pictured at his desk surveying a collection of clinical photographs which could just as well be stills from a snuff film. In photos on the same page, displaying examples of silicon handiwork, are Brigitte Nielsen (caption: 'silicon transformation') and the Italian, Carmen Russo (caption: 'artificial robustness'). Nielsen looks like she's giving birth to twins through her chest; Russo looks like she got a two-for-one package deal, 'robust' lungs and a permanent smile thrown in at cost.

While waiting for Shelley and Spock, I had imagined us on the verge of an era in which the surgeon's scalpel would overcome all obstacles to social mobility, and provide hope for those whose physical shortcomings kept them at the foot of the ladder to success. Massimo and his Brazilian colleagues have devoted themselves instead to the arcane practice of stereotype retrieval. 'There exists a movement among models,' according to style consultant Constanza Pascolato, 'not only in relation to bigger breasts, but also more pronounced shapeliness, and it runs counter to an image of wholesomeness'. But model Monique Evans shows that we're still at the mercy of the experts: 'In the consultation, they agree with every request, but on the operating table, asleep, they go ahead and do what they want.' Monique had asked for forty-four inches, but had to settle for forty-two. So, we're safe after all. The surgeons are still on the case.

In addition to such taxing research I prepared for this present excursion by telephoning the Brazilian consulate for information on hotels in Belém. The brochures sent were encouraging: even the 'traditional waterfront market' is declared totally lacking in tourist interest; and the Belém entry in *The South American Handbook* for 1986 hardly differs from that in the 1975 edition. Included in the package is a magazine, *Brazil, Tourism, the Land of Sunshine,* publication of which is sponsored by the Ministry of External Relations and the Banco do Brasil. Amidst the appealing beach scenes and standard-issue photos of parrots (the tropical fix) and skyscrapers (the modernization fix), and the rendition of minor cult leader J. Christ overlooking Guanabara Bay, there is no mention of plastic surgeons. What is provided, however, is a selection of female bodies. The photos of black women are frontal and the photos of non-black women are what I believe are referred to as bum shots. Can someone help me out here? In the face of an economic crisis for which no obvious solution has presented itself, the reality of tropical underdevelopment is mollified by projecting the familiar images of the imagined good life of sun, sand, sea and *tanga.* The message is, I think, that this particular path to modernization will be different from what happened in Europe and North America because it will retain authentic elements from the antediluvian era. Instead of having to reconstruct the past in the form of theme parks, historic monuments, Disneyland-style image castles, the new development path in the Third World – such tourist brochures imply – will include a have-your-cake-and-eat-it-too provision: the hot tang of sexy old South America with the best of the West thrown in. All this and Amazonia too. A blurb from an upmarket tour agency reads:

> Step through the 'green wall' into nature's most extravagant show-case, the Amazon Rain Forest. Peer through the lush green of a sun-dappled jungle canopy for the brilliant orange of a toucan beak. Listen to nature's drum beats. Explore the labyrinthine waterways and tributaries in nimble Zodiac landing craft. Exotic. Untamed . . . Expert naturalists and guides travel with you aboard the Society Explorer, the only expedition cruise ship to venture this deep into the continent, to bring insight and understanding to this magnificent, mysterious region . . . The Amazon: Some Dream of Adventure . . . *Others Live It!*

In specialist discussions of the Third World, modernization is so debased and problematic a term that it matters little whether one presents it in inverted commas in order to signify ideological soundness. In science culture techno-speak the term embraces the charm of white-wall tyres as easily as the throb of a hydroelectric dam in the middle of Eden. The thing about Eden, though, is that the fantasy is purely in the eye of the distant beholder. Up close, Eden is pastiche and turns out to have a bunch of earthly relations hanging off the front porch and grinning into the camera, distant kin who would love to tell you their stories but who are hard to hear over the chatter of development activities.

On my earlier trip through Eden, the captain of the *São Pedro* offered me some unexpected tourist tips. Taking a boat to Belém from an interior town, I was trying to find a way to pass time outside of the hammock which served as a cabin. The captain, realizing that someone from Europe was naturally hip to big-city ways, was telling me about all the fun he anticipated at journey's end. Cunnilingus. An opportunity to escape from the other-worldliness of life in the interior. A bit of muff-diving. A lie-down in the lap of luxury. More than a bit, in fact maybe a week's worth of serious tonguing.

I found it hard to hold up my end of the conversation. Here he was going on about stuff that men of the world could bat around for hours, and I wasn't helping out. I was helping out so little, in fact, that Captain Cunnilingus, doubting that I recognized what he was talking about, forsook words and provided a creditable Marcel Marceau version, acting out the spreading of labia and insertion of his alternative dominant signifier. I assured him I'd gotten the message, but feared that I was stuck in the wheelhouse with a certifiable case. Or maybe Belém was *the* global capital of labial encounters. Had I been so out of touch that I didn't realize that the major reason for heading for the big mouth was to get down?

This was a man who was not an extra in a Herzog film, nor did he have a lip-plug, receive Sting in his *maloca* or tread the boards as an extra in *Antonia das Mortas*. A working stiff on the Amazon, an *umbandista*, a Euro-Amerindio-Afro-Americano, but for all that not much different from the bellies propping up bars throughout the West: keen on sports, politics and pussy, in that order.

The city he was anticipating has many elements of postcard cliché. A picturesque waterfront and colonial architecture juxtaposed with neon beacons, skyscrapers and street beggars. Definitely Jimmy Reed territory, if you happened to come from an interior city where the street lights served mainly to keep the bats feeding well.

Although revealing my profound ignorance of the speciality offer-

ings of Belém, the discussion did serve to reinsert me into the world of hetero men, a not inconsiderable event after a year of discursive exclusion. Having been in Santarém for so long, the fact that June and I had failed to produce offspring was sufficient evidence of my impotence (or worse, lack of interest in having a family). I had descended in ranking from *vippy* (VIP – it took a while to work out that kids in the street were not haranguing me as a hippy), and after the six months during which the *haute bourgeoisie* waited for me to make a recognizable move (an entrepreneur lurks within all gringos), I was finally consigned to non-special visitor status.

That I could handle, but what was less easily bearable was being lumped in with the other gringo interlopers, the Franciscan brothers (Canadian, US) charged with the spiritual welfare of the region. Slotted into local possibilities I was either (1) impotent foreign anthropologist or (2) fallen-by-the-wayside Franciscan. Visiting an outlying town for the first time I found myself identified as a lapsed priest travelling in the interior with his dark concubine. Children seized his hand and asked to be blessed, *bensa papai*. How could I not oblige?

I have slipped into salacious ex-pat mode, positioning experience in relation to sexual mores, finding it more comfortable to accede to the demands of the big luso-tropical episteme in which, according to common wisdom, tropicalism is a fundamentally antagonistic (and transcendent) *mélange* of Afro-Euro-Indian brawn, brains and fecundity. In part, this reflects what others have written of Amazonia when, as in the case of being stuck in Manaus for instance, they are so bored that interest can be raised only by focussing on licentiousness. But it also reflects the fact that the image of the nubile is inseparable from the image of the forest. Full frontalism is cool as long as it's apparent that this is a 'natural' condition.

On this trip, the encounter of European with local conceptions of sexual naturalism was well illustrated in Santarém upon the arrival of a French geographer. We first spotted her at Bar Mascote (Santarém's uniquely with-it night spot), and later had it confirmed by the jack-the-lads that another *sociólogo* (sociologist: generic for foreign visitors with no visible means of support) had arrived to do 'research' (generic for what foreign visitors with no visible means of support do to pass the time). She was easily the most dramatic addition to what was an admittedly drab floating population of foreigners, stumbling in tight dress and stilettos down Rua Mendonça Furtado. However, she soon pulled a move which was to prove her undoing, namely, revealing her commitment to naturism, a hobby I had long assumed was restricted to the trailer courts of North America. It was, she later explained, a perfectly natural pastime suitable for free spirits of all ages. Short shrift from the locals, however, and she plummeted from exotic foreigner status to that of mere *puta francesa*. So much for going native.

In Belém it is an uncommon pleasure to shoot the breeze with a passing metropolitan, but lurking behind the hail-fellow-well-met introduction is a crucial question: What's your library like and can I have it when you're finished? Erich Segal's latest? Sign me up.

Without a print drip-feed it's hard to get through those twelve-hour-long equatorial evenings and the idea that by a simple embrace from nature in the raw one is happily going to part ways with the printed page is not on.

To take a cab out to the airport (the only reliable source of paperbacks) is to admit defeat. The problem is not the selection (execrable, but who's watching?) or the price (insulting) but the fact of actually having to choose. The reason for mentioning this is that if one goes in search of reading material in Belém, there is a lot to be learned about the way the printed artefacts of higher civilization are disseminated. On current evidence what gets disseminated is the flotsam, and if one takes that as in any way indicative of the way imperial cultures are actually represented on the ground, there is something sad and peculiar going on – sad in the sense that the artefacts on offer are so narrowly representative of what's happening in Babylon, or Mammon, or whatever this place is called; peculiar in the sense that some interestingly arcane examples are available for our critical scrutiny.

In the minor chattels section of Belém's second-hand bookstore, the Livreria Econômica, is a collection of English-language books which runs the entire interest gamut from A to B. They are well represented by sex and marriage guides, 'A Doctor Writes . . . ' style books of the

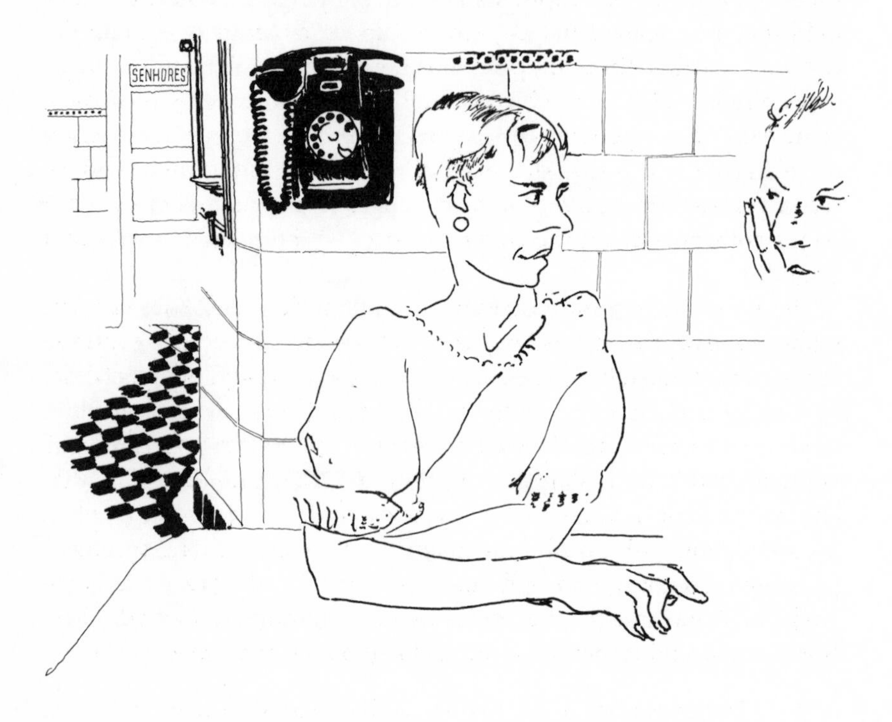

sort found before the sexual revolution became the launching pad for the new therapeutic culture. For the English-language student in search of supplementary pedagogical input, this sort of material hardly constitutes a major archaeological find. For the print-hungry traveller there is some compensation. Hidden amongst these self-help tomes are some good examples of the golden years of the paperback, as desirable for their covers as for their readability.

Four that I picked up were Charles Williams' *Hell Hath No Fury*, one of the hard-boiled contributions from that otherwise mainly nautical scribe; Hector France's *Musk, Hashish and Blood*; Somerset Maugham's *Up at the Villa*; and Margaret Mead's *Sex and Temperament in Three Primitive Societies*. The covers of all of these share a feature with the self-helpers, and that is that they are vaguely licentious. Prominently displayed on all are breasts. On Mead's opus they are unadorned, ersatz Mesopotamian; on Williams' is displayed, in what must at the time have been a reasonably racy manner, a pair revealed (in Ken Weaver's term) in a 'shoulder mounted boulder holder'; France's are near-East negligée; and Maugham's are dinner-party *risqué*.

In the excitement of finding an unexpected source of books in English it was easy to overlook what is a major mystery. Of all the titles published in English since paperbacks first surfaced, why should the holdings of this little shop in northern Brazil have such a high concentration of books which are either sex-related or which have (semi-)naked women on the cover? Is that all people read when travelling abroad? Is that all that is saved from the abandoned heaps of reading material? Is there some mysterious process whereby only books with breasts on the cover can survive the effects of heat and humidity?

This is not really a question that has much to do with Amazonia, but it does have bearing on the way certain Brazilian stereotypes continue to insinuate themselves, structured, as Said has argued in *Orientalism*, by a set of expectations which the West brings to bear on others out there. In a recent magazine supplement article in the *Independent* (15 February 1989), for instance, ostensibly about deforestation ('Bonfire on the Amazon'), there is a typical example of the non-Brazilian preoccupation with Brazilian sexuality. As I understand the argument presented, one of the underlying reasons for Brazil's rapacious behaviour in Amazonia is the widespread commitment to hedonism. Brazilians would rather, it is said, get a good tan than save a tree.

> The caricature of the hedonistic Brazilian is difficult to escape because there is so much truth in it, especially in Rio. These people are absorbed by their cheap sensuous dance halls, their alluring clip joints, their festivals and their carnival. Above all, they are absorbed by sex.

'Sex', according to the author,

> is the one reliable delight in Rio. Men and women are equally predatory and equally available. They believe that they are rather good at sex, which is probably true, and are not in the

> least prudish. Homosexuality, bi-sexuality and heterosexuality are all openly displayed . . . The Brazilians' interest in the bottom and their history of preference for making love from the rear has been the subject of several academic treatises.

And so on. Let's see if this reportage makes the same kind of sense if we perform some exploratory and experimental surgery on the prose:

> Sex is the one unreliable delight in London/Washington. Men and women are equally unenthusiastic and equally reclusive. They believe that they are rather poor at sex, which is probably true, and are not in the least adventurous. Bestialism, necrophilia, paedophilia are all repressed . . .

And so on. I don't have the appropriate clinical training to get too deeply into this text, but I think I can put my finger on a few lumps: sex is bad, dangerous and threatening, especially so when performed by passionate Afro-*latinos* who are wont to do it in public, and anyway, Brazilians have bum-chum tendencies because these have been documented in 'academic treatises'.

In spite of the subtlety of the author's analysis, I think it is possible to extract an unambiguous conclusion from his musings, and that is that the only way that Brazilians can save the forest is by using their woodpeckers.

This commentary on representation is all by way of an admission that I don't know what to make of the sensuality discourse that appears in so many portrayals of Brazil, including this one. I'm grateful for the version of viral civilization available in the Livreria Econômica, ecstatic at the portrayal in the *Independent*, disturbed at the kind of erotic utopia portrayed in *The Emerald Forest*, but can't see how the lubricious aspects can simply be overlooked as though they are not really central to the way in which representations are conveyed cross-culturally.

The books are finds as far as I'm concerned. I wanted the Mead book because it once belonged to Protasio Frikel, a pioneer of Amazonian ethnography. *Up at the Villa* has a cover by Charles Andres, an illustrator who frequently included a likeness of himself in the covers. In *Up at the Villa* he features as a satyr. He's best known for his Zane Grey covers.

Musk, Hashish and Blood is mega-purple: 'It was white and smooth, giving somewhat to the touch, soft and sweet to look at and of fine satiny texture, a young, healthy woman's body . . . something spurted up into my face and stung like a jet of scalding water . . . "You did wrong to give him hashish," whispered a woman's voice. "His brain is torn with delirium",' and so on. I quote liberally, but not that liberally.

Confusion is engendered by the fact that the interest which I might have in discovering a Charles Andres cover in a secondhand bookshop in Belém is beyond trivial. It is esoteric bullshit, part of a First/Third World non-contact routine, and of interest only because the discovery fortuitously reveals another tropical sexuality angle. On the other hand, however, it disproves the claim made by a number of mass media commentators that global cultural homogeneity is just around the corner, if not already squatting on the doorstep. For these experts, the issue of the underdevelopment (or non-development) of the Third World is either no longer crucial (because not much can be done about it) or no longer relevant (because symbolic strategies are more important – that street kid may be starving, but he's got a Mickey Mouse T-shirt, so he's part of the system). This is dangerous rubbish, but no less subscribed to for that.

The global village pronouncements by the mega-media operatives and their academic counsellors are, as is mandatory in the world of business, optimistic in the extreme. Given the incredible concentration of ownership (Orwellian translation: increased choice), they really have no alternative to braying that the vast apparatus is matched by vast cultural effect. On the ground, however, the ways in which people engage with these cultural products is far more diverse than the barons would like to let on. The terms of reference cited are, almost invariably, of the sort cited in the 'Bonfire on the Amazon' article: lowest common denominator, and all the traffic strictly one-way.

Ocean and I are on an interior flight. There are some family groups returning from holidays laden with gifts and consumer durables, but most of the passengers look like commuters quietly anticipating landing and getting to work. There are technocrats flipping through sheafs of reports. There is a crew of goldminers who look grim and morose as though they're being sent into space to renovate and clean up after *Alien* and glancing nervously out of the windows. And there is Ocean, hungry again.

In the seatback pocket is an in-flight magazine with the unreassuring title, *Icaro*. Amidst the usual ads for whisky, cars and ski holidays, there is a London fashion feature ('Modern, yet well behaved, the yuppies innovate only in small details') and, just to keep me happy, a feature on plastic surgery. Although some curmudgeons may raise a

dissenting paw, the article ('The Ugly and the Beautiful') declares that, '[It] would be difficult for anyone not to recognize the name of Dr Ivo Pitanguy, the renowned plastic surgeon.' Eyebrows also may be raised at the infelicitous translation provided for the non-Portuguese speakers aboard: when clients pass through his elegant waiting rooms each is 'searching for a solution, which can vary from the most commonplace wrinkles to heartbreaking deformities'. If these are 'solutions', what's the problem?

Pitanguy, following in the footsteps of Lemuel Pitkin, got his start in 1961 while helping to cure the wounded from a circus fire in the suburbs of Rio. The article does not mention whether he was restoring freak performers to their former states of ungrace or afflicted members of the audience, but it doesn't matter much because Pitanguy reveals that beauty has little to do with appearance. It is 'something which shines from within when a person has discovered the serenity which stems from an inner peace of mind and a complete acceptance of the way he or she is'.

The interview is disappointing because the doc rarely gets down to concrete examples, preferring to soar in the logorrhoeic and – need we add – ozone-deficient stratosphere where 'spirits of a certain era' stroll hand in hand with a 'young beauty who symbolizes the handsome racial melting pot which represents Brazil's heritage'. When harsh reality penetrates, the contents of the melting pot precipitate into racial stereotypes: Anglo-Saxon women want larger breasts; Latinas want smaller breasts; Japanese 'have localized weight problems as well as features they feel can benefit from surgery, such as broad noses'. The punchline, however, is that 'there is more adding than taking away'; Pitanguy is a body-builder.

Among the many curious aspects of this body-renovation discourse is the denial of sexual attraction as a prime feature. 'Big breast' in the abstract is pretty, how shall we say, disembodied. What we have here is a generalized wanna-be syndrome. Plastic surgery is good for you not because you get laid, but because you feel better about yourself if and when you do. One of the appealing twists which comes with reading about this body-beautiful fine tuning is that it is so remote from most people's lives that it assumes the character of a museum exhibit or time capsule, but one which comes from the future rather than the past. The number of Brazilians for whom such transforming desires can be realized is minute, and reading about the goods on offer is like browsing through a mail-order catalogue from another planet.

'Hey, buddy, can you lend me a spleen', is one of those good ol' songs they sing when times are tough and the tough, rather than getting going, get technical. Far removed from points on the social scale where plastic surgery is an option are Brazilians for whom Pitanguy's observation of a preference for 'more adding than taking away' is turned on its head, for the modern Feuerbach's aphoristic output is not 'You are what you eat' but 'You are what you donate.' These are the organ donors who, denied even the opportunity to dispose of their labour power, attempt to sell the only resources they have – the odd kidney or otherwise redundant vital innard. The New Constitution includes measures to restrict such extreme forms of self-employment, but the fact that people are driven to such acts enfeebles the legislative devices. This modern Burke and Hare routine is the logical extension of plastic surgery, and provides the expression 'gut rehabilitation' with a new set of meanings.

III

STRANGERS AFOOT

A number of defensive measures are required of the foreigner strolling down Presidente Vargas, Belém's main drag, if only to ensure steady progress. Although difficult to blend in entirely, it's possible at least to pass as some kind of 'other' Brazilian and thereby get rid of some of the magnetic forces which draw those for whom foreignness is synonymous with an open-wallet policy: a briefcase rather than knapsack, sandals rather than Doc Martens.

Ocean is a case study in the opposite approach, more thoughtful than the yob we saw in Recife – tattoos, tweed cheese-cutter cap, Union Jack boxer shorts – but resolutely impervious to the temptations of disguise: tan Airey and Wheeler seersucker suit (with underemployed Swiss Army knife in pocket), Hawkins Astronauts, red Yamaha Loctite T-shirt, straw hat, and Globetrotter valise. Another ten stone and he could have been Sidney Greenstreet's nephew. It is an honest approach, but one certain to provoke occasions of social intercourse from which withdrawal is possible only via invocation of the '*Eu não intendo Portuguese*' clause. A last resort. It was required only for the resolutely persistent, such as shoeshine boys attacking under café tables and the drunken pool player in Santarém who insisted he recognized Ocean from Guyana, where the two of them had worked at a remote botanical research station. 'And where are those postcards you promised to send me from London?'

There are not that many foreign visitors in Belém, certainly by comparison with Brazilian cities in the north-east and south, and not much diversity within that small number. There are entry-level student tourists and off-the-beaten-track older couples, and there are those who stay at the Hilton or Novotel. For both groups Belém is effectively the main shopping district which sits above the port. The city is a stopping-off point on the way to the south or to interior Amazonia and almost all immediate tourist needs can be met within a ten-minute walk of Presidente Vargas. The extensive market on the waterfront reflects the low priority which tourism has. Aside from one gentrified craft enclave it is devoid of any facilities not related to the sale and purchase of local produce, clothing, hardware, prepared food and the odd tropical throwback or songbird. Unless you promised to bring back a sloth head, you're unlikely to have made a fashionable score in the Ver-O-Peso market.[1]

Alongside the colonial backdrop of the Praça da Republica and the Teatro de Paz are a few reminders of a harsher legacy. Situated next to a telephone exchange at the lower end of Presidente Vargas is a human being missing three-quarters of its body. S/he is a head, soup bowl haircut and torso down to the point where most people's ribcages would end, and that's it. Red biro in mouth, s/he draws pictures on sheets of paper laid out by the keeper. Further up the same block is a crotchety woman with black-framed specs and a tin cup. Non-ambulatory, skirts splayed out, she rattles the cup and screeches at passers-by. Yet further up is a codger in a straw hat who looks like any number of men humping and selling produce on the waterfront. This guy, however, has mega-legs, red, scaly and swollen like inner tubes, each toe the size of a banger.

There is a dry stretch until one gets closer to the Teatro where, outside a bank into which he's carried when it rains, sits Albertus. He has a beaten, angelic face, a bit like the young Brando recovered from worrying about how he might have been a contender. Albertus is growing out of the pavement, a flat-based torso pushed up from the mosaic. He smiles and, holding in one lobster-like maw a roll of cruzados, gestures faintly with the other. He winks and tips his head and when passed a note the soft extensions close and shift it to the one pincered claw.

It's not that different from the pavement outside Finsbury Park except for the presence of so many small children among the relegated. When friends ask why I don't take my kids on the next trip, I'm stumped for a quick and non-apologetic reply. Amazonian children not cosseted in Goldilocks settings and supervised by teams of

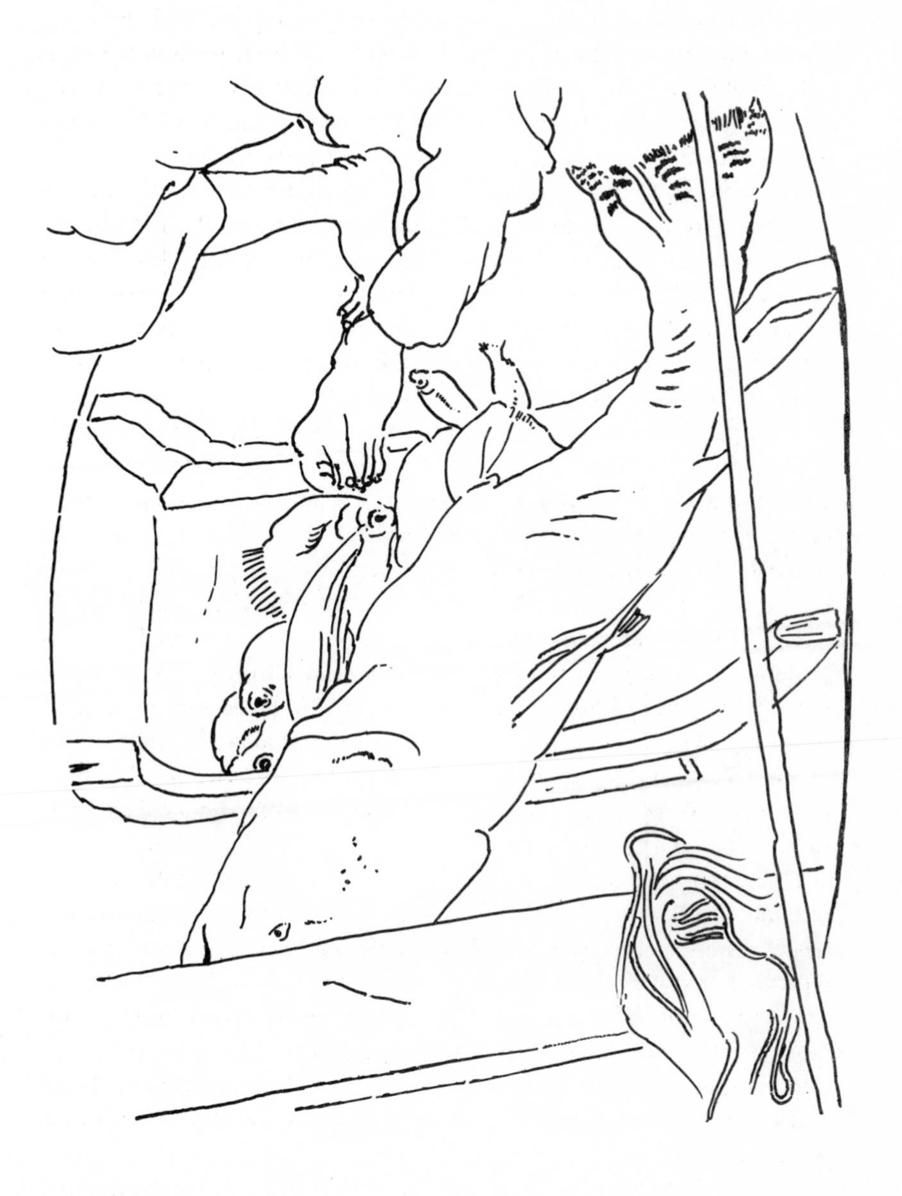

domestics are not exactly lolling around in a tropical playground, splashing in streams and pausing only to scale a palm or mango tree for a quick snack. They are early-entry candidates for the University of Reality, a demanding course leading to postgrad work in sustained underemployment. They aren't children, but adults in small bodies.

What you won't find outside Finsbury Park are peripatetic street traders who look like extras from *Mad Max*. They prey on tourists, offering a range of unprepossessing artefacts: knives in sheaths made of the remnants of tropical fauna, pen and lighter cases, necklaces, knick-knacks. The dominant style is neo-tropical gothic and features gargoylish figures moulded in green or brown epoxy. 'Hey, English, French, German, you buy this knife. It remind you of the tropics when you cold back home.' Actually, all I need is the sight of the gates at Finsbury Park.

The traders occupy a specialized fringe world. On the one hand they are traditional migrants compelled by remote forces to make a living on the move. On the other hand, however, the look is late-hippy nomad, and many are deeply infected with New Age discursive routines picked up from their better-heeled, First World analogues. It is an Altamont vibe: hip threads, low street values.

An atypical example is Nilton, a traveller of the old school, whom we came across later in Santarém. We are sitting outdoors at a quayside restaurant as the street lights come on. There is something forbidding about sunset on the equator. In temperate climes, a day of heat and sun implies a fairly long coast into the gathering darkness, but at zero latitude dusk is cut short and the sun hardly bothers to tip its hat before dropping off. As the street lights come on moths roll out of their hammocks en masse and rush to judgement. Hot on their heels are the bats, after humans the major beneficiaries of street lighting. For twenty minutes there is major chowdown as the bats pack away the calories in an aerial version of shark feeding frenzy.

Once the bats have finished, there is not a lot to watch. At an adjacent table, two slightly overdressed European women – guests at Hotel Tropical, Santarém's class crib – are eating slabs of meat cooked at their table by deeply committed waiters. Other tables are occupied by local businessmen. A table of three heavy imbibers is reduced to two. The departing member of the troika seems to have become dyslexic at the wheel of his car. As he painfully manoeuvres his vehicle from the space, he manages – slowly and with deliberation – to crease the door of his companions' car. They watch, but do nothing until he has pulled out on to the road, then they make their way over – it's a good ten yards – to examine the damage, laughing and shaking their heads. Ocean and I are almost comatose.

We are approached by a Sergio Leone extra: shapeless felt hat decorated with the skin of a jungle cat, grizzled and dentally retrograde visage. Nilton is from interior Ceará in the Brazilian north-east and is staying in a hammock-flop out on the Santarém–Cuiabá highway. He joins us and fends off two other sellers, one offering the standard-issue *Alien* motif knife, the other offering sniffables. Nilton accepts a *caipirinha* and chats while HO draws him. The waiters flick their towels and keep the other two traders at bay.

Forty years old, Nilton has travelled throughout South America and as far north as Acapulco. His dream is to settle in Tijuana where, he claims, the tourist pickings are so good that he'd be willing to forgo the travelling life. He can write his name, but is illiterate and ashamed of it. He attributes his great mobility to his passport, which ensures that he is a real person, not a *Zé Ninguem* (Joe Nobody), and is treated with a degree of respect by border officials and federal police. His destinations are determined by tourist fashion. Ecuador is best, he says, Colombia is pretty but tough. He lives by fashioning bits of dead animals into trinkets. From his bag he extracts the skull of a small deer which is half transformed into an epoxy gothic icon for somebody's mantelpiece. The finished pieces he's carrying are amulets made of cows' teeth and we trade him an autographed Philip Larkin postcard for an assurance that we don't have to look at the rest of his wares. He's vaguely apologetic about his offerings: it's just a way of making a living while travelling. The pieces mean nothing to him. A way to pass the time.

If he could go overseas he would go to England ('I take my hat off to England'), but Germany, France and Italy suck. Going to the States is unthinkable, a monstrous place whose only value is the contribution of tourists it makes to this projected Tijuana paradise.

A few doses of *pinga* into the evening and Nilton is trying to account for his wanderlust. Part of it is due to the hardship of backwoods life, but that's true for everyone where he grew up and not all of them left. He says the main reason, however, is that 'I like to fuck,' announced with a sheepish grin. After a long consideration of the virtues of women from different countries, he somewhat reluctantly – in light of his vast international experience – confesses that at the end of the day, when all is said and done, in the final analysis, he still has a special fix on the girls back home in the north-east, especially the black beauties

of São Luis: short stature, hairless, tight pussy. Embarrassed at this crude avowal, Nilton is quick to retrieve a more modern position. He is, in the end, a New Man, loving them more for their minds than their bodies. It is a view, he says, which he has had to cultivate in the era of AIDS. Nilton is the perfect chat-show guest.

I was surprised at his mention of AIDS, and he was one of the few to show any consciousness of the virus during our time in Amazonia. We did sight a poster in a public building in Belém: 'Love them, don't kill them'. Also, a Japanese farmer used an AIDS metaphor when accounting for the previous year's disastrous black-pepper crop. The colonization of upland forest in the region south of Santarém has been oriented towards several unfulfilled agricultural and pastoral goals. Production of poor quality foodstuffs has resulted in extensive deforestation and little profit. Subsequent use of cleared forest for cattle pasture has been only marginally successful. Black pepper is the most recent cash-crop entrant to the system, but after a couple of years of reasonable harvests, many farms have been hit with a leaf disease apparently resistant to any remedy. My Japanese friend, a garden-vegetable farmer and owner of a small pepper plot – and somewhat bitter at incursions into his specialized areas of agriculture by *caboclos* and *nordestinos* – referred almost gleefully to this leaf disease as 'pepper-AIDS'.

The 'needle-culture' focus on the spread of HIV in North American and European populations is mostly limited to drug-users. The prospective Brazilian dimension is entirely different. In the absence of accessible medical facilities, many people diagnose and treat themselves for a variety of unspecified illnesses (liver complaints are the most common), and injections – self-administered or given by specialist entrepreneurs – are regarded as particularly effective. The contents of the syringe are almost irrelevant. When I was first in Santarém, a neighbour told me he was treating himself for a liver complaint: 'This week I'm having ten injections of the blue medicine, next week ten of the yellow, and after that ten of the red. I'm feeling better already.'

We didn't, I'm sorry to say, get a chance to meet many more people like Nilton. He was a clued-in conversationalist, maybe a bullshit artist, almost certainly a lost statistic, but a walking-talking refutation of the 'lost people in a lost land' characterization according to which Amazonia has to be saved from itself by clear-sighted technocrats and go-go speculators. Nilton traverses that false landscape much as recruits to the Wobblies (International Workers of the World) traversed the US economic frontiers in the early twentieth century, riding the rails, living by their wits, invisible as long as they weren't organized.

Living in public, as tourists do, Ocean and I were never short of self-selected companionship, almost invariably well intentioned but almost as invariably short-lived. Bar room chit-chat. Returning from a party in the Belém suburbs, we are dropped off at the Hilton at about midnight and cross the street to the *praça* bar freak show. At this hour it is usually unpleasantly crowded, but for some reason most of the patrons have decided to call it an early night. The combination of diminished custom and our more presentable than usual appearance leads to an all-out shoeshine assault. Ocean, particularly sensitive to the danger of his Astronauts being touched by anything other than Wren's dubbin, is having some difficulty in dislodging an enterprising limpet. A woman at an adjacent table intercedes and the kid departs, muttering darkly.

The woman is sitting with two other prostitutes whom we have regularly seen in the bar. One of them is pretty if street-worn. The other is an unusual beauty. Approaching dwarfdom, oriental-looking, she wears a bowler hat and green evening dress. If Fellini got a tropical bug, she would feature prominently. They slide off and our friend is left to pay her share of the bill – sixty cruzados. She produces a thousand-cruzados note. Ocean acknowledges the ruse, pays for her, and she joins us.

Having seen us sitting in the bar scribbling and drawing over the past couple of weeks, she seems to have written us off as potential clients, but in the absence of a better offer is willing to talk. Periodically she checks us out to see if we may not be game after all, dropping heavy hints and then smiling and staring to see if they've clicked in anywhere. I ask what she's been doing in Belém: 'I spend my time at the beach, just walking around, and with my lovers . . . ' Smile and stare. When we talk about local food and I mention *tacacá*, she says it's like drinking sperm . . . Smile and stare. I ask about places to hear music and she says, 'Let's go to a nightclub. I will do striptease for you . . . ' Smile and stare. Finally realizing that she's netted a pair of dead fish, she orders another Coke and loosens up.

Lucia is from Maranhão and is in Belém on a working holiday, having left her child at home with her mother. She finds Belém a pretty dull place and work-wise things are slow. All of the people she knows in Belém are casual acquaintances whom she has met at places such as

the *praça*. Conversational gambits pretty well depleted, we are joined by one of her acquaintances from another table, a camp fellow named Paul who describes himself as basically French – 'My grandfather had a French restaurant in Itaituba.' (This is a bit like a Thai restaurant in the Outer Hebrides.) He is a masseur and can do 'wonderful things to your body', a claim bolstered, he thinks, by frequent unsolicited knee squeezes. Thanks, Paul, but I'm into maintaining my personal space if you know what I mean. Paul, being an ostentatiously cosmopolitan kind of guy, is perhaps more emphatic than many other urbanites in his disparagement of all things Amazonian: 'So primitive, so crude, not good for the soul. But the beaches, I adore the beaches, so white and clean and invigorating. You must come to the beach.' I explain that both Ocean and I are high-risk melanoma candidates and that in any case I like the forest better. 'The forest? But it has Indians. Ooh, I hate Indians. You can't mean it. The forest?'

There is a direct relationship between Paul's tedium factor and his delight in himself as he rails against the incredible awfulness of all things Amazonian bar the beaches. After half an hour the demi-monde chit-chat has got boring. But so, apparently, have we. Paul and Lucia lapse into a bitchy, foreigner-baiting routine which spells evening's end.

Or so we think. But two foreign males walking Belém's streets at two in the morning can have but one thing on their respective minds, or so thinks Ferdinand. As we cross the park near Eutíquio – sole occupant a military policeman straightening his socks – a guy comes out of the shadows and falls into step as we head down Mundurucús.

'What time is it please?'

'Two-forty.'

'It is dangerous here.'

'Oh, why's that?'

'There are many abandoned houses, thieves wait in them. You should walk in the middle of the road. I will keep you company.'

There are street lights and taxis pass frequently. Ocean and I normally walk in the street anyway, to avoid the garbage, dogs and chasms in the pavement. The guy himself looks harmless, but is probably not a freelance Samaritan.

'You are not from here, are you?' he asks.

'No. I live in England, but I'm not English either.'

'Your friend?'

'No, he's English and doesn't speak a word.'

This guy is hard up for conversational gambits.

'Where are you going?' I ask.

'Just down there,' he says and gestures towards Arsenal.

'What do you do?' I'm pretty sharp in the conversation department as well. I should be more interested, or at least mystified, but it has been a long day. Is he a cop? Does he want to change money?

'I study business administration. My name is Ferdinand –' and now that we're on a first-name basis – 'what is your hotel room like? I would enjoy seeing it.'

Sorry, pal. Another encounter underscored by sexual prevarication. The evening has been jam-packed with stalled come-ons culminating in this incredibly languid and far-fetched pitch. This sort of would-be monkey business happened frequently enough in both heterosexual and homosexual modes. The gay buy-in was encouraged, I suppose, by the assumption that two foreign males travelling together were basically cruising. The fact that Ocean didn't speak any Portuguese was a factor which enhanced assumptions of predation: when importuned I would turn to Ocean to explain in English what was going on, keeping him abreast of the myriad offerings. A quick reality check. For the importuner of any sexual persuasion this translation confab seemed to imply a consultation: shall we go with this one or not? The translation was tantamount to a counterbid and was an unwanted complication. What we needed – perhaps worn around the neck – was an update on the shopkeeper's defensive homily: 'Please do not ask for custom as refusal often offends.'

The party we were returning from on the evening when we bore the full attentions of Lucia, Paul and Ferdinand was one of the few occasions when we fell into serious ex-pat company. It was a gathering of various people who had participated in the First International Congress of Ethnobiology (see Chapter VIII), and it took place in a Belém suburb favoured by foreigners – in part because of its shortage of inner-city drawbacks, in part because it is close to the maritime complex which doodlebuggers call home port. Committed to the ragged-trousered mode, we went by bus, sardined for an hour, and emerged to find ourselves embraced by a Boi-Bumba dance which the host had arranged with a local troupe. The spread reflected the host's assimilative tendencies, local foods and firewater cut with tropical juices. Members of the local press were engaged in gate-crashing forays, hoping to pad out stories concerning the host's forthcoming court appearance on sedition charges. With the dance troupe, the press and the cosmopolitan guest list, we had entered a new Lost World.

Snaking through the assembled researchers and lobbyists from indigenous and environmental groups was a representative of the 'global media', a journalist/producer whose brief was to rope in a few talking heads for a Turner Broadcasting Inc. eco-series. She and her crew had shown up at the conference and were mightily disappointed. 'You guys are talking above people's heads, you know. What we need is stuff that anyone can understand. If you could just stand in front of the camera and explain it simply, that's what we need. I mean, environmental issues are real important, but if you can't put it in language that people can understand, it's just not gonna get anywhere. We'll be shooting from about nine tomorrow morning. Sure hope you can be there.' Well, sure.

Fortunately, she seemed to be getting few takers for her eco-destruction as entertainment show. She might have been fooled into thinking she was on to a cheap source of talking heads by the fact that a large number of the participants were staying at the Hilton (a hundred bucks a night) and so had at least a toe-hold in her real world. For the Brazilian researchers who live and work in Amazonia, the cost of a night in the Hilton is equivalent to a large chunk of monthly salary. That appearing in optical muzak was a less than appealing prospect for the assembled experts was hard for her to swallow. I'd like to think that the would-be participants' reluctance represents an internalization of *caboclo* views about the value of outsiders' representations of what is going on in Amazonia, but I know I'm going to be disappointed.

A decade before in Santarém, the fact that June and I were doing research cut little ice although few were so impolite as to impugn our good intentions. The problem was that *pesquisas* (research) just didn't make any sense. Lots of researchers had passed through Santarém and passed out again without leaving any clear evidence of accomplishment. As far as Santarenos were concerned, 'research' was part of 'development', if not patently detrimental then certainly obscure. Research away, but please don't ask us to believe that it has any direct bearing on our lives.

There was one notable exception. In Mujuí, Santarém's main plateau satellite, the outbreak of a mystery virus had led to an invasion of medical technicians briefed to take blood samples. The locals' view? These technicians were using the blood to make rocket fuel for the US space programme. Much as it sounds like a tabloid headline, it made just as much sense as any claims that the research had direct relevance for the health of people in Mujuí. (Mujuí has a propensity for extraterrestrial news. When I asked a journalist friend if he had been to Mujuí in the ten years I had been away, he scoffed, but then remembered that he'd been sent there the previous year to check out reports of UFOs.)

One of the background elements in Amazonians' belief in the efficacy of injections (or in the case of Mujuí, in the rocket-fuel-boosting applications of infected human blood) is that even if alternative explanations are available, they can't be put into practice. Most Amazonians' health problems are not caused by trauma, but by the absence of a basic public-health apparatus. Affliction by intestinal parasites can be alleviated by widely available pharmaceuticals, but as soon as you eat your next meal the worms are back in the groove. In this setting, you might as well spend fifty cruzados for a spirit-possession cure as a hundred cruzados on a pukka medical remedy: they're both unlikely to affect the real cause of illness, and one is a lot cheaper.

I'm feeling guilty about the eco-series producer and her project. I don't know what a 'good' film about Amazonia would consist of, but it would have to capture the peculiarly fragmented nature of the region. It would have to draw attention to the fact that cinematic representation of Amazonia has played a big part in creating the fragmentation which makes it so difficult to get a clear view of the place. Some exotic locales seem to be capable of simultaneously embracing visions of paradise and deprivation. Hansen's Disease adds to Hawaii's colour, for instance: Father Damien brings succour to Polynesian Hansenites who nevertheless remain capable of being rendered in heroic historical or romantic form. The simple suffering complements rather than detracts from the background of a ten-foot break on the North Shore and legions of garlanded *wahinis* watching Don Ho work out on *Tiny*

Bubbles. Down south, for some reason, the romance of Hansen's Disease just fails to get a leg up. Armadillos burrowing down to slurp some of that ripe flesh in deep-forest leper cemeteries, fake street lepers extending bandaged limbs from shaded doorways – it's just not sexy in docu-drama terms. Foucault may have secured leprosy's place in the periodic table which includes syphilis, tuberculosis, cancer and HIV, but in Amazonia the theme just stands there on its own, a pathology emblematic of little more than nature's perversity.

This is not to say that there isn't an exotic wholeness to Amazonia which can't be captured on film, it simply isn't one which includes the leper-licking armadillo. It is either the intact-but-threatened nature plus Amerindian film or it is the ersatz Western artefact film, the one in which 'A Whiter Shade of Pale' slops out of a riverfront trading shack and Yves St Laurent shades peek from under a straw hat.

In both, symbols speak louder than words, and Amazonia needs a bigger voice, not a silent one.

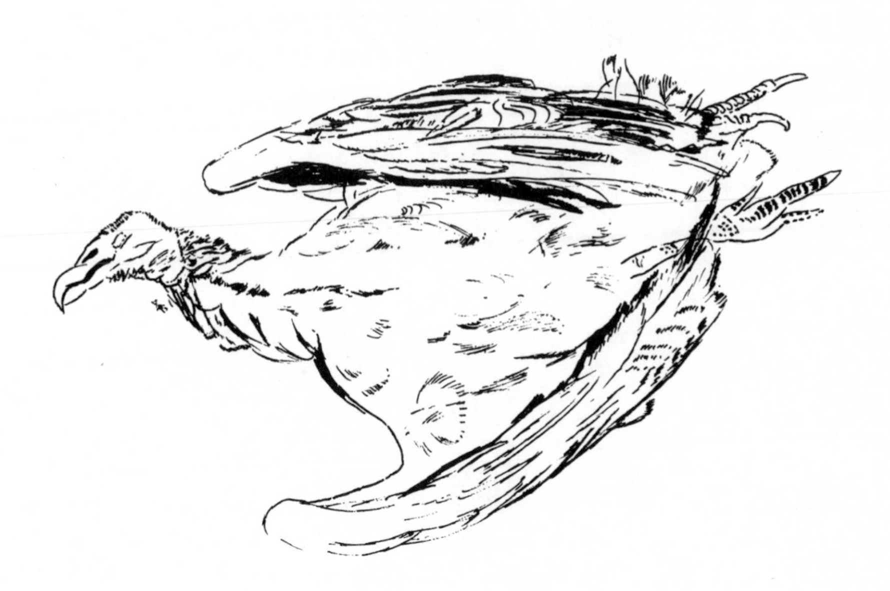

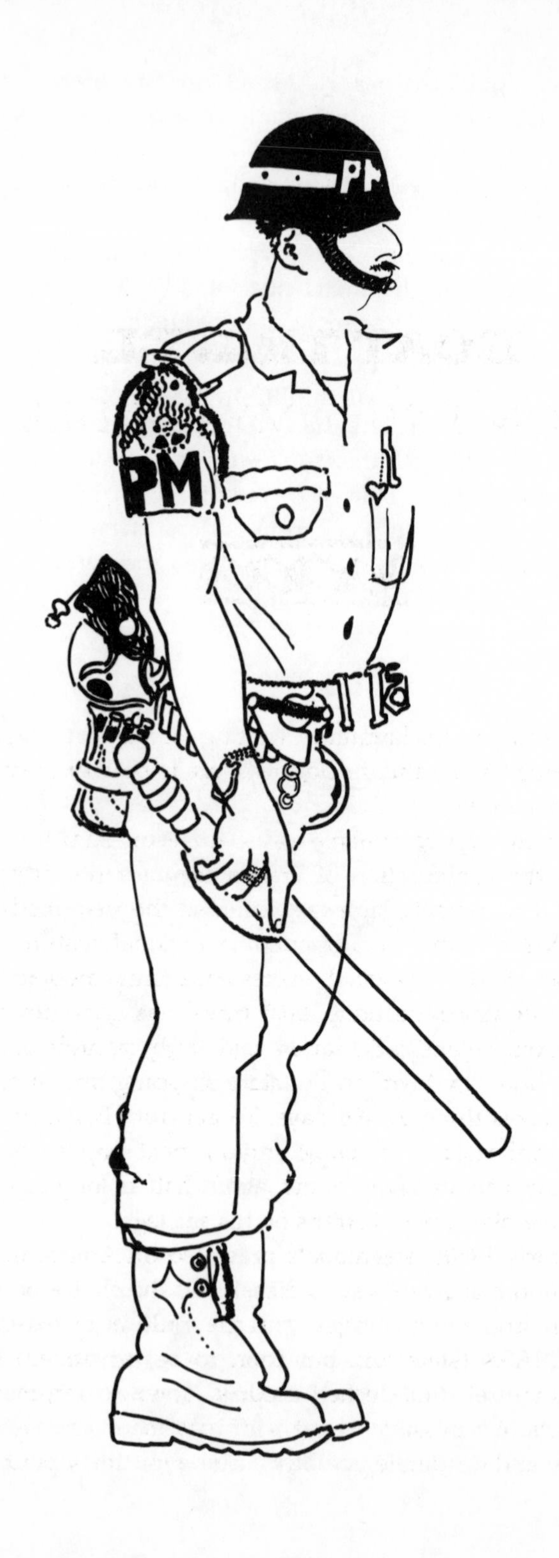
PM
PM

IV

BOAT TRAVEL
DON'T PULL MY PADDLE

Ocean is curled up in his hammock waiting for the text to get back to something recognizable and the boat to Soure to pull up. I leave him to snooze on for a while.

Historically, the only reasonable way to travel in Amazonia has been fluvial. With the construction of Transamazonica (its direct predecessor, the Belém–Brasilia highway, initiated the neo-dustbowl process which has become so prominent a regional feature) and the system of tracks and roads which makes Amazonia 'modern', and the improvement in air connections, boat travel has gone downmarket. The air trip from Belém to Santarém costs forty pounds and takes a little over an hour; by boat, on the state shipping line, it costs nine pounds, but takes three to five days. To get from Belém to Soure, a major town on the island of Marajó and our next stop, costs only one pound and takes about seven hours, about half as long as it takes to queue. Ocean wakes up and straps on his sea legs.

Until the early 1960s, steamboats prevailed on Amazonian waterways. Fuelwood has given way to diesel, and the choice of vessel for trips between large towns ranges from the multi-hundred-passenger scheduled ENASA (state-run, but soon to be privatized) boats, to smaller (fifty-metre) dual-decked models, down to ten-metre petty trading vessels. It's possible to get a lift just about anywhere, but if you're hearty and desperate you buy a canoe for thirty pounds.

Marajó is an island which sits on the mouth of the Amazon – though the island's size (that of Switzerland or Wales) militates against any perception of isolation. It's more like a large plug. The channel running between Belém and Marajó is wide enough for one to feel always on the verge of losing sight of land, but not so wide that one ever does. At the western end the channels narrow dramatically and riverbank foliage is just beyond arm's reach.

The island was the site of Marajoara culture (or Arua, two of several disputed terms) which represents the development of a kind of society largely unrecognized in Amazonia: centralized, relatively complex, sedentary.[1] The distinctiveness of Marajoara culture depends, however, on what would seem to be an incorrect characterization of Amazonian Indian societies generally as small-scale, itinerant, forest-dwelling and hunter-gathering. Evidence from Marajó and Santarém – another site with large prehistorical sedentary populations and a high level of craft manufacture, as well as burial practices suggesting something quite removed from savagery – complicates the picture of pre-colonial Amazonian life.[2] Even the supposed isolation of interior forest groups has been successfully challenged through the discovery of evidence of large-scale *farinha* production which can only have been useful if fairly long-distance trade was possible.

However, contemporary Marajó's direct connections with Indian antecedents are fragile to say the least. There is a type of pottery produced by contemporary peasants which employs Indian motifs, but the island is mainly known for its extensive cattle and water-buffalo industry based in the swampy interior grass fields. It also supports a large number of fishermen divided between inshore crabbing and netting – from canoes or small boats – and offshore activities where river meets sea. Unlike other fishing folk in Lower Amazonia, some Marajoenses can survive as year-round specialists.

If you were being singled out for river-travel punishment, you'd be forced to travel in July, the holiday month. The boat to Soure leaves Belém two or three times a week, and to get a ticket there is the initiation of a day-long queue. The noticeboards contain contradictory information and the ticket operatives lock themselves behind glass, so travellers, porters and guards become founts of highly speculative information. Each customer can purchase up to five tickets, so it's a matter of finding a willing compatriot. A fellow in bright yellow shorts and vest offers to buy our tickets and tells us to come back that evening.

Late afternoon and we are sitting quayside. A trio – semi-flash sinister guy with shades and a briefcase, two stout minders – chat with a pair of policemen examining the shoulder bags of a pair of youthful vagrants. From the adjacent market comes the hiss of stallholders; then shouts, and the two policemen are off. Others run from elsewhere in the market, and in a few minutes a fellow is pushed out, rubbing his jaw and looking doleful, Popeye style.

Pre-prandial entertainment under our belts, we retire to a restaurant to wait for our tickets. A smooth salesman spots two likely characters and opens his briefcase to dazzle. A bottle of Logan's Scotch, starting at four thousand cruzados and knocked down to three and a half. A bottle of Johnny Walker: '*Pinga* is bad for the liver, but this is good for the heart. What about some eyeshadow and a blusher kit?' 'Sorry, I've given up using it. Sweat too much.' 'For your wife,' he says, maybe less trusting now.

It is hard to fathom what he really thinks the selling prospects are. The products are too expensive for any but a seriously comatose local customer to contemplate, and any foreigner hanging around that particular dive is not the sort to be buying Johnny Walker or eye-liner from an ambulant trader. Sometimes the sales pitch is just a pretext for talking to the foreigner, but the foreigner has been through this particular routine so many times that camaraderie finds little nourishment in the subsoil. Far and away the most persistent are the hippy sellers of handicrafts which, they are convinced, are absolutely unmissable exotic mementoes of real Amazonia. The basis for the 'special relationship' mistakenly perceived to exist between the traveller from another country and the traveller within his own country is hip marginality. We've both placed ourselves out of the mainstream, the sentiment seems to be, therefore: buy my bloody trinkets.

The prominence of the cattle industry on Marajó seems to have affected the way human boat cargo is treated. The path to the ticket collector looks like the sort of maze used in abattoirs to get the quadrupeds cued-up for trepanning. Once aboard, I notice with dismay that the old-style open deck where you simply sling your hammock has been outfitted with banks of plastic chairs designed by an osteopath trying to drum up business. All seats taken, we retire to a hold where hammocks can be slung and where the last breath of fresh air departed at about the same time the toilets were cleaned. The soundtrack is engine throb and screaming kids.

Ocean, who has yet to be *forced* to spend any time in a hammock, is seriously unenamoured of the steerage prospect and retreats to an

upper deck. I am mulling over the concept of boat scheduling. The posted time of departure is eight o'clock, and fortunately we showed up early because it actually leaves at seven-thirty. The posted journey time is four hours; actual time is seven. I've done this before: sat in a hammock thinking about who I complain to and who will care.

When June and I arrived in Leticia several lifetimes ago, we heard that there was a boat across the river which was heading for Manaus. We hurriedly bought hammocks and caught the ferry. Securing places, we put up our hammocks and got ready to travel. Ten days later, they cast off the lines. I look upon the time spent in this particular cloacal site as a major formative experience. The hammock I had bought in the ill-informed rush was designed with someone smaller in mind, say about half my size. I had to lie in it with legs crossed and my head balanced on the cord, a duck egg in a quail's nest. After several days subsisting on supplies of biscuits and the captain's promises of imminent departure, we went in search of a solid meal and found, late one night, something warm which at one time, we were told, had wings. Thoroughly unsated, we stopped in a *taberna* and by candlelight purchased a packet of sweet biscuits. Making our way back to the boat in heavy rainfall, balancing umbrella and torch, we ate the biscuits, pausing only when an unexpected texture – crunch with a liquid punchline – registered itself. Turning torch to biscuit we saw that we had interrupted someone else's dinner, a family of weevils who had made the same menu choice. A mix-up at the serving bay.

The ensuing voyage had several high points. There were some keen card players. There was an assistant district attorney from Sacramento who had brought some quality Californian pot with him. There was a Frenchman working in Peru who, lumbered with toothache, had attended a clinic announcing that whatever the dentist did he was not to remove anything, just patch up the pain. After explaining several times and reassuring himself that the dentist realized what the brief was, he settled back in the chair, opened his mouth and let the man get to work. The dentist re-emerged minutes later with the offending tooth gripped in his pliers. The Frenchman could not believe it. For almost two weeks he retold his story, his cheek bulging as he checked the space with his tongue. He had come to help the poor and a backwoods dentist in a spotted tunic had done the dirty on him.

These were the high spots. Most of that trip I spent doing what I like to think was a good rendition of a suffering person. Our major splash-out meal in Benjamin Constant had left me with dysentery. While everyone else was lounging around in the heat, I was down below standing next to the engine in a sweater and raincoat, desperately trying to get warm. When forced into the smallest room on the boat, I squatted on the toilet resting my feet on a senior member of the tortoise faction. Incarcerated in the loo, this poor innocent was waiting to be several days' main course. I don't know if it was a hundred years old or two hundred, but much as I sympathized with its plight, other demands were then being made. As I perched there, feet resting on its corrugated back, wondering where all this fluid was coming from, far from feeling a oneness with all things great and small, I thought that I'd just about had it with boat trips. Ocean, for childhood reasons I felt were too delicate to explore, was as I've said looking forward to river travel. Under the circumstances, I thought he was getting far too easy a deal – not nearly enough suffering.

One of the advantages of taking an ENASA boat, especially during July, is that it is less likely to be overloaded and therefore less likely to turn turtle. During the holiday seasons – especially July, December and January – passenger demand is so heavy that it is not unusual for a boat to carry twice the permitted number of passengers as well as extra loads of holiday consumables. Top-heavy and wending its way among sandbars, such a ship is ripe for the headlines, and passengers aware of the danger keep their eyes peeled for a possible sandbar collision. Having eyeballed the immovable object, they rush to the other side, ensuring catastrophe. In mid-July such a script went into production near Belém. A boat with capacity for sixty passengers was carrying a hundred and forty. It turned after hitting a submerged object in the Bay of Guajará off Belém and seventy people drowned. Weegee would have had a field day. In fact, many admirers of Weegee have found work in Belém. The day following the Guajará sinking, the quality daily ran a full back page of photos of twisted corpses – on the dock, on the deck, being lifted into boxes or hoisted over gunwales – and weeping relatives.

The underlying cause of all this – holidaymaking – is also portrayed, albeit in a different set of photos showing be-*tanga*'d *moças* catching some rays on the beach. The beach and body equation is a venerable tradition, but it is surprising how much attention is focussed on so ordinary a part of daily existence. It is one thing for North Europeans to make a big deal out of melanoma holidays in the Mediterranean sun, but for those for whom sun-worship is as accessible as a grim February day in London . . . A typical daily paper in Belém in July is padded out with more mammaries per square inch than you could, well, shake a breast pump at. I take the society page of *O Liberal*,

18 July, and count nine five-by-three photos of individual bathing-costumed lovelies, three massed breast photos, and another thirteen photos of beauties posing with local dignitaries, for a grand total of some fifty brace of Amazonian bosom. The journalistic passion for bathing beauties hardly does justice to the beach obsession, misrepresenting, for one thing, the place of sexuality in all this. Beach-going is family business as much as it is the preoccupation of the would-be pussyhounds and their quarry. Narcissism not nookie is the subtext.

We are on board and steaming. The boat to Soure is filled with large working-class family groups for whom Soure is simply a place with beaches. It has no resorts as such, just a little collection of ratty riverfront bars with sound systems, and a few palm-shaded beer stalls on a couple of beaches out of town. There is little in the way of hotel accommodation, few restaurants. The several hundred or so passengers disembarking each trip are swallowed up in the homes of kin or friends.

Arrival in Soure is disconcerting. After entering the narrow river which connects Soure to the branch of the Amazon, hours of dark end in a raucous party-time dock scene; but having emerged from the crowd of merrymakers we find dead streets, bedraggled dogs, and a torpor too thick to budge. Only the mosquitoes break the state of suspended animation.

The hotel could have been described in one of those dissembling ads for north London Victorian terraces: 'In need of modernization', perhaps with the 'For Sale by Auction' tag which indicates that only the desperate need apply. A similar room in Belém would have cost a fifth the price. Torn, mosquito-friendly screens, bed-bugs, water pressure in the lavatory too low to dislodge earlier offerings, and party animals keeping things going until the early hours.

The next day we bump into the fellow who bought us the tickets, Marcos, and his cousin Mauricio – the former a secondary-school student in Belém, the latter a clerk at one of the mining operations in Macapá opposite Marajó on the north bank of the Amazon. The M&Ms are, like virtually all visitors to Soure, staying with relations, in this case an aunt. She lives in workers' barracks attached to a small fairground where there is an annual water-buffalo exposition and auction. The building is stucco, has a cement floor, and is roofed with corrugated iron. The kitchen area is in a corner near a little bedroom made of screens. The M&Ms' (and other relations') hammocks, a table with three broken chairs and a bench are the only furniture. On the walls there is a religious poster advertising a saint's day, a photograph

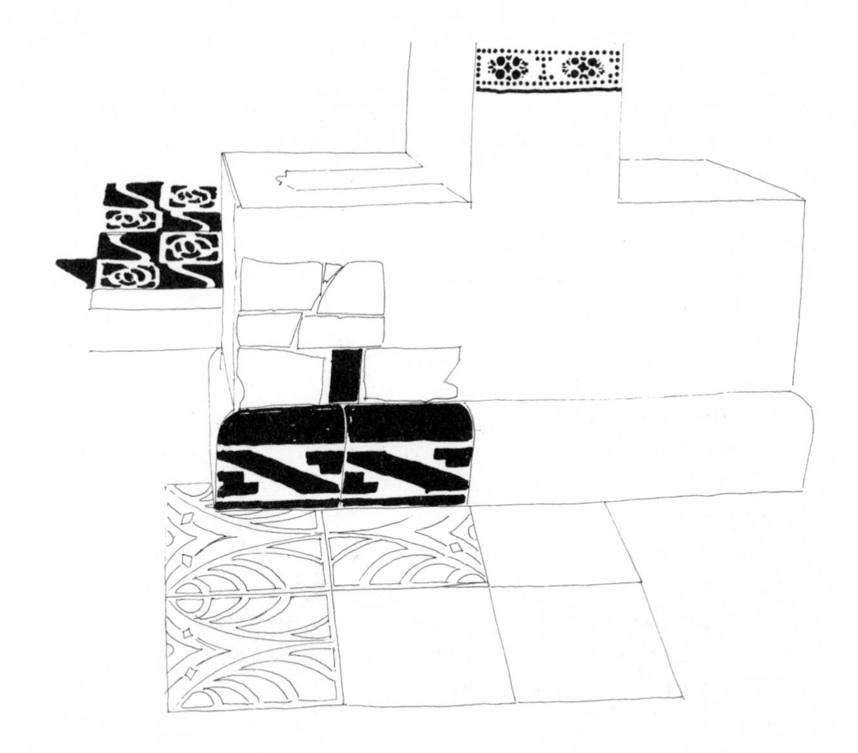

of a former state governor, a petroleum-products poster featuring, in universal auto-products style, women whose breasts are falling out of their bikini tops, a number of out-of-date calendars, and a radio which sounds due for a trip to Kwik-Fit Euro. But even through the thirty-hertz burble comes the kind of music which turns up like a bad penny. While elsewhere in the world hoovers are hoovering and ducks are being dusted, aunty is chopping wood for the fire in the company of Rick Astley and Kylie Minogue.

Although hardly the Margate of Marajó, it looks as though a fair proportion of Soure's service population counts on doing the bulk of the year's business in the holiday month. A municipal bus carts day-trippers to beaches virtually abandoned the rest of the year, little commercial enclaves which have nothing to do with the lives of the smallholders, ranchers and fishermen who live there. The quayside disco conurbation provides the only evening entertainment.

The beaches look like they were imported from the Caribbean, long swatches of white sand with palms and mild surf but lacking the smell

of salt. The attraction, however, is less the meeting of sand and water than the combination of beer and fish. Sheltered under pavilions in the style of Indian *malocas* and embraced by generously specified sound systems, fun-seekers eat, drink and dance. Barely out of earshot of the sound systems are fishermen's houses set just back from the tideline. Craft are moored offshore or in the mouth of a small river several hundred metres up the coast. Herds of goat feed at the waterline.

In one of the beach houses I find a capsule portrait of social mobility. Wandering around a river mouth, I ask a guy unloading ice from a boat where I can find someone to talk to. He points me in the direction of his boss, a 'big fisherman'.

My *modus operandi* is pretty opportunistic: settle on anyone who will talk to me. I figure that a gringo out in the middle of nowhere who looks like he just stepped (grimly) off the Victoria Line and who collars a guy taking five under a palm tree is going to be taken seriously. The big fisherman, unlike almost anyone you are likely to meet on the Victoria Line, is unfazed. 'You want to talk? Talk.' That established, it all falls apart. He professes to know nothing. 'Oh, I couldn't say, *senhor*. No, I don't know anything about that. You better talk to my *patrão, senhor*.' Rarely do I encounter this kind of respect, and I'm happy to take it. In London I'm forced to put on a tie before going to the hardware store for a box of screws, otherwise I'm likely to be asked insultingly phrased questions and then told they don't make them any more.

The boss's house looks like the sort of thing you see in before-and-after photos of New Jersey hurricane devastation. This is 'after-but-repaired'. No longer a working ranch, the old homestead has become the holiday cottage of the *patrão*'s children. Although he still keeps a boat and nets there, he and his wife live in town. Far from gringo-ing my way into a peasant-turned-property-speculator scenario, I simply find myself at a holiday season beanfeast for extended family plus servants. They are hospitable and make nothing of it. That a Portuguese-speaking foreigner wandering around this particular stretch of beach should drop in for a chat is taken as perfectly reasonable. It's never happened before, but why wait? In one sense it's good that Ocean isn't present because then I would have to spend a lot of time translating and we'd get bogged down in the reality of the situation, i.e., 'Come on, what are you guys really doing here, this far off the track?' Instead, I can do the loopy researcher act ('Mind if I take notes?'). On the other hand, in such circumstances Ocean tends to get a full-access backstage pass. Whatever problems are thrown up by his being a linguistic null set are more than compensated for by the fact that he can sit down and draw a picture, something far more tangible than my 'research' account.

The protocol is that a chair is produced, food is forced on me, and life goes on. I am given crab, several kinds of fish, rice, beans, *pimenta* and *farinha* and told to get on with eating. Within the three generations represented there is a native couple whose living has come directly from what they have fished or grown. Their eldest son, educated in Belém (engineer), is a government employee whose connection with rustic livelihoods is limited to sport fishing. The eldest daughter has married into the dominant rural social group, the large-scale ranching and farming fraction. While father may have paddled his canoe to work, his children fly out for holidays. The grandchildren are Benetton urbanites. They know little about the fish and plants which have been the focus of their grandparents' livelihood and regard my interest in the fishing and agriculture of the local peasantry as seriously wayward if not positively backward. They'd rather talk about teen culture in London. Even for their parents, raised on Marajó and knowledgeable about fishing and crabbing, the 'peasant livelihoods' business is not the reality of modern Marajó. For the old man, the future of Marajó lies with his fisherman son – bigger boats and bigger markets – and his daughter's husband. The son who has carried on as a fisherman is completely dependent on iced-fish sales to Belém and beyond.[3] For the daughter, Marajó is the place where her husband's business is located. In Belém, they go to the yacht club. For the teenagers, Marajó is simply the place where their grandparents live. As far as this family goes, I got there twenty years too late. Whatever peasant livelihoods were once enacted here have been transformed and the family farm is just a *memento mori*.

For the poor urban folk partying down at the other end of the beach this example of social mobility is irrelevant. Praia do Pesqueiro is just an extra-urban pleasure, an accessible holiday bolt-hole whose residents are an inconsequential part of the backdrop. They're here for the party. What I'm up to is regarded with bemusement: 'When we have a holiday, we go to the beach. What's the mystery?' That there are people living and working in Soure is just a background detail, a backwards reminder of what Amazonia has been, not what it is to become. The abject normality of Amazonia's relationship to urban holidaymakers is underscored when we eventually return from Soure to Belém. It's a midday sailing, the sun is out, beer consumption is high, and the river bottom for the full course of the voyage is marked

by the no deposit–no return spoor of that recent product of unconstrained industrial speciation, the Amazonian lager lout.

One day I miss the bus from the beach and have to wait at Praia do Pesqueiro an hour for the next one. Walking up the beach from the fishermen's settlement, I find myself in an out-take from a remake of *Lord of the Flies*, turning out of the tideline scrub to be presented with the best facsimile of civilization that can be created with the resources at hand. I'm braced by two drunken youths who look like trouble, one standing in front blocking my path, the other just to my side.

'I speak a leetle English. What you, French, German? I understand. What you do here? We have holiday time, dance until three in morning. It good. Down at wharf, many *moças*. You have good time . . .' Slow down, Joe Bob.

He's an inebriated tape-loop who looks like a sawn-off Lionel Richie. His pal to the side looks psycho-fierce, young Richard Widmark. It must be the sun. I can't tell if the smile is intentionally maniacal or not. He wants to know where I come from. I mention

London, Connecticut and Arizona to cover a number of bases. He has studied his geography text, telling me that Connecticut was one of the thirteen original colonies and that it's bounded by New York, Massachusetts and Hoji Island. Bonus marks and next question please.

Although my Portuguese is passable, any self-nominated conversationalist with a grasp of a few English phrases prefers to struggle through some pretty tortuous linguistic terrain before conceding the advantage of a viable lingua franca. Like the two guys above (whose apparent ferocity was the result of sitting in an incinerator and drinking firewater all day), students who have been exposed to some English (and many make considerable sacrifices in order to pay for private lessons) seem to be checking out if they've been conned. Have they endured the special pain of language tuition without getting the real goods? A few minutes of chat later they seem convinced that the training offered was in English and not Urdu and things have improved. But stage two is: 'Will I get on in life? Can you get me a job in London?'

There is something especially tiring about trying to communicate without a fully functioning life-support language for both parties. In Soure we kept bumping into the M&M twins, but really had nothing to say to them. Ocean, however, since he could speak even less Portuguese than the M&Ms could provide by way of English and sign language, was better company. For me, there was little to be discovered about Marajó from the M&Ms and partying down at the riverside was like travelling to Amazonia only to find that I was trapped between stations on the last Friday-night train from Leicester Square.

One evening I booked out early, leaving Ocean in the bar in the company of the M&Ms. Four hours later, at two o'clock, I went in search of the expedition artist. The bar was packed in the aftermath of the week's big event, a fashion-cum-dance show to celebrate the summer in Soure. Ocean was encircled by a troupe of drag queens and their rough-trade minders. He looked like a big white cake surrounded by vultures. Gamely carrying on with his drawing and buying beers to keep the lads sweet, he was overdue for rescue.

Mauricio, after some words with the river queens and an informationless explanation to Ocean, had shoved off, leaving aforesaid explorer in a dead orbit, fending off drunken interrogation with a few ineffectual tools: 'Me painter, from England. *Não intendo Portuguese.* You want more beer? Again? No money, don't have any more cruzados, flat, skint, mate.' I think Ocean must have been more distracted

than he realized, wasting valuable sketching time fending off the circling vultures by throwing out scraps of beer money. As sketch manager, I was responsible for making sure that he met his daily quota of artistic output and in hyper-situations such as that presented by the Soure Dance and Fashion Show, I'd have expected a fairly thick wad of product. But all we got for four hours' work was a couple of sketches and an expedition budget shrunk by defensive philanthropy.

Next day, shot of the M&Ms for good (big M was treating himself to a series of injections, and we were cheering for the opposition), Ocean received a more viable proposition, an offer of marriage from a young woman from Belém. In an overloaded bus with old ladies and young children jammed in the aisles, who should be offered a seat but the six-foot-tall Englishman? The seat in question was, realistically, more an incipient space, a hint of hope, a tiny slot between Frances and her mother which in the end became a cushion built of thigh wings. Still, any port in a storm. Using me as *ad hoc* heartsearch interpreter, it was established that a natural bond existed between Frances and Ocean, her uncle having been a professor of art in Lisbon. Trying to slow things down, Ocean pointed at his wedding ring and tried to get across the message of 'two little daughters back home –' pause – 'with the *wife* . . . ' But to little avail. Frances knew when she'd found the right man. Warm *abraços* at the bus stop and see you at the chapel in the morning.

Miffed at not having been blessed with such attentions (even Frances' mother turned a blind eye), I could console myself with but a single licentious but non-marriage-invoking approach from a girl who worked at night in front of the Belém post office. Each night as I walked back from dinner at the Hotel Central she spoke to me from the shadows, a different temptation on offer each time. The first was simply to go to a nightclub; the second, some smoke; the third, straightforward 'fuckyfucky' complete with suitable hand gestures in case the thick stranger couldn't track the lexemes.

Her office in front of the post office is just out of range of the street lamps which mark the centrepiece of Avenue Presidente Vargas and not far from the Belém Hilton. Whether true or not, the Hilton is popularly regarded as an action spot; and across the road in the *praça* bar in front of the Teatro da Paz is its street-level analogue, within whose penumbra lurk members of Belém's downtown demi-monde: transvestites, dealers, scene-makers. There's a neatness about the arrangement which conjures up images of Henry Ford's version of what a proper town looks like, something he tried to install upriver in the 1920s consisting of a neat grid of streets, the filling station on the corner, a hospital, a town hall, and so on.

The Hilton itself – of which more in Chapter V – is a modern version in that it contains within one shell (rather than within a town framework) all the facilities required by your modern corporate traveller. Just beyond its boundaries lie not only an earlier imperial model – the grand buildings, wide tree-lined boulevards, liveried waiters – but also the terrain of the marginal Brazilians whose position within the 'Order and Progress' motto of national development has yet to be secured.

If there is a bottom to the social scale in the *praça*, it is probably occupied by the shoeshine boys and street urchins, whose miserable proximity to absolute street level accurately reflects their prospects. It is such a commonplace pathology that the reality of young children having to subsist on the leavings of an already impoverished mass becomes unremarkable. The treatment meted out to such children varies. They may be tolerated by waiters and patrons, paid for their services, or kicked away like dogs. Waiters required to remove gangs of begging children may well once have been such themselves.

The ecology of the *praça* bar – outside with no covering, patronized by the hip and the seedy and by adventure-seeking scam artists, located between the major monuments to the imperial good life and the modern era – ensures a high activity level. The problem for the casual tourist is that the *praça* bar is actually a place of work, an office for those whose livelihoods propel them into the street. This is enterprise culture with a vengeance, including among its many organizational innovations the creation of the sort of University of Life playground where disenfranchised kids can really get to grips with the enterprise culture.

Escaping from Soure, entrepreneurialism rears its head again. There was congestion in the ticket queue, but after paying off a person near the head of the line, I only managed to get tickets for the sailing at three in the morning, eighteen hours later; given my growing if not quite fully mature antipathy for all things Sourean, this was a bit like having parole revoked. There were, fortunately, a number of scalpers dealing in 100 per cent marked-up tickets for an earlier sailing. They were, unfortunately, deeply enamoured not only of enterprise, but also of its cultural trappings. Simple payment was not enough. We had to plunge all the way in and pretend that the forces of law and order were about to descend upon us, haggle in the shade of a palm and invest a trivial transaction with as much meaning as could be found. From Soure, the only way is up.

TONIO FAGUNDES
VEREADOR POR BELÉM
LUTAR PORQUE ASSIM NÃO DA
PSB

V

BANKING ON THE HILTON

The Belém Hilton, in the summer of 1988, was site of the First International Congress of Ethnobiology, a gathering of some significance for Amazonian studies in that it combined presentations of research from a group of anthropologists, botanists and biologists from as far afield as the People's Republic of China with an opportunity to establish an overt political link between academic studies in Amazonia and the consequences of development for the most shabbily treated of all Amazonians, the Indians. Prominent in the proceedings were contributions from Kayapó Indians who, having forsaken a decided coolness towards collaboration with white folk, had decided to make a broad-front move.

There were undeniable – and awkward – ironies in the meeting, not least of which was the sight of Kayapó Indians parading before the Chinese contingent assembled, cameras at ready, in a reception room of the Hilton; and it was evident from the newspaper and TV coverage of the issues that they were as exotic for Paraenses as they were for the foreign visitors.

Escaping from the confusion of the opening conference arrangements, I sat poolside watching workers on a rickety wooden cradle trying to reassemble the Bank of Amazonia sign ten storeys above Presidente Vargas. Hilton poolside is a cheap exit from the cardboard-box existence of the surrounding streets. On weekends, white ex-pats

can easily stride into the pool changing rooms, grab a hotel towel and check out the chlorine. *Feijoada* (the Brazilian national dish of black beans and meat) is served on Saturdays for those wishing to synchronize their gastronomical clocks with the rest of Brazil. A body-beautiful crowd hangs out there. Limitless supplies of deferential hotel staff live to serve.

At ten in the morning, I'm sitting at a table adjacent to Fernando Rey's understudy: baggy white suit, white patent-leather slip-ons with tassles, chin-warming beard with grizzly, goaty bits creeping out from a dye job that needs an update, heavy spectacles attached with a gold chain. As he raises his paw yet again, a waiter comes over, laden with Smirnoff. His partner, who sits most of the time with her hand rested on his forearm, is a striking *mulata*: denim halter top, white shades, pedal-pushers, red pumps, and earrings big enough to use as quoits. I think they're in love.

Across the pool there are several sunbathers, but the wind is up and poolside recumbency doesn't look all that pleasant. I spot a couple of reps from the World Wildlife Fund catching some rays. When in Rome . . .

One bather, a fat guy in his late fifties with big breasts and belly flopping over the rim of his Speedo, has a rug whose non-organic nature is revealed by its perversely good behaviour in such a coif-demolishing breeze.

Viewing the proceedings at the Hilton, it's striking how convinc-

ingly and professionally First World the situation is. In spite of the fact that the Congress is taking place in a pretty exotic locale, inside the lower lip of the Big Mouth, not exactly the Sioux Falls Holiday Inn, the Amazonian-ness of the circumstances has to be laid on, coaxed into place. A Kayapó *maloca* is built in the Hilton basement; Indians are shipped in; feathercraft is on sale; boat trips to see the 'real Amazon' are advertised. All these add-ons are a distillation of *that* Amazonia, the one which is so heavily telegraphed that any danger of misapprehension about which exotic other is on offer is suppressed. No, it's not Bali, Bangkok or Burkina Faso, but I don't think it's really Belém either. In fact the Belém within which this all occurs is in a different order of otherness. It can't be comfortably summed up as parrots, *pinga* and purple sunsets; nor, apparently, should it be allowed to distract from the carefully constructed normality of the big hotel.

For example, barring access to Hiltonish switchboards, any gringo seeker of direct-dial access to home turf heads to the TELE-PARA office on Presidente Vargas. In the international calls end of the office the aquarium-style windows and doors make it impossible not to notice the character doing a good to excellent imitation of an enraged beast suffering from the kind of illness frequently seen in animals confined to the zoo – ritual pacing of cage, random violent outbursts, a distraught working out and replaying of an immutable condition: I am fucked. I know it, you know it. I can't do anything about it. You can't either. Or won't.

Unlike a lot of street cripples, this guy is a large, vigorous, fit human. He just happens to be short one leg from the knee down and seriously pissed off. He's enraged the way Rumpelstiltskin was, but he can't stamp the ground without falling over. Pushed up against the locked rear door of the TELE-PARA fishbowl is his suitcase, stuffed with clothing and papers and bound with ropes. He has a diary/notebook which looks like a Filofax and from a distance, when you see him hopping around raging with black book in hand, he could be a street-corner preacher trying to get a part in a Flannery O'Connor short story. He is an object of amusement and ridicule. A well-dressed student couple strolls past, and the guy (they are a 'guy-and-gal' kind of couple) tries to impress his squeeze by pretending to pick up Rumpelstiltskin's suitcase and run off with it. The gal isn't too amused. In fact, she gives her significant other a withering look which spells big trouble in the long-term-relationship department. Rumpelstiltskin's pulse heads towards two hundred and steam comes out of his ears. Everyone on the street stops to look: someone's put a coin in the machine. But, as is the case with the psychotic polar bear scraping its muzzle as it makes the turn at each end of the enclosure, the performance is too well known, too regular. It's a big play, but it doesn't go anywhere new.

In a less dramatic key, there are other active players similarly overlooked: the occasional entertainer; the longshoremen in singlets and turbans who hump hundreds of thousands of feet of timber from barges to loading bays; the self-nominated parking attendants who direct cabs into the angled parking slots and then try to get work washing them; the people with sweets and cigarette stalls whose turnover couldn't be less if they were posted to Antarctica; the ladies who sell *tacacá* in late afternoon and don't want to sell you a second bowl because one is plenty for the health-conscious. They're all out there in the street for anyone who wants to see.

Returning to the lobby, I speak briefly with Darrell Posey, the anthropologist from the Museu Paraense Emilio Goeldi who has organized the congress. He has just returned from his second interview with the federal police. He'd been anticipating that they might drop the charges against him; instead he found himself fingerprinted and mugshot. Normally equable, Posey looks on the verge of a bit of cudgel-throwing.

Although Posey's case[1] attracted a fair amount of attention outside of Brazil because of its link with the proposed Xingu hydroelectric project, the circumstances in which he found himself are by no means unusual.[2] In January 1988, invited to attend a conference in Miami on the Wise Management of Tropical Forests, Posey accompanied two Kayapó Indians and acted as their translator. Posey has worked with the Kayapó since 1977, during which time conflicts over use of Amazonian resources have intensified. The Kayapó, located on prime real estate in the state of Pará, have found themselves in a particularly exposed position – especially in relation to the Xingu hydroelectric dam, which will flood vast tracts of their territory. Having made their case in Miami, Posey and the two Kayapó, Paulinho Payakan and Kube-i, were invited by lobbyists to visit Washington DC to present their views to one of the project's major funding bodies, the World Bank. Although there was little hope that construction could be blocked, enough attention was paid the gathering to ensure that threats of withholding some funds were raised.

Upon return to Brazil, Posey found himself *persona non grata*. He was eventually charged under a Brazilian statute designed for unwieldy foreigners and faced imprisonment and/or deportation. The substance of the charge was untoward involvement in national affairs and 'denigrating the image of Brazil abroad'. In addition to threatening the easy implementation of a hydroelectric project supported mainly by the government, the contractors and the banks, the scandal yet again revealed pointedly – and in an international setting – the failure of Brazil Indian policy. What meagre concessions have been made to Indian groups in Amazonia have been poorly protected by the national government. Official boundaries have turned out to be permeable[3] – cross-cut by highways, invaded by miners, farmers and timber extractors – and when members of the official Indian service, FUNAI, have done their jobs too well and actually defended Indian rights, they have found themselves eased out.

Paulinho Payakan, in a conversation in Belém in July 1988, said that because no one in Brasilia, either in the government or in the Bank, would talk with him about the proposed Xingu project, he had to go outside the country to make his case. He and Kube-i have been charged as well, although their position is awkward for the government. Officially, Indians are protected from criminal process because of their status as quasi-citizen wards of the state. The charges eventually lodged were even more perverse than in Posey's case. Over the summer, the smart money was on the government's declaring the two to be 'acculturated Indians', and thereby removing their statutory protection. It would have been argued that by making a case in

Washington for Indian rights, Payakan and Kube-i would have demonstrated that they no longer deserved to be treated as 'real' Indians. Instead, the government decided to prosecute them under the same statutes applied to Posey, the 'Law of Strangers'.

There is another, more widely political dimension to this. The much vaunted redemocratization of Brazil following the protracted decay of the generals' cabal which ruled Brazil from 1964 to 1985 raised the expectations of many, but little that has occurred since has confirmed those early hopes. Inflation is pathologically high and the 'trickle-down' benefits of modernizationist development would disgrace a micturating rat. While there were few delusions about easy accommodation of the macro-economic pressures afflicting Brazil, there was at least the feeling that return to civilian rule would carry with it a measure of the freedom of speech vanquished in the name of national security during the generals' reign.

Amazonia, however, is not really part of the political constituency. It is treated as a 'resource'. Basically, the argument of the state is that, for the common good, Amazonians must face up to the fact that they will remain subservient to a greater need.

If there is any apparent reason in this argument, it is derived from the underlying assumption that rapid and large-scale exploitation of Amazonia – via hydroelectric power, timber, iron ore, gold and bauxite extraction, to name some of the most destructive enterprises – will permit a significant reduction in the size of Brazil's foreign mega-debt. Even if, however, estimates of 1990 mineral exports from Pará – the region in which the major projects are concentrated – hold true, this sum (£1 billion) represents only one or two per cent of Brazil's foreign debt. In any case, the history of foreign investment in Brazil, and Latin America as a whole, offers little evidence that the promised 'development' effects please anyone quite as completely as they please the lending banks whose G-spots have been maintained in an orgasmic state for some time. As Branford and Kucinski present the case in *The Debt Squads: The U.S., the Banks, and Latin America* (1988), of the $272.9 billion which was borrowed by Latin American countries between 1976 and 1981, most was returned directly to the banks in the form of debt servicing (62.2 per cent) and capital flight (20.5 per cent), or used to build up international reserves (8.9 per cent). Of all the money borrowed, only $22.9 billion (8.4 per cent) actually went into producing anything. In 1985, Brazil's foreign debt as a percentage of gross domestic product was 47.8 per cent.

The Posey/Payakan/Kube-i case is but one demonstration that the political will of the civilian government concerning Amazonia differs only marginally, if at all, from that of the generals. The long-expected addressing of the problems of agrarian structure has come to a similarly dismal end. Particularly galling to those who work with Indians is the fact that the government has made it increasingly difficult for researchers even to get permission to work in Amazonia, much less criticize developments there. According to Posey, since December 1987 no permits have been granted to researchers in the Xingu area threatened by the proposed hydroelectric schemes; yet at the same time, in the area of forest from which Payakan and Kube-i come, there are 6,000 goldminers and several hundred timber-cutters, none of whom is excluded for want of a permit.

A story in the *Jornal do Brasil* of 4 August 1988 typifies the experiences of many Indian groups with the judiciary and governmental bureaucracy over the years, as well as illustrating the piggy in the middle role which FUNAI, the national agency of Indian affairs, has frequently played:

> A federal judge in the state of Minas has decided that the

remaining 150 Indians of the Krenek tribe will have to leave the 212 hectares of the Resplendor Indigenous Reserve, 290 kilometres from the state capital. The judge's decision, made on 28 June, delayed by a judicial break, instructs that the withdrawal of the Kreneks be effected 'without any type of violence'.

'Is there violence greater than the expulsion of Indians from lands which they have occupied since time immemorial? Is there violence greater than denying them their means of livelihood?' protested yesterday the Coordinator of CIMI [Indigenist Missionary Council] in Minas, Fabio Alves dos Santos. The judicial decision was in favour of the rancher Balbino Laigner de Lacerda who has occupied the area since the 1950s, in permanent litigation with the Kreneks.

According to Fabio Santos, there remain only about 60 hectares of Indian land of the 4,000 hectares originally granted the Indian reserve in 1920 by the state governor, and demarcated in 1942 by SPI [the forerunner of the current Indian agency, FUNAI].

Since the 1950s, fifty invading colonists have settled on Indian reserve land leading to a case successfully brought by FUNAI in 1971 in which, according to CIMI: 'FUNAI arranged with the government of Minas to transfer the reserve to the invaders in exchange for moving the Kreneks to the reserve of the Maxicali, their enemies. The result was that the Kreneks returned to their own land.'

The exchange was illegal and was rescinded, but the state land title agency went ahead and granted titles to the 52 colonists.

End of story. The current dilemma facing such groups as those making up the Kayapó (a name used to cover several different peoples in Xingu) represents a new chapter in Brazilian development policy: interior lands are now being opened up not for agriculture, but for large-scale extraction and – in the case of the Xingu basin and in line with what has already occurred on the Tocantins River – hydroelectric development. In these circumstances, the connivance of the government in the invasion of Indian lands by colonists is only a transitional crime, and one which has at least two longer-term objectives. In the first case, land invasions permit the government to assume extraord-

inary powers when it comes time to end the disputes and be seen to have achieved, in that chilling and debased phrase, law and order. Second, casual land invasions permit the private colonists to act as shock troops who effectively subsidize secondary 'improvements' to land. A typical pattern is for agricultural colonists to clear virgin forest, fail to subsist on it for more than a few years, and so leave the way clear for cattle ranchers or other large-scale users to buy up, invade, or otherwise procure such land free of the major improvement cost, clearing the forest. In such a setting of chronic conflict, government development plans benefit by appearing to be thoughtful, long-term resolutions of the kind of social strife which is only to be expected of lumpens and Indians.[4]

The proposed Xingu hydroelectric project would inundate approximately 18,000 square kilometres, a tidy piece of land.[5] Eighty-five per cent of this land was nominally granted to indigenous groups. The figures themselves are not easily digested because they are on an unfamiliar scale. Imagine that Britain's hurricane of October 1987, instead of felling just a few million trees, knocked down every tree and building and was followed by a flood which left the entire population of Britain bobbing in the North Sea. Get the picture?

There appears to be an inverse relationship between the decentralization, which certain ideologues claim to support, and the amount of economic centralization achieved by the very same people. Britain and the US are obvious examples. Brazil and some other semi-peripheral states seem designed to aspire to a kind of divine overachievement in this regard. Given their lamentable record of satisfying even their own acquisitive bourgeoisies, one can only surmise that they are doing it on someone else's behalf. God forbid that we speculate about the identity of such beneficiaries. We may, however, draw together some observations . . .

In the search for some coincidence of scale between Amazonia-the-vast and the kind of investment which is so large that it is invisible, eyes are drawn to such financial entities as the European Economic Community and the World Bank. A concrete example of collaboration between such entities is the Carajás iron-ore project in Pará. According to Treece:

> the General Assembly of NGOs passed a motion calling on the EEC to reconsider its support for this investment and to impose conditions with regard to the protection of the environment and the Indian peoples of the Carajás region. The contract[6] actually contains a vaguely worded clause requiring respect for human rights, but this is tied to the provision for the Indian communities which the World Bank demanded as a condition of its own loan. Thus the EEC, despite being the biggest investor in the Project, has no independent observers and relies on quarterly reports from the World Bank, in addition to what they are shown on specially arranged visits. (1987:22)

It might appear to the concerned reader of the Third World page of the quality dailies that every effort – in these green-conscious times – is being made to ensure that even such mega-projects as Carajás have the benefit of environmental impact experts commissioned to 'soften the landing' (post-astronaut-as-hero vernacular). The actual situation may be somewhat different, as K. Taylor observes:

> The main funding agencies of international development that have U.S. financial support are the multilateral banks (MDBs), especially the World Bank and the U.S. Agency for International Development (AID). The World Bank has recently set new policy for the treatment of those indigenous peoples

> affected by development projects that it funds. One of its key provisions calls for the recognition, demarcation, and protection of indigenous lands 'containing those resources required to sustain the . . . people's traditional means of livelihood.' Demarcation is to be completed before any funds are disbursed. Unfortunately no project funded by the Bank has yet respected this provision and, in fact, several current projects are allowing the opposite process to occur, with considerable loss of land and natural resources as a result.

Whatever the Bank's faults, it is not guilty of dissembling. In spite of the journalistic conviction that it is basically a philanthropic organization, the Bank makes no effort to disguise its bottom-line commitment to its stockholders. Nor can it be said that the Bank has not covered its ass. In the 1971 edition of *World Bank and IDA : Questions and Answers* – an autonomic call and response publication covering the gross operating features – the answer to a (self-inflicted) question (page 34), *56/ Why has so large a proportion of the Bank's lending been for the development of transportation and electric power?* runs as follows:

> An improvement in basic services such as transportation and electriç power has been a primary requisite for faster economic growth throughout the developing world. That is why the Bank has devoted so much of its attention to these two sectors since it began to assist economic development over two decades ago. At that time, the inadequacy of basic services was the chief physical barrier to increasing production in the developing countries. Since then, considerable progress has been made in reducing this obstacle to development. But, although much has been achieved, the need for further investment is still pressing. In these as in other sectors, the Bank provides not only finance but also a substantial amount of technical assistance.

And just to make it perfectly clear: *57/ Doesn't the Bank's industrial lending assist the industrialization of countries with cheap labor, which will compete unfairly with the industries of the countries which provide the Bank's money?*

> The rational use of the world's resources suggests that each country, rich or poor, produce what it is best fitted to produce. . . . (p. 35)

There is, in addition to the bland and pernicious assumption that what is rational is that which is best fitted, an assertion of unity of interest which is daily contradicted by the social configurations of 'each country'. For the Kayapó, the rationality of the Xingu project is hardly obvious, nor is it apparent to them that they require technical assistance to overcome obstacles to development. In fact, as recent work undertaken by the Kayapó Project has shown, even the kind of 'management' criteria so boldly proclaimed by the technocrats as falling exclusively within their special province are far more scrupulously pursued by the Kayapó than by anyone else; but the goals of Kayapó environmental management fail to fit within the larger development profile envisaged by those for whom Brazil presents an ideal investment climate.

Ocean has read this and what follows and has raised the white flag and shaken the red – the former in the name of the Mogadon clause, the latter, I think, to encourage me to justify myself. His line is that no one wants to read *that* much about macro-larceny. A bit of lively illustration will suffice. But the sad fact is that the activities of 'aid agencies' simply aren't on that many agendas. The so-called quality papers, however commendable their analyses, tend to place 'aid' stories in special-interest weekly supplements. It's not news, it's for the devoted. While there is no point denying that any coverage is welcome coverage, it is also the case that these activities do not just take place in some remote region called the Third World. Where do all those readers of the 'quality' dailies think that their banks got the cash to promote their development policies? I take Ocean's point that it doesn't make for reader-friendly reading, but there's a good reason for that: it's plug ugly. Horses should bolt, dogs howl, mothers wail . . .

The scale of foreign investment and its consequences in Brazil have been documented in numerous books and articles in the context of Latin American or Third World overviews and case studies, but the special relationship between Brazil and foreign banks is somewhat obscured by the welter of statistics unavoidable in such comparative studies. One important indication of the magnitude of that special relationship can be illustrated by the activities of the World Bank in relation to Brazil. The Bank, formerly the International Bank for Reconstruction and Development (which also includes, for specialist lending purposes, the International Development Association) provided Brazil, for fiscal 1987, with loans totalling $1,261,500,000 to be spent on thirteen projects. Brazil's cumulative borrowing from the

IBRD as of 30 June 1987 was $14,346,100,000 spread over 162 projects. Impressive though these sums are on their own, they gain greater luminescence when viewed against the background of global bank lending.[7]

Of all the loans outstanding in the fiscal year 1986–7, a total of $120,488,073,000, those to Brazil accounted for 10 per cent ($12,702,731,000, a figure smaller than the $14 billion cited above because some funds had yet to be disbursed), making Brazil the largest borrower (just ahead of India with $11,375,647,000). Brazil also has the highest percentage of loans outstanding, 10.57 per cent (above Indonesia with 7.94 per cent).

If the 161 subscribing members of IBRD/IDA/World Bank are ranked in terms of IBRD voting power (percentage of total number of votes), those countries with more than 1 per cent are a mere twenty, with the US at the top of the heap with around 20 per cent, followed by Japan with 5.5 per cent receding to Kuwait with just over 1 per cent.

I guess this is what is called pluralism: to each according to ability to pay, from each according to how hard they can be squeezed. Amazonia's place in these calculations is obscured by the convention according to which World Bank loan approval is contingent on assurances from the borrowing country that proper safeguards (as regards the rights of indigenous peoples and the environment, for example) are being maintained.[8] The Bank line is that it lends the money to the country in question, and can't get too involved in precisely how it is spent. This is analogous to the situation prevailing in Britain where, until recently, home-owners could borrow money cheaply by increasing their mortgages yet spend the money on new cars.[9] Some of the money used in the construction of Transamazonica, for instance, was originally part of a loan to a Brazilian highway improvement scheme, yet the Bank has steadfastly denied that it participated in the construction of Transamazonica.[10] 'I only sold the guy the gun, I didn't tell him he could kill anyone with it.'

With the opening of the Berlin International Monetary Fund and World Bank conference in September 1989, it was apparent that criticism of Bank policy vis-à-vis loans which threaten indigenous people and tropical forests had been forced on to the agenda. An interview (Radio 4, 23 September 1988) with a Bank official on the eve of the conference, however, revealed the difficulty the Bank has in sustaining its claims to political neutrality. On the one hand, the Bank has been forced to review its environmental policies and has agreed that 'there have been some problems', and that it 'is determined to have environmental issues as important as other issues'. On the other hand, however – and as the interviewer pointed out – the Bank has some difficulty in enforcing laws in borrowing countries. It is, after all, just a bank. The Bank official's reply was simply that borrowing countries have laws, and 'we can assist them in enforcing the laws'.

Worthy as this may sound, someone has switched on the noise-reduction system. A recent example of how 'laws have been enforced' is provided by the Posey/Kayapó case. The statutes acted upon are those dealing with the legal suppression of dissenting voices. The laws which protect the rights of Indians (and other objectors) are in effect concessionary laws: only applicable as long as they don't protect resources someone else wants.

An early example of this was the Xingu National Park in northern Mato Grosso, proposed in 1952 and finally made legitimate in 1961. Although created by a federal act, the government of the state of Mato Grosso carried on granting land within the proposed reserve to non-Indian speculators. The federal government eventually intervened to protect the reserve boundaries. In subsequent years, however, the integrity of Indian reserves was demoted. Under a new Brazilian Indian Statute of 1970, invasion of Indian land and relocation of Indians became permissible for six reasons:

(1) to end inter-tribal fighting;
(2) to combat epidemics;
(3) to maintain national security;
(4) to carry out public works in the name of national development;
(5) to suppress public disorder;
(6) to develop mining.[11]

Hardly pausing for breath, the government approved the building of a road which would pass through the Xingu Reserve, an act which in fact created the conditions outlined in items (1) and (2), and was justified by the prescriptions in items (3) to (6).

It is hardly coincidental that such a move should take place under conditions of military dictatorship, and as Davis has argued, the success of the highway assault on Amazonia owes much to the combination of business and military rationales unified under an advanced bureaucratic apparatus. He notes five factors of particular importance. One, Brazil's National Highway Department 'was one of the most modern state agencies of its kind in Latin America'. Second, construction of the roads was largely the responsibility of the Army

Corps of Engineers, backed by technical resources sustained by the public purse. Third, there was generous provision of funds via USAID and the Inter-American Development and World Banks. Fourth, the building of the Transamazonica network was accompanied by an aerial-photographic and mapping survey which revealed, among other things, such mineral deposits as those in Serra do Carajás. Fifth, manufacturers of heavy earth-moving machinery were enthusiastic participants. According to Davis, 'Between 1970 and 1972, Caterpillar Brasil sold over 700 pieces of equipment worth $47 million to the Brazilian Army Corps of Engineers and to the seven private construction companies that were contracted to build the Trans-Amazon Highway.'

Davis points out in his conclusion that there is a contradiction in perspectives on Amazonia, one which unfortunately survives ten years later:

> The reasons for this widespread destruction are *not* to be found in a lack of concern for the environment on the part of the Brazilian people . . . the causes for the rapacious destruction of the Amazon rain forest are to be found in the same set of factors that are uprooting Indian and peasant populations in Brazil.

He has this to say of the matters raised by indigenist and environmental groups: '[To] date . . . the issues raised by these organizations have hardly penetrated world opinion and have only received slight notice in the international press'. Today, little has changed. Coverage of Amazonian events tends to emphasize the relatively trivial effects of what Amazonians are doing to their environment, while the external causes of the depredations tend to be overlooked.

As I write this, there are periodic radio reports from the Berlin International Monetary Fund/World Bank meetings. Quoted several times are pleas from the president of the Bank to do something about the world's poor. Asserting the 'moral outrage of poverty', he suggests higher rates of economic growth, greater investment in education and curbs on population growth.

The naive or casual listener might find it difficult to recognize the occupation of the quoted speaker. Is he a preacher, a politician, a demographer? No, he's a banker, and his seemingly anodyne prescriptions, when lowered to the ground in Amazonia, are not only cynically devoid of relevance, but in fact will achieve – in the Xingu complex for example – something quite different from the good life on offer from the Bank: higher economic growth will be obtained outside Amazonia, not by the targeted poor; nor is investment in education likely to reach them, though it has produced research which contradicts the claim that Bank-funded projects have no environmental impact; curbs on population growth are likely to be made redundant by the absence of any population at all.

The desecration which has occurred and shows every sign of continuing is carried on under a banner so opaque that only sophisticated folks can't see it. How else to explain the gullibility with which the Bank's (and other lending agencies') pronouncements are consumed? The 'minimally acceptable standards of living', 'the waste of precious resources', the vicious cycle of poverty and environmental degradation' (all catchphrases employed by Conable, the Bank's president, in his oration) are not original conditions of the Third World. If one asks why they prevail now and regularly finds the presence of 'aid' agencies, even those observers whose noses have been designed to screen out offensive odours may smell a rat. If that reads like a heavily qualified statement it is only because, regardless of mega-scent evidence, the preferred reading of 'aid' stresses its philanthropic connotations at the expense of facts. One widely cited (and even more widely ignored) observation draws attention to the positive correlation between the extent of foreign aid/investment and the degree of political repression. Ignoring the discredited (but still often proclaimed) notion that 'aid' is designed precisely to bring democracy to the barbarian peasant, it would appear that the ideal conditions for aid/investment provision are those which most completely exclude any notion of democratic process – the Philippines, Chile, Brazil, Indonesia . . . [12]

For the Bank to survive it will have to maintain its undeniably distinguished record of prestidigitation: being a major Third World player, being a profitable enterprise, yet distancing itself from any culpability when the outcome of development schemes is manifestly deleterious to the alleged beneficiaries of aid. If journalistic coverage provides any index, the 'world's' dismay at the withdrawal of a steroid-motivated Olympic gold medal is the week's big heart-tugger.

The bureaucratic apparatus within which the Brazilian state consummated its holy alliance with major world players is still in place; so too are Amazonians' perceptions of their role within the larger scheme of things as subordinated to the overriding demands of national progress and integration. Compounding the pessimism with which Amazonians contemplate their objective position within state plans is the realization that those plans catering for the despoiling of Amazonia are being overtaken by a succession of crises.

Of increasing importance in the debates over eco-destruction/development is the contribution made by non-governmental organizations (NGOs) such as the World Wildlife Fund, Friends of the Earth (merged in the US with the World Resources Institute and the Environmental Protection Institute), Amnesty International, Survival International and Cultural Survival. (The latter three have a markedly lower profile due to the fact that they are primarily concerned with a mere subset of 'the environment', human beings.) Debate here currently focusses on the concept of 'forest management'. Leaving aside the fact that 'forest management' has already been part of the technical arsenal of Indians for a couple of thousand years, one faction of the debate's antagonists proposes to promote the sensible exploitation of the forest by recognizing that bans on logging are unrealistic (security overheads too high) and that what should be done is to allow the business community to organize the felling of the forest. This amounts to little more than an increasingly administered (for instance by World Bank technocrats) replication of what is already occurring. Leave it to the experts. This style of forest management is presented in the World Bank's Tropical Forest Action Plan:[13]

> Properly used and managed, the tropical forests constitute a massive potential source of energy, a powerful tool in the fight to end hunger, a strong basis for generating economic wealth and social development, and a storehouse of genetic resources to meet future needs.

Aside from asking 'what else is new', the sceptical listener might well wonder who is to be the beneficiary of all this nature lucre.

On the other wing is a more diffuse group which consists not only of 'leave the forest alone' lobbyists, but also of researchers who, unlike a number of spokespeople for 'the rain forest', have some practical experience of forest management. The lobbyists in favour of leaving the forest intact can point to the historical record: the business community's commitment to the rather diminished profit levels which result from development go-slow policies is not exemplary. In fact, it stinks. Taking into account the fact that much of current Amazonian development is already administered by this selfsame business/bank community and is hardly replete with enviable examples of environmental sensitivity, it is not surprising that when asked who's afraid of the big bad wolf, a lot of little piggies put up their hands.

Researchers on this side of the forest management debate are themselves divided. On one hand there are those who recognize that there is very little standing between the present situation and even wider-scale efforts at securing forest resources, and one view adopted is that the only way to mitigate these effects is by demonstrating that the forest contains profit possibilities other than those residing in timber extraction. Publications from the Kayapó Project headed by Posey have presented versions of this argument. Another research project which aims to prove that there is more in the forest than money-trees is Project Combu near Belém, where botanist Anthony Anderson (and forester John Rombold) have worked with a group of *caboclos* whose income is almost entirely forest-derived, but comes from forest products (primarily *açai* – a palm fruit) other than timber. The viability of this livelihood depends on managing the forest by selective and diverse forms of extraction.

Unfortunately, the forest management notion has already been appropriated by First World agencies whose basic argument is that management is too important to be left to locals. What does represent an advance within the local-expertise forest management proposals and those of the 'intactness' lobby is the recognition that the structure of the contemporary forest is in many respects a social product. Any reasonable proposals for sustained yield, forest management, wide-base resource use (and other euphemisms) development must take account of the fact that the forest environment is subordinate to the social environment. It is noteworthy that even in these days of hyper-consciousness of Amazonia so much otherwise well-informed literature on the rain forest should rarely deign to mention its actual inhabitants. (For more on this debate, see Chapter XI.)

There's a document called *World Bank and IDA – Questions and Answers* which – overlooking, if permitted, the human toll exacted on behalf of the organization – is pretty funny. The issue I have, a collectable September 1971, is a sub-species of the agony aunt confessional: the Bank asks itself some tough questions and provides suitably no-punches-pulled answers. The format is: *27/ How often do you beat your wife?*

> The WB does not beat its wife. Wives are treated under the special provisions agreed in Geneva in 1970 concerning the disbursement of domestic funds under the rules of which all wife-beating is confined to member countries contributing more than 36% per annum of funds earmarked for Dinner Expenses. Under such rules, wifebeating is virtually disallowed.

Nonsense of this kind is presented po-faced, and the document as a whole is certainly one of the minor unread documents of our time. The Bank has no serious opponents (it is the *World* Bank after all). What you try to do with the Bank is make it answer to the public, a task to which it responds with the alacrity one has come to expect of an institution so sure of its place and mission that it is known simply as 'the Bank'.

The Bank responded to environmentalist lobbying in the 1970s by appointing personnel responsible for reviewing the environmental impact of Bank-funded projects, a gesture which ensured many sleep-filled nights on the PR front (about ten years' worth). However, it apparently achieved little in the real world, judging even by the Bank's rather sanctimonious but appropriately detached recent admission that environmental considerations have had too low a priority.[14] Staffed by upwards of one to five people,[15] the environmental impact unit was responsible for reviewing hundreds of projects a year, and did so at the end of the assessment chain, thereby ensuring a pass rate that would satisfy the most parsimonious quality-control manager. It also hired one of the most competent ecologists it could find, a man whose credentials and skills are so impeccable that many critics are eaten before they're out of the pan.

Appendix 3A of the 1987 edition of the *World Bank Annual Report* shows that environmental considerations did not rate an officer or department director. Appendix 3B, however, which lists officers and department directors after reorganization (30 June 1987), contains an entry for 'Director, Environment Department', but the position is vacant (as are only three other of the eighty officer and director positions). Over the past few years the Bank has found itself under enough NGO pressure to be forced to review its 'commitment to environmental problems' (though it is careful to merge them with others under the catch-all title 'the vicious cycle of poverty and environmental degradation').

This interest in things the colour of money may be viewed, charitably, as a bullet-biting exercise. But as even Mrs Thatcher has come out of the closet and donned the green shroud, one might reasonably wonder if the choice of the green bullet is made over one with a slightly heavier charge. Two examples of eco-political collaboration are Indonesia and Brazil, and horrendous as the eco-effects of these projects have been, the fact that both development strategies have been pursued in concert with repressive political goals has not escaped everyone's attention. What's likely to change in the near future is that the eco-excuse will be increasingly relevant to the politics of necessity. The choice after all will be: Look, the future of the planet is too important to permit our worrying too much about political rights. Let's get our priorities straight.

Poolside at the Hilton may not be such a bad place to button up against the chill. And maybe the guy with rug has the right idea: just because the fact is bald doesn't mean you can't still cover it up.

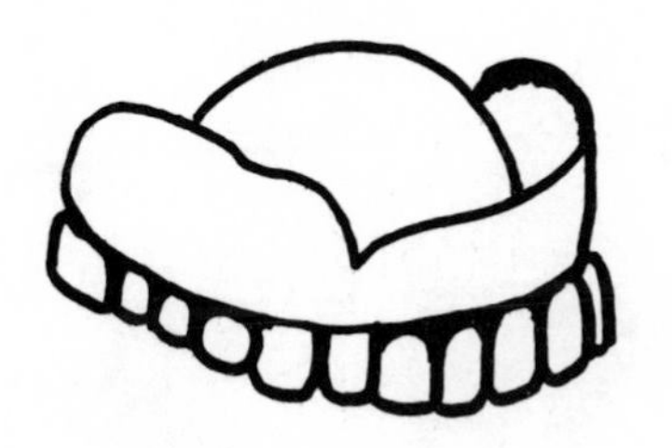

VI

SANTARÉM
IN THE SHADOW OF EDSEL

Santarém was a semi-scheduled stop for our fact-finding mission. I had been away a long time and things Santareno had assumed a well-rounded memory shape which I did not feel comfortable disturbing. My reluctance to return was reinforced by the difficulty of getting there by boat. At the end of the July holiday boats were overcrowded, the queues were many hours long, and the food was bound to be inedible except under conditions of violent hunger. Ocean was a counterpressure, however, and his enthusiasm for river travel had all the signs of dementia. Even after the trip to Soure he showed no willingness to believe that three or four days sitting in a hammock was one of those experiences which can be imagined as well as it can be endured.

I was also dismayed at the prospect of finding myself on a Möbius strip, acting out a postmodern refutation of Thomas Wolfe: not only can you easily go home again, you can't leave once you're back. Furthermore, I had seen a 1982 article in the *New York Times*, 'The Sorcery of the Amazon', which advised travellers not to settle for anything except the Hotel Tropical: 'It is air-conditioned, and has two swimming pools and a restaurant that specializes in tambaqui and other local fish. The hotel will book city tours, tours to beaches or a two-hour river excursion to the junction of the Amazon and Tapajós rivers.' That was about as much advice as I could take.

Tambaqui probably sounds pretty exotic, but really, this is like recommending that when in Texas, check out the chili con carne. I couldn't find the second pool at the Tropical. It must be the one people swim in. In 1976, as I looked out from the rear balcony, all I could see was a local photographer doing a fashion shoot. In 1988, they were at it again. I leave the Heart of Pankness for a decade and return to see a local yokel instructing parvenu jailbait how to strike absurd 'swimsuit' poses. This is not a Möbius strip, this is just pure Möbius.

Santarém is the third largest Amazonian city in a two-city race, Belém and Manaus being win and place respectively. After winning the flip of a coin, I managed to haul Ocean aboard a jet for Santarém. As we landed and I was fitting in my Santarém memory chip I saw from the window scenes which were not recognizably Santareno. There were trees, for one thing, and no houses.

Until the late 1970s, Santarém's airport was just shy of downtown, a great convenience and of limited aural damage potential as hardly any planes landed there. The new airport was kilometres outside of town towards the Tapajós edge of the plateau. The cab which took us into town was driven by a man who chuckled over all the changes which had occurred in the previous ten years. 'Yeah, it's really growing. Lots of activity.'

One thing which had grown in particular was the use of asphalt. What had previously been a rutted grid of cement-like laterite had been transformed into something approaching the seriously smooth. Whatever the real reasons for this infrastructural largesse it could not have gone unnoted that during the period when Santarém was a National Security Area and overseen by military forces the one thing which everyone approved of was that they had tarmacked the roads. They might have been an invading force (few would have dared say so even if they'd thought it) and they might have been the hand inside the Prefect's glove, but even so, smooth roads were crowd-pleasers.

The last time I had stayed there, a room in the Mocorongo Hotel had cost very little. The driver, still chuckling, informed me that the Mocorongo was long gone and had been a dump anyway, certainly beneath our consideration. The spectre of urban development quickly reared its head again as we approached my old house. Gut rehab with extreme prejudice – it wasn't there. We'd lived in it for more than a year, guarded at the front by a chained monkey – Christian name, Chico – and enclosed rear and sides by fences and palms. The house

was stucco, had two rooms, a standpipe under the cooking awning, and a jerry-built shower cleverly positioned in the middle of what seemed to be a migratory route for troops of fire ants. A neighbour's marmoset visited in the mornings to clean insects from the rafters. When it rained heavily, a stream passed through the garden and the bolt-hole became a rivercraft.

It was located on a political joke. The triangle of turf in front of the house was laid around a trio of cast figures alleged to represent the three branches of the armed services. It would be nice to believe that the lifelessness of the figures was a sculptural insult, but there are other examples of this sculptor's work scattered around town which suggest a degenerative optical disorder rather than subtle political insight. The accompanying plaque commemorated the coup of 1964 and the three figures were known as The Three Stooges. Now they had disappeared, whether ripped from their base with the return of civilian rule or torn up in a fit of aesthetic pique I don't know. I asked the driver, just to hear him chuckle.

Santarém is a place which is not noticed very much. It was the site of one of the largest Indian (Tapajós) settlements at the time Europeans first passed down the river, but they have been erased (there have been no Tapajós Indians for about a century), and what examples of Tapajós culture might remain lie under the city. Santarém is a place people pass through on their way west (immigrants) or east/west (tourists), not off the main routes by any means, but hardly a major pulse-taking site either. It's on various borders: geologically, those of both the Brazilian and Guiana shields; geographically, lost somewhere between Lower and Middle Amazonia. In terms of 'national integ-ration', it is connected to the Transamazonica via a spur, and is considered a site of upland colonization, though it remains the focal point for river-based inhabitants. It doesn't epitomize anything. It's a collection of default values. Returning twelve years later, it's difficult to get too excited over the concept 'social change' as exemplified by Santarém.

It's terrible to describe a place, especially one you have some attachment to, as the urban equivalent of a used car (and in this case an Edsel), but . . . Santarém is best known outside Amazonia or Brazil through its various foreign connections, illuminated briefly by the attentions of modern conquistadors: the naturalists Wallace and Bates, US Confederate refugees, and Henry Ford. Wallace and Bates mention Santarém frequently in, respectively, *A Narrative of Travels on the Amazon and Rio Negro* and *The Naturalist on the River Amazon*, and while commending its climate, neither gives the impression that he will be racked with sorrow upon departure.

The connection between Santarém and US Civil War refugees is more unusual. It's truly a minor form of celebrity, but one which still delivers a bit of cachet to some of the older Santareno families. The central characters in this are members of the Riker family, Missouri Confederates who left the US after the war in search of a place where they could maintain themselves in the manner to which they thought they were accustomed. From all accounts, things didn't work out terribly well, although Santarenos don't hold it against them. There are Santarenos who still correspond with Confederate brethren up north.

Henry Ford's story is better known. Although he, like the Indians and the Rikers *et al*, did not see his intentions fulfilled, his monument on the outskirts of Santarém is far and away the most durable (or at least most commonly cited) link with the world beyond and acts as a reminder of what happens to those whose eyes are bigger than their stomachs.

There are numerous, mainly sketchy accounts of Ford's Amazonian scheme(s),[1] most of them pursuing a 'Ford's Folly' line: North-American industrialist tries to transplant factory techniques to the tropics and takes a bath. There is some truth to that line, but it is misused. Instead of appreciating why it is that the form of extraction attempted by Ford (and others looking for their own personalized El Dorados, like Ludwig with his Jarí project) was inappropriate for the ends sought (jungle bulk-buying) and not in any simple sense plainly wrong, the story is presented as a tale of Man Beaten Back By Nature (Read All About It). Such treatment merely reinforces the myth of the forbidding forest/amazing Amazon/green hell/land of adventure where men are men, women are welcome and children are kidnapped by Indians etc., etc.

The Amazonian rubber industry – or 'boom' in the naturalizing jargon of those for whom social processes are better expressed as subservient to remote and mysterious processes – began roughly in the latter half of the nineteenth century and ended during the First World War. It was based on tapping naturally distributed trees, but with the successful plantation cultivation of the major type of rubber tree, *hevea brasiliensis*, in South-east Asia, the monopoly was dissolved overnight.[2] South-east Asian plantations, however, found their output rising just as the First World War was constricting the market. The rubber glut at the end of the war led to the formation of an Anglo–South-east Asian cartel and prompted renewed interest in developing plantation-based production in Amazonia. Ford's venture was a combination of corporate planning – of the kind for which the US has since become increasingly infamous as its central position in the world economy is eaten away – and public relations eco-bumbling. Ford hoped not only to be able to produce cheap rubber, but also to enhance the vertical integration of the Ford Motor Company, i.e. make their own tyres.

On the eco-front,[3] Ford was at the mercy of a number of managers and sharpies who were, respectively, under-trained in tropical agriculture and over-trained in spotting generously stuffed corporate wallets. The one million hectares of land which Ford bought on the Tapajós could probably have been acquired for close to nothing (the man who chose the spot just happened to have purchased it earlier under a Brazilian government incentive scheme) and was less than ideal for purposes other than lining the seller's pocket. A few years later, in 1934, Fordlândia operations were dropped, and the plantation moved downstream to Belterra, close to Santarém. At the new site efforts were renewed to combat a leaf blight which had thus far dramatically disrupted efforts to establish a rubber factory in the field. Ultimately, the leaf blight proved resistant even to the blandishments of FoMoCo cash and early fears in the South-east Asian cartel that a New World rival was on the horizon proved unfounded. Planting at the Belterra site proceeded at so slow a rate that it would have taken 1,000 years for the whole concession to be placed under cultivation.

Much of the blame for Ford's disaster has been attached to that traditional nemesis of failed entrepreneurs, labour; and although responsibility for the failure has been convincingly shown to have resulted from many factors amongst which labour is virtually inconsequential, it is a myth which endures and is employed currently to help justify the hi-tech/low-labour character of contemporary large-scale projects. In fact, wages paid by Ford were three times higher than those on offer in Belém at the time, and living and working conditions in Belterra – potable water, electricity, schools, a hospital, eight-hour working day – were vastly superior, according to Dean. The real problem was that after thirteen years, $10.5 million, and the planting of 3,650,000 trees, there was little rubber to be tapped and no one had a convincing excuse (being 'beaten by nature' was not on the agenda in those go-go times).

The impact of Fordlândia/Belterra on Santarém was modest in terms of transforming the local economy, but of considerable consequence in transforming Santarenos' perceptions of future possibilities. Like the US Confederates' efforts, the Ford failure conferred on Santarém the air of a bride abandoned at the altar. Many years later, in the 1970s, the long-delayed opening of the Curua-Una hydroelectric dam east of

town only confirmed this dismal reputation; and even the completion of the Santarém–Cuiabá highway, bisecting the Transamazonica, was less an act of professed 'national integration' than a sluice whereby the miserable drop-outs from Transamazonica could slide into the relative comfort of a big town. All in all, Santarém lives within the shadows of others' failings, and while Santarenos display a degree of regional chauvinism, they are also realistic enough to recognize that in terms of the pie-in-the-sky promises thus far made, the track record leaves a lot to be desired.

The airport cabby (called into service here as the man in the street) displays a lot of this sort of disenchantment and ambivalence about what the future holds. This is not a 'cultural feature' of Santarém, it is simply a realistic assessment of what is likely to happen in Santarém (and elsewhere in Amazonia) based on what has happened so far.

As we drive along the airport road he notes with some pride that as a member of the army battalion of engineers he helped build both this and the Santarém–Cuiabá highway. The experience was horrific. A year of suffering, and for what? All the agricultural land has been wasted. We could have been the richest country in the world. His work party, he claims, was attacked by Indians, who killed a sergeant and a corporal. Others died of malaria and hepatitis.[4]

His spleen is shared out equally between the Brazilian government and foreign governments en masse, the former for being a pack of thieves and the latter for being the skilled beneficiaries of such thievery. Speaking of thieves, I ask about the governor. 'The worst.' And how will he do in the upcoming elections? 'He will win because he can pay more than anyone else.' And just for the record, a naive question about political opposition. A derisive snort: 'This country can't be managed by civilians, only the military, and they don't want to take it on again.' (This faith in the military option is shared, according to a poll taken in São Paulo in late 1987, by 32 per cent of the population.)

An example of good government, says the cabby, occurred in an unnamed African country which, having basically an English system (generic for 'good'), recently jailed, fined then executed an Englishman caught with two hundred grams of smoke. We finally sort this one out and settle on Malaysia as the more likely candidate and heroin the more likely substance, but these details are irrelevant. 'We need this in Brazil. We need a new constitution, one like the English constitution. It's a little country, no? You could fit two of them into the state of Pará, but it's still rich.' I mention that there is no constitution in Britain. 'What? Just the monarchy? Well, that's even better.'

There is a problem here: I am presenting the views, quite widely held I think, of a semi-literate, unskilled Amazonian and he sounds like a leader writer for *The Sun*. It would be a mistake, however, to think that the cabby sounds the way he does because he embodies the quality of *Sun*-ness. Where he's coming from, as people used to say in California, is a place racked by frustration of a very high order, a place where for twenty years the suspension of political rights was accompanied, quite logically, with the engineering of what now seems to be an unbridgeable gap between those with something – and a lot of something – and those with nothing.

His choice of abusable substances as an example of a desirable area for 'strong' government action was not casual. He, like many other Brazilians, has been subjected to a barrage of drug-menace hype. Amazonia, according to the cabby, is filled with cocaine labs. The north-east is covered with marijuana plantations. And, it goes without saying, the cities of Brazil are *de facto* ruled by a pharmacologically inspired and depraved population. 'Everybody knows this. The whole place is falling apart. Listen, I only have five years of schooling, but I can see things and I understand what's happening. I'm like a lot of people here. We want to do well, but what chance do we have?'

The cabby, for all his righteous grievance at being at the receiving end of a social system which specializes in placing poor people at the foot of a cascade of effluent and then complaining that they smell bad, is a close relation of Captain Cunnilingus and his friends – belly up against the polished mahogany of the Bar of Experts and dishing the truth on politics, football and sex. Coca production, which has slipped firmly into Amazonia, presents itself as the reasonable way for the reasonable peasant to go. According to Hecht, while maize might bring in $150 an acre, cocoa $150–200, and livestock a few dollars, coca will bring in $5,000–10,000 an acre. This does not mean a rush on places at English public schools, but it does mean the possibility of mitigating the poverty endemic in the region. In 1988, the north-east of Brazil, for example, (the source of many Amazonian smallholding 'pioneers') contained approximately 30 per cent of Brazil's population, yet accounted for only 15 per cent of its GDP. North-easterners have a life expectancy of fifty-one years (compared with a national average of sixty) and 45 per cent of them are illiterate. There also, 224 large farms control more land than 1.7 million smallholders, while two million peasants control no land at all. These are motivated Amazonian 'pioneers', and in spite of the cabby's finger-wagging it doesn't take a cunning peasant, just a rational one, to see how the books balance.

While we're on a numbers jag, in the country as a whole, 60 per cent of workers earn less than $100 per month, this in the eighth largest economy in the world. *Brazil 2000*, a national social profile published in 1986, recorded that the richest 1 per cent of Brazilians earn as much as the poorest 50 per cent (which amounts to 13 per cent of total income). Put another way, 1.4 million Brazilians make as much as 65 million of their less well-off fellow citizens. And just to give some idea of what pluralistic poverty really means, 15 million Brazilians do not even officially exist because their parents could not come up with the

five dollars necessary to register their births. Without birth certificates they remain non-persons.[5]

In spite of what the cabby is struggling to get off his chest, drug business in Santarém is far above street level. Although the line in newspaper stories between a simple thief and a druggie is a slim one, the real action is upstream on the Tapajós, where the cocaine moguls have entered the gold business to launder their money. Itaituba, the main upriver commercial centre, is more deserving than most of the 'asshole of a turkey' appellation – it's so unpleasant that even the gold traders have shifted their operations back to Santarém. Itaituba's main product, aside from gold, usury, and a nice line in Purgatory simulation, is mercury-laced effluent, a by-product of gold-mining. The Tapajós has never been a particularly bountiful river, but the mercury is putting paid to what little it offered. The presence of such a concentration of industrial pollutants on the Tapajós is hard to take in. It's as though having wandered for months across pristine Arctic tundra you come across a Kentucky Fried Chicken container filled with plutonium.

Around the corner from Santarém, tucked inside the mouth of the Tapajós, is a village called Alter do Chão which in microcosmic form illustrates the central importance of the class struggle in modern Amazonia to the issues that currently obsess the eco-lobby in Europe and North America. Once a deep coma village (it didn't see the twentieth century coming around the bend and was on life-support for quite some time), it is now the site of the country-home *ne plus ultra* of Santarém's *haute bourgeoisie*. Precisely the same forces which have led to the mercury pollution of the Tapajós have resulted in the emergence of Alter do Chão as the spot that's hot. The forces derive from the growth of a parvenu faction in Santarém – one which has to a considerable degree displaced the older traditional mercantile parasites, although there is some overlap – whose wealth is based on Santarém's position at the gateway to the gold-mines of Jacareacanga/ Itaituba (although the opening of the Transamazonica diminished Santarém's trading importance). But as elsewhere in the apparatus of Amazonian gold production, the place to be is not thigh deep in mud waiting for nuggets as big as hens' eggs to fall into the basket, but to be supplying the goods and services required by those waiting to catch a glimpse of the chicken. These supply-side operators belong to the Santarém Yacht Club and have beachside country houses in Alter do Chão. As their ability to pay fees at the club improves and the lavishness of their country retreats advances, so will the aqua-domain increasingly resemble an experiment in chemistry.

When June and I had been living in Santarém, a Frenchman called Julien pulled up, the parachute spinnaker on his yacht having failed to attract enough wind to take it further. He and a friend had crossed the Atlantic from the Azores, then moored for a while at the Belém Yacht Club. Downstream, at Almeirim, he and his companion Michele (she flew to Belém, a sensible move) had met a Franciscan brother on the verge of packing it in after twenty years' service. Based in Santarém, Father John had invited J & M to visit him there. Living a few hundred yards away were these two other gringos, making a perfect guest list for brunch.

Father John was in crisis. Accused of being a Charismatic and rolling down the aisle while sermonizing, he was being retired to Omaha. Although we had lived within shouting distance of each other for a year or so, there had been no contact. The assembly of guests was peculiar enough, but that paled in the face of the menu.

Getting from our crib to John's involved walking across the little grass triangle on which were displayed the poorly executed statues of representatives of the three branches of the Brazilian armed services, the earlier mentioned *praça das tres patetas*. The street was lined with mango trees and a mixture of decrepit stucco and thatch houses, some with gardens, a couple with fruit stalls. Emerging on to the square which embraces the church, we were on the verge of stepping into the world as conceived and constructed by Sears Roebuck, Montgomery Ward and Henry Ford. Being intractably naive, I figured that anyone who had spent twenty years in Amazonia must have forsaken most of his roots material, but far from having gone native Father John was still locked into Velveeta cheese and cocktail gherkins. From his generously proportioned and eclectically stocked Frigidaire he produced item after item bearing the marks of a serious late-night shopping habit satisfiable only at Food Giant, Gristedes, El Rancho, Safeway and other monuments to the big belly. That morning I had brewed coffee over an open fire and here I was being offered chilled Cheesewhip and whipped cream from a nozzle. Like a few stuffed olives with that waffle? What about some more strawberries? Come around for fondue tomorrow?

Perplexed was the look on the faces of Michele and Julien: Who are these lunatics supping with the mad priest? This is all very nice, it said in the cartoonist's balloons in the background, but we have crossed

the Atlantic and sailed up the Amazon in our home-made boat and now we are eating *le brunch* with Americans so heavily addicted to convenience food that no expense is spared in ensuring a continuity in diet even while camped in lower Amazonia. This is serious refusal to face cultural detoxification.

What was on offer at Father John's was a little corner of the American Dream (pre-OPEC, pre-privatization of the money markets, pre-being chased out of South-East Asia) which is part of the Amazonian development package. On a small scale there is the appropriation of Disney motif paper plates and cups[6] at children's birthday parties, as well as the ubiquity of the 'Pepsi Generation'. Brand-name fixation is the base currency in the fetish battle for hearts and minds, and almost everywhere you look there are juxtapositions of local forms and up-to-the-minute image imports.

I'm afraid that discussion of the spread of mass cultural artefacts and symbols has built into it a fairly heavy sleep factor. One more photograph (caption: 'It's the Real Thing') of a tribesman with a bone in his nose quaffing a Coke and you're still none the wiser.[7] Much liberal indignation has been focussed on the evils of commercial culture, the way its brightly painted detritus pollutes 'traditional' societies. By way of liberal reaction, primitivism and 'ethnic arts' are promoted as somehow superior, untarnished cultural products.[8] This argument is replicated in many seemingly different consumer spheres: the 'superiority' of cotton over polyester (and all possible extensions – wood over plastic, Tuscany over Costa del Brit, and on and on); in the popular-music branch of the culture industry, 'World Music's' authenticity is supposed to represent a genuine relationship between ethnic performer and world audience. This is all familiar territory to experienced consumers, fashion victims, and representatives of the taste-developed end of the First World cultural sphere. When you talk to representatives from other spheres, say 'French' Paul, the surreptitious knee-squeezer, there is astonishment – Get hip, man, get modern – and not a little indignation that the well-travelled visitor is so seriously retro. The point here is that the high-culture (loose usage) critique of the predatory expansion of the worst on offer from the overdeveloped consumer centre is contradictory: on one hand it wishes to say, 'Look, all this stuff you're taking on board is garbage, it is not what "civilization" really has to offer'; but on the other hand, it deigns to offer this view on the grounds that it has the authority (as provider of all these representations of its culture) to attribute real meaning to these objects and images, and reveal the misconceptions of the uninitiated. The contradiction is revealed in the answer to the following question: If all this stuff we (the unformed frontier marginals) are taking on board, all this cultural garbage, is so far removed from what is really true and important about the offerings of your civilization, why are you getting so het up about it? Well, the reason is that it's really important, it's integral to the myth of culture and absolutely essential if the distinction between us and the other is to be maintained. It's embarrassing and annoying, apparently, to see even civilization's garbage simply appropriated without any appreciation of the logic according to which it has been assembled and configured within the larger scheme of things.

An example of this untoward appropriation, albeit not a very straightforward one, is the Santarém Yacht Club. When we first arrived in Santarém, the yacht club was just getting off the ground. In fact, when we left Santarém it was still getting off the ground, if the presence of yachts is any criterion. Physically, the yacht club was a row of poured concrete moorings around a roofed bar and dancing area, a *maloca*. Socially, it featured more prominently than the nautical lacunae might suggest. It was the élite club for those who had grasped the future, although what took place there was little different from

what occurred in Santarém's numerous other social clubs: people of similar class or residential or occupational orientation carved out a little space where they could do business after business hours.

It is defiantly oblivious to the irony which embraces the notion of a yacht club as processed by the First World cosmopolitan, for whom a yacht club is a sub-type of social club which emerges after a relatively long period of cultural speciation and is positioned within a grid which also contains golf, tennis, bridge, squash and beach clubs – all markers of the careful domestication of leisure pursuits for which the good life of advanced civilization is so revered. You cannot, according to this received cultural wisdom, do as the Santarém Yacht Club does, have a club with no yachts and locate it in a neighbourhood of squatter settlement.

For most people to whom I have described the yacht club, or even mentioned it, the very idea is comic and/or disorienting – 'You can't be doing fieldwork in a place five hundred miles up the Amazon which has a yacht club.' It confounds belief not because it is a physical or social impossibility, but because it has no precedent in First Worlders' expectations of this part of the Third World.

Within the apparatus of the yacht club, members carried on doing pretty much what they had done before without the benefit of the new institutional trappings. People ate and drank, had parties, waterskied, and went out in power boats from which big-game hunters could blast anything foolish enough not to recognize that a boat full of people who didn't have to hunt in order to live was a boat full of people ready to shoot anything which looked remotely in range.

If I approach this whole question of yacht clubs in Amazonia from the perspectives provided by modern social anthropology, I find myself addressing a number of disbelieving factions. On the one hand there are those for whom the presence of an interior Amazonian yacht club, properly, and let's not quibble, is about as far removed from the agenda as, say, the colour of the Queen Mother's latest hat. On the other hand – while we're still counting – there is an eco-domain group for whom Amazonia is pretty devoid of all but the grossest social ills and to whom actual Amazonian societies (i.e. those which include Captain Cunnilingus and crew) are an irrelevance which will eventually find a place (if they're really lucky) in the archaeological record. On the third hand – since we're still counting – there are the modern chroniclers who are only too happy to find evidence which supports the notion of cultural homogeneity. If it looks like a Madonna T-shirt, walks like a Madonna T-shirt . . . we must be home.

Since we've stopped counting hands, I might as well introduce number four. Number four says that what happens at the Yacht Club isn't any of your business (or mine, but they had the grace to let me hang around and get a feel for the place). I didn't feel any more comfortable hanging around the late Clube do Santarém, to give it its proper name, than I would hanging around any other, but at least at the late Clube it was evident that everyone was making it up as they went along. If asked, I'd recommend burying the place, but I won't be and they wouldn't anyway because they've committed themselves to 'the future' and the Late Clube is one of the vehicles taking them there. In the future, by another view, all this stuff around the edges will disappear. Mercury schmercury, I hear the old ones say. That cabby should be happy to have a job at all. And so on. All the bad stuff will be consumed by the engines of progress and deposited elsewhere. But most observers have pencilled in a different scenario, one in which the conspicuous consumption which the Yacht Club represents has a vastly shorter half-life than club members would like to believe; and if, as some observers believe, mercury pollution in Amazonia is on such a scale that it is affecting hundreds of thousands of people, then third and fourth hands jokes may have an unpleasant basis in fact.

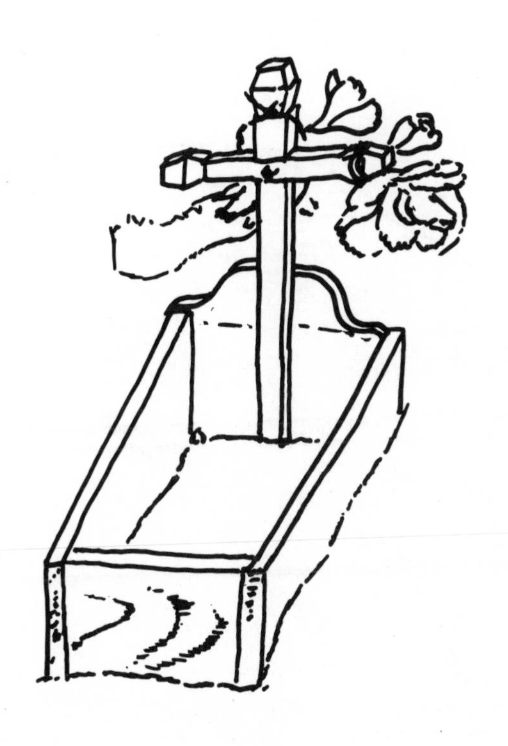

VII

LITTLE MONSTERS

Ocean and I are in relaxed tourist mode, hanging around the central market trying to acclimatize. Ocean is beginning to tune in to the concept of wildlife. His main object of desire is the *urubú*, the street-cleaning vulture whose studied pose is that of a bitter and twisted bachelor uncle – standing quietly in the parlour corner, but coming forward quickly enough when food is laid out. The market surrounds a fish hall in which is displayed a range of river and marine specimens, some recognizably fishlike, others looking more like prototype dinosaurs which fell off the evolutionary conveyor belt. Among the most colourful specimens is the piranha, the poor fish burdened with more symbolic weight than any animal should have to endure.

> **11.5 Piranha.** Bradford Dillman, Heather Menzies lead jolly Jaws spoof, made in 1978, with a mutant freshwater fish picnicing off unwary river bathers. News headlines.
> (*Guardian*, Friday 3 June 1988)

Why is the piranha so appealing? Two reasons, I think: as Lévi-Strauss might have reminded Radcliffe-Brown, it's good to watch film actors being eaten by them and therefore they are good to eat. Second, its big mouth is not just hot air. It's a stand-up kind of fish, a motormouth with menace.

There is, viewed from the comfort of the Barcalounger, also the appeal of comic overachievement: what makes the fish so endearing is the ludicrousness of a hand-size, hyperactive carnivore being capable, as pulps and Bs would have it, of stripping the flesh from cow or human in a matter of minutes. The closest domestic analogue would be a frenzied assault by massed budgerigars or a troupe of Mexican hairless chihuahuas.

In Amazonia, the piranha's real danger profile is pretty slight and the fish is better known as a nice pan-fry or barbecue item, easier to catch than be caught by. The crucial symbolic underlay of its celebrity is its carnivorousness. Just as lampreys in England and Wales were esteemed for their meat-like flesh (thus making it possible to fall off the Lenten wagon while seeming to adhere to a restricted piscatorial menu), piranhas are usefully ambiguous: if head-on cannibalism is too much, the piranha provides a gastronomic half-way house, anthropophagy at a civilized distance, having a neighbour for lunch.

Far more threatening – although hardly a common aquatic mugger – is the candiru. Among the many unfortunate consequences of overconsumption of Biblical texts is the fact that the lexicon of officially exotic beasts is limited to those easily rendered in cartoon form ascending the gangplank of the Ark. Excluded are a great number of interesting species. There is the frog used in various recipes for *curare*, a plant extract which, applied to the tip of a blowpipe dart, relaxes the muscles of the struck monkey so that it falls from its tree rather than rotting uselessly in the canopy. And there is the aforementioned candiru, a tiny (matchstick-sized) fish with barbs on its gill covers. It likes a warm place to hide, say a penis, vagina, nostril or anus, and is not removed with a gentle tug. I've never seen one of these things, nor have I met anyone with direct experience of its effects. But like everyone who has heard of the fish I'm something of an expert, thanks to the fact that almost everyone who has heard of it has written about it, and I believe everything I read.

The degree of fascination with the fish is out of proportion to the actual danger. Leaving aside – just for the sake of comparison – the far greater likelihood of being run over by a skateboard or hit by a falling piano, even the common or garden threats on offer in Amazonia – malaria, chagas, schistosomiasis – seem to pale in the presence of the candiru. Obviously, he says, poking the ground with his cane, it is the candiru's specific fascination with an organ of great significance that enhances its celebrity. The emasculating ability of the candiru is the real finger on the volume knob in as much as – in one of the most commonly cited scenarios – the fish may only be extracted by sacrificing the host itself. At some point the afflicted has to decide whether the pain is extreme enough to justify the analgesic which spells *sayonara* to the organ of great significance, and at the hands – it goes without saying – of a knife(rusty)-wielding dreg. If you're not man enough to stand the pain, you don't deserve to keep it. Faust had it easy.

The interest in candiru may also simply be a result of the fish's perverse predator profile. Sharks bite, rays sting, the octopus fondles and cuddles and gets the beak in, moray eels do a fair imitation of piranha, barracudas bump and bite, but the candiru is subversive, literally strikes below the belt, and pointing Percy at the porcelain becomes more an act of faith than an autonomic obligation.

Other celebrated aquatic species include the electric eel whose eyes are bigger than its stomach. The eel's power provision (500–1,000 volts) is capable of stunning prey – cattle and humans for example – far larger than it can consume. There are also a number of shark-sized catfish reputed to have savoured the delights of human flesh.

The most appreciated of the large edible fish is the pirarucu, a fierce-looking but relatively benign animal whose preference for nesting in lakeside shallows has made it vulnerable to the harpoon-bearing canoeist. Specimens of ten feet and 400 pounds are still captured. In addition to its tasty flesh, the pirarucu also provides scales of a size and quality permitting their use, *à la* Dr Scholl, as callus buffers and nail files.

The most dangerous fish by far, however, is the terrestrial *tuberão* – the shark – the land speculator for whom Amazonia is a realm of untold incentives and speculative possibilities. The terrestrial proclivities of *tuberoes* are matched by another of the larger aquatic species, the *boto* or river dolphin. Two types of *boto* are common throughout the Amazon – the *tucuxi,* which looks like a marine dolphin, and the pink river *boto* – but in spite of their abundance they are definitely off-limits as far as hot meals are concerned.[1]

Not only forbidden food, *botos* are also capable of assuming human form, typically dressed as *Miami Vice* extras in white suits and borsalinos. They are particularly irresistible to comely virgins. For a young girl a quite reasonable excuse for not boarding the boat back to work is menstruation and the enhanced susceptibility to the lures of the *boto* that it brings.

In Amazonia, belief in *botos'* trans-species activities is a serious topic and although stories of their quayside posing are told with a smile, there is no doubting the sacredness of the *boto* domain. Although not eaten, *botos* are hunted for their eyes and genitalia, which are used as amulets by adherents of spirit possession cults common to Amazonia and Brazil. While the male *boto* is mythologized as a riverine entrant into human affairs, the female is, perhaps only apocryphally, the victim of human reciprocity. A friend (former Franciscan novice turned pimp and compensating for years of carnal deprivation by structuring his secular recovery entirely around sexual themes) told the widely recounted tale of the fisherman who slept with a *bota* which had got entangled in his nets. On a later fishing trip, a baby *boto* hopped into the canoe saying, 'Hi, dad.'

Although this kind of belief is a common starting point for anthropological digression, studies of *caboclo* classification schemes (involving flora and fauna as well as such supernatural entities as the *cobra grande*, *curupira* and the *tapire-iauara*) are not terribly developed. Maybe one of the reasons for this is that when people talk about *botos* it sounds too much like listening to discussions about the origins of Santa Claus. The inescapable image is of tumescent dolphins cruising the riverfront, magnetizing pre-pubescent Amazonian genitalia and generating classificatory disorder. The *boto*'s ambiguous character reflects an accommodation to principles of classification which clearly steer the *boto* into the fish class (and indeed *botos* are, in the vernacular, 'just another fish'). On the other hand, possession of salient fish qualities cannot obscure the presence of significant human attributes: live birth, breathing, pink skin as well as, of course, a commitment to polymorphous perversity.

Although the *boto* and beliefs associated with it are prominent aspects of *caboclo* culture, it's hard to go on from there and present a social apparatus which can confidently be identified and described. It is hardly a victorious culture (if it were, there would be no need to 'conquer' Amazonia, an endeavour national politicians are constantly proposing); rather, it is an assemblage of leftovers. There is nothing as useful or comforting as an origin myth for *caboclo* culture. For Indians, Europeans provided one by transposing the Greek myth of Scythian women who removed the right breast to facilitate the use of a bow and arrow (*amazos* means 'without a breast'). With its connotations of aggression and self-dismemberment, this was hardly a propitious send-off for Amazonia. *Caboclo* culture emerged as a combination of various despoiled Amerindian cultures, the various colonial enclaves that replaced them (no one of which is so dominant regionally that it can be spoken of as archetypal) and a received, naturalistic wisdom that defined Amazonia as an assembly of rivers, trees, animals and equatorial exotica. Because *caboclo* culture is so amorphous a thing, beliefs associated with it tend to be shoved into a storage locker labelled 'folk culture' and left there, emerging only when they can be used to illustrate some general point about New World syncretism. (The veteran example of this process is provided by Haitian voodoo.[2]) Maybe a better way of putting this is to say that rather than being amorphous, structureless and in most respects incapable of humming a simple tune, *caboclo* culture has too many structures – traces of several histories which overlap and interpenetrate and generally misbehave, making it difficult to get a grip on guiding principles. *Botos* hark back to the abominations of Leviticus and in that sense are 'proper' (*cf* Douglas) quarry, but since they are known to haunt the quayside in gigolo whites they move downmarket on the folk-object scale. In real life, they also scramble for space in the symbolic free-fire zone where the Church and various non-aligned belief systems make their pitches for new constituents. At one point, for example, while I was living in Santarém, the cathedral's display cases of saintly figurines had to be closed to the public because too many Santarenos were attending church, but not for mass: they were ignoring the Big Three in favour of minor-league patron saints.

This confusion of religious priorities is common and revealed nowhere better than in the practice of *umbanda*. When attending (in the name of science only) spirit-possession workouts in Santarém and locked at night into Santa Barbara's sweatbox while the mediums tried to send letters poste restante to the panoply of Catholic, Indian and Yoruban spirits, I used to keep my eye on a particular item in the altar display – a plastic doll's-house-sized TV set with an image of a Mona Lisa-smiling Jesus. It reminded me, in circumstances bound at either extreme by boredom and trepidation, that I was still in a familiar place – that is, where the distinction between religion and commodity is vague, to say the least.

The impression of an erstaz folk culture operating on the fringes is hardly unusual, but typically such folk cultures are represented as interlopers, perhaps evidence of resistance, as in the case of Rastafarianism in Britain – or Mormonism in the Rocky Mountains, for that matter. *Umbanda* (or *macumba*) in places like Santarém or Belém doesn't have that alternative feel. Rather, it's part of the mainstream, not 'official' perhaps, but certainly not optional. *Umbanda* crosses over confidently into desanctification of supposedly untouchable domains. Church officials, for example, deny that *umbandistas* can be practising

Nas ruas de Belém,
o Círio

Catholics, but among *umbandistas* themselves, no problem: sacrifice a chicken to Exu (the devil) at midnight, and it's off to mass the next day. Since the Church can't exactly go with this flow to any degree (especially in an era when the Pope himself has brought back into Vatican HQ the operatives of Opus Dei), all it can do is resort to ever more rigid doctrinal poses. They may have lost control of the flock, but they can still beat them when they get within range.

European interest in syncretic culture systems in Brazil – of which *caboclo* culture is a rough gloss on one – pales in comparison with the nature study compulsion, and the plight of human Amazonia has only intermittently distracted a public gaze beamed in on flora and fauna of exotic demeanour. It is significant that the fascination of outsiders with Amazonian life forms centres on those species which have highly-charged implications for humanity's self-image, as king of the global campus: piranha and caymans because they eat people; parrots because they 'speak'; *botos* because they are pink, warm and foetal; candiru because they are (like David Cronenberg's venereal vectors) remorselessly attention-grabbing genital parasites; electric eels because they pre-date the Age of Duracell; monkeys because we covet their prehensile tails; pythons because, like electric eels, their eyes are bigger than their stomachs.

Unfortunately, viewing such animals is not a casual matter. Some visitors to Amazonia, trained through zoo visits to expect the big cat house to be just an ice-cream kiosk away from the aquarium, are distressed at the seeming shortage of high-profile wildlife. One of the reasons for this shortage is the absolute reduction in animal numbers due to the 'development' of Amazonia. Aside from that, different species tend to be widely dispersed and getting around to see them is not easy. My own perception of Amazonian life is flavoured primarily by Geoffrey Household's *Dance of the Dwarves* (in which demonic otters run riot terrorizing a solitary gringo whose tale comes in the form of a diary discovered after his demise) and the comments of Wallace and Bates – the former in his description of a vampire's attack on his brother's nose, poking out of the hammock and making an irresistible focus for the vampire's spinning, blood-lusty gyrations, and the latter in his no-punches-pulled, let's-call-a-spade-a-spade account of the same creature:

> Nothing in animal physiognomy can be more hideous than the countenance of this creature when viewed from the front,

> the large leathery ears standing out from the sides and top of the head, the erect spear-shaped appendage on the tip of the nose, the grin and the glisteny black eye, all combining to make up a figure that reminds one of some mocking imp of fable.

Somehow, 'mocking imp of fable' fails to justify the horror story build-up, but the impression of plug-ugliness still comes through.

Ocean's interest in visiting Santarém had been generated by stories a sculptor friend had told him of a visit to forests in Brazil where he was fortunate enough to view a number of suitably tropical big animals. Ocean, faced with a choice between the feeble imagery of my faunal experience of Amazonia and that of his sculpting friend chose, not too surprisingly, the latter.

My earlier time in Amazonia, while hardly animal-free, was not exactly riddled with dramatic encounters. *Tucuxi* and *botos* were commonly sighted: in forest far from human settlements there were various types of monkeys; an interior colonist once showed me a brace of peccaries he had managed to trap without wounding; we had a sloth (the smaller, three-toed variety, *bradypus tridactylus*) living in our garden for a while; there were plenty of vampires; the only cats I saw had been trapped and skinned (aside from a *maracajá* – which looks like a normal jaguar afflicted with psychosocial dwarfism – tethered in a jungle diorama in the lobby of Hotel Tropical); and there was a steady flow of strange-looking fish. But in the main, encounters with exotic or large beasts took place at the end of a fork. A *várzea* (flood plain) family I was staying with caught and cooked a manatee, a major gastronomical event but hardly eligible as a communing-with-nature entry. In fact the meal was the conclusion to a bit of petty poaching, perhaps not in the category of filching ivory or rhino horn, but hardly benign. As it happens, the prohibition on eating river turtles is widely overlooked and the real rule of the jungle is indistinguishable from that adhered to in North America during deer-hunting season: if it moves, shoot it. If it doesn't move, shoot it just in case.

Though pretty innocent of forest things, I was still obliged to take Ocean on his tour. The forest settlement on a plateau where I had worked ten years earlier can now be reached by bus. In the old days the only transport was in so-called parrot-perch trucks,[3] pick-ups with wooden benches installed in the back. They were cramped and uncomfortable and followed no schedule. Before that there was just a dirt track and produce came in on horseback.

Setting off from the central market in Santarém the truck used to pass through the squatter fringe of the city, letting passengers off at a complex of smallholdings and city-dwellers' weekend cottages before climbing the escarpment to the plateau. Although all the land on the margins of the road was being worked in some way, the secondary growth beyond was substantial, and at some points unmodified forest could be glimpsed. An hour later the road veered off to the west and deposited passengers in a *nordestino* (northeasterner) enclave called Mujuí.

Mujuí was colonized in the 1950s by immigrants from Ceará and in subsequent years wavelets of *nordestinos* settled in or passed through (Plan B). For many Santarenos, Mujuí epitomized a *nordestino* colony: the settlers were 'fierce', they were 'believers' (*crentes*, i.e. Protestants), they were rootless (and so likened to a bird, the *arigó*, which flits from bush to bush). Evidence for this caricature could be found anywhere, in town or out, but the ethnic stereotype reflected more the feeling that Santareno style (use of riverine and terrestrial resources according to seasonal climatic shifts) was being cramped by the rapid clearing of upland forest. There were some good grounds for this resentment, but being an upland farmer was hardly a cause for celebration. Hampered by shortages of water, roads, transport, literacy and familiarity with local eco-expertise, many Mujuí colonists were one step away from packing up their tensions and heading for another oblivion address. Few people I had known there in 1976 were still there in 1988. I think the chickens and dogs were the same.

Ocean's hopes of a walk beneath a monkey-congested canopy were dashed as soon as the bus started out of Santarém. What in my time had been a breathing space of secondary growth connecting town and country had since been transformed into an abandoned building site

É PROIBIDO CONVERSAR
COM O MOTORISTA

littered with sawmills and scrub. Along the once thinly populated road were tavern-centred settlements of shacks, complete with last-legs dogs and child mortality statistics playing in the dust. Mujuí itself now extended half-way along the length of the feeder road, but the town centre, plucked whole from *Antonio das Mortes*, looked just as devoid of hope as it had a dozen years earlier.

When I had lived there I always looked forward to getting back to Santarém. June and I lived in an abandoned shop which overlooked the stream which passes through the town. The stream looked like a tributary of Love Canal, with fluid the colour of molasses.

The shop consisted of four walls and a tin roof. At night the rats would run along the beams from which the hammocks were hung, scattering something other than moonbeams. Traps set on the beams were effective, but after the snap and descent there would be furious screechings and thrashings until the animal went under. It was easier (and safer – they might have dropped into your hammock) to live under sheets and let them go about their business.

At that time peasant dreams of a successful agricultural career had been usurped by visions of Marlboro Country. The forward-looking Mujuí colonist was the guy with his eye on a cattle ranch and life in the saddle, but all the land accessible by road from Mujuí was either under claim or under cultivation. Typically, an agriculturalist would rise at five o'clock to walk an hour to his patch of land, travelling with a group of men and children (or, very rarely, women) who would drift off as they came to the tracks leading to their plots. They carried pots of prepared food, farming implements, and – occasionally – rifles (you never knew when something might move).

Those with their eyes on hamburger farms were playing a difficult game: trying to calculate how far they should go into the forest beyond the end of the road, with the expectation that the road would soon be extended to meet them; and how much land they could clear without the risk of invasion. These were very small players in quite a large game. Brazilian tax law has long encouraged what can only be described as a parking lot policy vis-à-vis the forest. In fact, given the very generous inducements for felling forest (tax credits, tax relief, tax havens, various subsidies) as well as the near complete absence of voiced objection, the forest is not just threatened, it has virtually been declared the vegetation equivalent of a non-person. It's being 'disappeared', as they say.

I used to follow around a pair of Mujuí brothers who had seen the future in cattle and had committed themselves (quite unrealistically as it turned out) to a remote, undocumented stake six hours' walk south of town. Having cleared twenty hectares, they soon had a decent crop of rice – most of which rotted in a shed because they couldn't haul it out. Twenty hectares is a fair amount of agricultural land, but in pasture terms it is barely sufficient for twenty head of cattle. Their enterprise was the sort which might appear in an agricultural textbook in the 'How Not To Do It' section. My most vivid memory of this ranch is the sight of dead chicks lying on the ground beneath an *urucú* bush in which mother hen had sought a safe roost. Victims of blood-draining bats, according to a cowboy *manqué*, their flattened bodies looked the results of an encounter between a wet newspaper and a lawnmower. Wildlife out west.

Ten years is a lot of development time, especially when the woodman is practically being force-fed steroids to keep his work-rate up. Mujuí didn't have much going for it to start with; as a minor outpost in the 'conquest of the tropics' it was beneath attention, hardly even worth a statistic. As Ocean and I disembarked from the Santarém–Mujuí bus any illusions I had that the limited appeal of a place such as Mujuí would spare it the full effect of progress disappeared. Certainly the scene before us was devoid of even a gentle hint of pristine forest – no troops of howlers, no gently browsing tapirs, a sky at no point obscured by swarms of parakeets. The Douanier Rousseau tableaux had been sent packing to be replaced by a landscape from which hope had been milled into obscurity. All that was on offer was the standard issue 'shoot me if I'm dying because I can't tell' dog, some feisty chickens, and *tabernas* selling warm Pepsi. Going into the interior to find some forest for Ocean, all we'd come up with was infant desert, the edge of the Amazonian dustbowl where all the signs were vintage despair. In the US of the 1920s, 'Dear Okie, if you see Arkie, tell him Tex has got a job for him out in Californie' may have rung hollow and not a little ironic, but in Amazonia the new dustbowl has opened branches not only in the west, but in the south and east as well.

It was August, and in Santarém the river was unusually high. Normally at that time of year the western stretch of riverfront is a wide beach filled with produce brought in from *várzea* settlements. Instead, boats were double-parked against the quay and the *várzeas* were awash. In a last-ditch attempt to provide Ocean with exotica, we tried to hire a small boat and visit the *várzea* complex east of town. We ended up with a riverine equivalent of a heavy-goods vehicle. The boat had just been overhauled and the owner was not going to use it for several days, so he sent us out with a truculent crew who had been counting on a day off.

A few minutes from the dock and it really is hard to believe that a city of 100,000 inhabitants is hiding behind us. To the north the silty water of the Amazon is mixing with the blue water of the Tapajós; to the south, the escarpment – the northern extension of the Brazilian shield – rises dramatically; to the east, the river flows past the flooded forest. A few miles downstream the boat enters a narrow channel and is lost in a network of lakes and islands. There are some houses still above water, most with shrimp traps out front and a few head of cattle. In the narrower passages, water buffalo can be seen or heard. There are egrets and kingfishers and occasionally *botos* surface. The crew have never been involved in this kind of tourism before. What do we want to do? I explain that the expedition artist wants to get in touch with nature, but they seem to think that sketching is just an early form of photography and can't get the hang of the long pose. We move eastward and after an hour or so tie the boat up on a tiny island. Three of us go out in the canoe with nets and lines in search of piranha. The net is ten metres wide and a metre deep. We tie one end to a floating mass of greenery, paddle around it to secure the other end, and take the canoe into the flooded forest. As in upland forest, there isn't much by way of a soundtrack: a few birds, the sounds of animals surfacing, but hardly enough to disturb the VU meter. It's too subtle for ears accustomed to screening out noise. It's visually overwhelming, yet aurally disconcerting, as though someone pulled the plug. Making our way back to the net we find it empty and have to resort to solo mode. The poles are Tom Sawyer style, but require wire leaders. Bits of beef are the bait, and after a few seconds the piranha are on the case. Even a pissed-off and vigorous trout seems languid in comparison with a hooked piranha. The word 'strike' evokes a sense of purpose, game fish cruising and measuring the quarry before moving in. It doesn't suffice for what happens with the piranha. It's more like combustion, and you sit there holding the rod as far away as possible while the fish goes through its baddest-fish-on-the-block routine. Manuel the mechanic is particularly wary. His right hand bears a suppurating wound from an avenging fish caught the week before.

Returning to the boat we find that Ocean has lapsed into a nature coma, sprawled in a deckchair and apparently barely capable of putting pen to paper. At midday, the glare is strong, the water as calm as a glacial lake. The cook has prepared some pieces of beef which we eat with rice, *farinha* and peppers. The peppers are a life-threatening species, the size of a fingernail but packed with high-concentration pain juice.

On the return trip, a fellow in a canoe emerges from a channel and we stop to give him a lift. Stuffed into the canoe is a *jaú* catfish which weighs about thirty kilogrammes, half as much as his captor. He's a weekend fisherman, who sets out each Saturday to paddle two hours east from his home in Maicá, where he has a smallholding effectively insulated from Santareno development. The only modern predation he has to put up with is the increased use of *várzea* cattle pasture and, of course, the occasional sight of magenta-hued gringo tourists. Unlike the fishing family on Marajó, the *jaú*-man is still an enthusiast, pleased at the opportunity of describing where, when and why he uses the various combinations of tackle lying amidst the selection of fish gasping in the swill at the bottom of the canoe. Nobody has told him yet that subsistence is out, the big market's where it's at. Ditto for our crew. Although the boat is driven by a Japanese diesel, has a pricey German sound system, and is mainly used for transporting manufactured goods from the Manaus free-trade zone to small interior communities, it's still working within the limits of a petty merchant routine established in the nineteenth century. The *patrão* is a Santareno businessman, member of the yacht club, Ford Escort driver; the crew live on the boat – whether it's working or not – receive a small wage, and are always on call. The mechanic is from a *várzea* settlement near Santarém; the cook and dogsbody is from the interior of Marajó, an itinerant who has been on his own since he was fourteen. Neither slaves nor wage slaves, they are minor *bricoleurs* in a system in which no serious alternative to *bricolage* has yet been presented.

Wallace wrote in 1852 that:

> Thus we find the province of Pará overrun with traders, the greater part of whom deserve no better name than pedlars, only that they carry their goods in a canoe instead of upon their backs. . . . There is a kind of gambling excitement in trade which outshines all the steady profits of labour, and regular mechanics are constantly leaving their business to get a few goods on credit and wander about the country trading. . . . It seems a very nice and easy way of getting a living, to sell goods at double the price you pay for them, and then again to sell the produce you receive at double what you pay for it. (1972:261–2)

And on and on. Similar sentiments are voiced by contemporary

Santarenos who are both mystified and miffed by the durability of trading as the focus of life. Santarém's development path is parallel to that of the suburbanized generic West, but while back home the shopping mall – an appropriately contradictory icon of centralization and decentralization – represents a new kind of social space, for Santarém the shopping mall *is* society; and unlike the disenfranchised metropolitan hanging out on the edges of the bright commercial glow, subsisting on leavings, Santareno marginals, like the *jaú*-man, just check out altogether.

The only animals Ocean captured in 'the forest' were some chickens. The best animal we saw on the trip was in Belém. Standing on the verge outside the Museu Goeldi campus waiting for a bus, we watched three youths emerge noisily from a *taberna* waving a bottle of *Tatuzinho* at us and jokingly challenging us to join them for a brain-shrinking session. On one of them was attached, over the liver, a handful of light brown fur as if the guy had leaned up against a shedding angora. A few days later, near the Ver-O-Peso market I saw a similar hank of fur stuck to another guy's liver. As I approached him he clearly thought his day was made: 'Only 4,000 cruzados and he's yours. Well, OK, 3,000. I really need the money.' 'I'm interested, but what is it?' 'A baby anteater.' Well, of course.

It looked like a customized mole, expensive dye-job, cut and blow-dry. A mature anteater is far from cuddly looking, more like a furry sabre with huge claws and Cyrano-proportioned hooter. I explained about Britain's quarantine laws to little effect while the seller gave me a quick run-down on the care and feeding of the anteater: 'He eats just what you do, some potato, some greens. It's as easy as keeping a bird.' I then revealed that I lived in Islington and what with the stripped pine and pasta machine, an anteater would just about seal my fate. He said he understood and moved on.

While writing about one poor bastard walking the streets of Belém with another poor little bastard clinging to his side, I am kept in touch with the unreality of it all: Sting appears on the box saving, so it is said – and apparently merely by saying so it is true, such is the magic of television – the Amazon rain forest. My day is complete, but there is more to come if I stay up late:

12.5 **Killerfish** A gang raids a Brazilian mine, escapes with a multi-million dollar haul of emeralds and hides them in piranha-infested reservoir. Lee Majors, Karen Black, Margaux Hemingway and Marisa Berenson lead this 1979 film which should have been eaten by its own title.

1.40 **Weather; Close.**

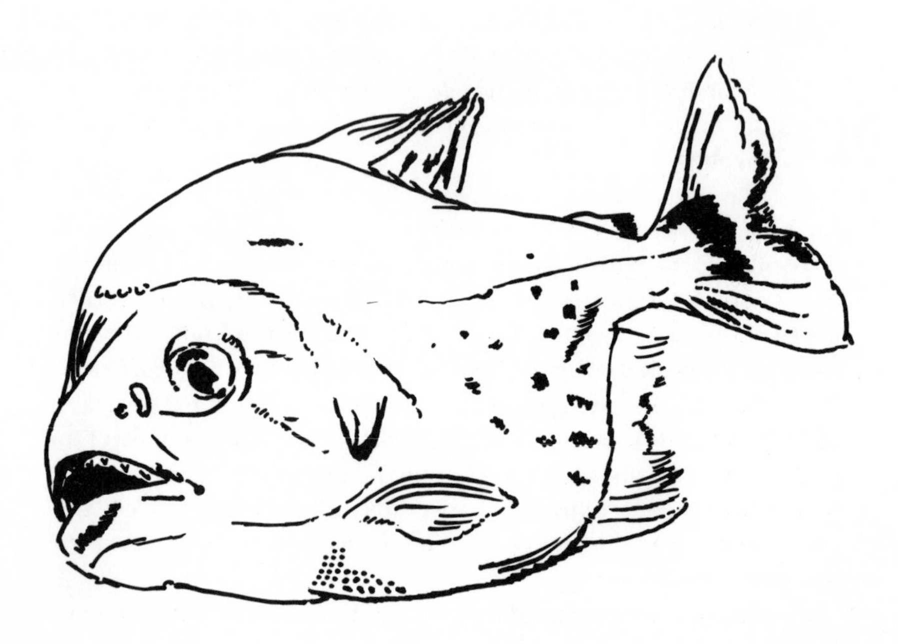

ANTARC

VIII

AMAZONIA AS ECO-DOMAIN

IS IT SAFE TO GET MY FEET WET?

An Easy Score

There are a number of reasons for the relative ease with which large-scale expropriation of Amazonian resources has been effected. Examples of these large-scale projects include the Serra do Carajás iron-ore mine, the bauxite mining on the lower Trombetas, the Tucuruí hydroelectric dam on the Tocantins River, coffee plantations and cattle ranches in Rondônia and Acre, the proposed Xingu hydroelectric project and manganese mining at Macapá. On a smaller scale but just as predatory and destructive are the various gold-mining centres as well as the numerous timber-felling and milling operations.

The first reason is that during the period of the National Security state (emerging in the years following the 1964 coup and lasting until 1985) Amazonia was effectively internationalized and made accessible to foreign and transnational capital.

Second, the suspension of political rights and a free press during the generals' reign precluded an open and critical discussion of the rationale for rapid Amazonian development.

Third, the resources on offer were most appealing to very large investors or consortia who, able to take advantage of economies of scale, could most profitably co-ordinate Amazonian extraction with their other enterprises. Small investors less capable of implementing such vertically integrated operations were squeezed out or, more typically, resorted to a strategy provided for them by the state – land speculation.

Fourth, Amazonian hyperbole (the biggest this, the longest that, like a sub-equatorial version of Texas) provides a constant background of mystification against which more discreet – and perhaps significant – factual matters appear drab and uncompelling. Accounts of the actions of such entrepreneurial swashbucklers as Ford and Ludwig are much more easily assimilated than are accounts of the tropical forest's closed nutrient cycle, and they sell more newspapers.

Last is the fact that much as Amazonia might epitomize for Europeans the locale of 'the other', it does the same for Brazilians. Implicit in Brazil's self-image as standing resolutely at the cutting edge of Third World capitalist development is its own sense of maintaining a periphery so vast and exotic that it cannot fail to suggest unlimited potential.

Some Gross Facts

The Amazon River is 4,000 miles long; a fifth of all the land-based water in the world is flowing in the Amazon; its outflow is twelve times that of the Mississippi and sixteen times that of the Nile; ten Amazon tributaries are larger than the Mississippi; it has more than a thousand tributaries, seventeen of which are more than a thousand miles long; more water passes out of the Amazon in a day than passes in front of the Houses of Parliament in a year; the outflow is 7 million cubic feet per second; approximately 15 per cent of all the water entering the Atlantic comes from the Amazon, measurably lowering the salinity of the ocean over an area of 2.5 million square kilometres and adding each day approximately 1.33 million tons of particulate matter; those tributaries of the Amazon which drain the interior basin (total catchment area: 6 million square kilometres) are largely nutrient free; the gradient of the Amazon is very mild, a fall of only a hundred metres over 3,000 kilometres, and the difference in river height from low to high season may be as much as thirteen metres (as in Manaus in 1953 and 1963); Amazonia contains about a tenth (500–880 thousand) of all the plant, animal and insect species of the earth; the Amazon Basin covers about 60 per cent of the eighth largest country in the world and is about the same size as continental USA; the island of Marajó in the mouth of the Amazon is the size of Switzerland (or Wales, or Denmark); Amazonia contains half the total bird species of the world; it has the largest parrots, rodents and ants, the longest snakes, and more species of bats and monkeys than any other forest; it has more species (2,500) of fish than there are in the Atlantic, including 500 species of catfish alone; the average rainfall is eighty inches, in some places 390 inches; the major Amazonian state of Pará is larger than Portugal, France, England, Italy, Belgium and Holland combined; Brazilian officials claim that 5 per cent of the forest has been cleared, World Bank researchers claim 12 per cent, and most of this has been destroyed in the past ten years; the first nine pig-iron smelters around the Serra das Carajas mine will require 1.1 million tons of charcoal each year, an amount which would fill a building 100 metres wide, 100 metres long, and fifty storeys tall; in 1985, 18 million live aquarium fish were exported from the state of Amazonas; in 1987, Brazilian scientists estimated that the amount of forest burned that summer was 77,000 square miles, an area one and half times the size of New York state; the same satellite data indicated that there were, conservatively, 170,000 individual fires (virtually all fires are illegal); the forest service has 900 wardens for an area larger than Europe; 16 per cent of the students at the University of São Paulo, one of the best, have Japanese surnames; 70 million Brazilians (i.e. half) are black or 'mixed race', but none of the governors of Brazil's twenty-three states is black and only seven of the 559 members of Congress regard themselves as black; 81 per cent of Brazil's farmland is held by 4.5 per cent of the population; Brazil's foreign debt is more than $100,000 million; gold fetches about $10 a gramme, of which the putative mine-owner receives 55 per cent; the remaining 45 per cent is divided up amongst the panners, diggers, hosers and guards such that an individual worker receives on average only 2 per cent; in Roraima, a territory in which the threatened Yanomami live, 45,000 miners produce three tons of gold each month.

Too many facts about Amazonia are recognised only in a broad sense. Almost all researchers in Amazonia agree that qualified ignorance is the only identifiable starting point. The developmentalist response to this lack of knowledge has been to raise the level of ignorance to previously unimaginable heights. The call goes out and they are queueing up to 'harness' Amazonia, 'meet the challenge of the tropics'. It is a conjurer's trick: while the eye is drawn to hi-tech investment, attention is distracted from the fact that it is an old routine which is being run, the extraction of raw materials.

In simple terms, there are only two broadly held views of Amazonia's place in the larger scheme of things economic. The first of these (the institutional voice of hard realities of the 1980s and beyond) is the familiar one that Amazonia contains a lot of valuable resources which are going to waste and Amazonia must be 'developed'. The second is that Amazonia is unsuitable for the application of the kind of development envisaged by its philanthropic developers. But while these opposed positions are easily recognized in journalistic and scientific publications, the idea that they are jostling for the front seat is a misrepresentation because the development view is matched by action while the non-development view is just that, a view. Transamazonica has been built; Serra do Carajás is a reality; forest has been felled to permit the grazing of generic Big Macs;[1] the Tucuruí hydroelectric dam has already flooded much of the Tocantins; the planned smallholder peasant recolonization of Transamazonica has been abandoned in favour of large-scale extractive enterprise. In the words of the 'scientist' Henrique Pimenta: 'Either the businessmen conquer the forest or it will disappear by the force of its own nature.' (*O Estado de São Paulo*, 18 August 1973). Because the developmental go-ahead was granted within the apparatus of the National Security State, Amazonian development is effectively institutionalized. The views of critics of 'development' have no comparable base.

That's the good-guy bad-guy scenario, and on the evidence the bad guys are winning hands down. Left out of all this, of course, are the invisible armies who are by and large excluded from both pro- and anti-development prescriptions and denunciations. They are known to be lurking in the background, but generally get relegated to 'backward peasant' or 'ignorant victim' slots.

Less simply, the argument concerning the wisdom of subjecting Amazonia to the kind of unregulated exploitation witnessed today breaks down into a number of well-represented views, and it's as well to know what they are.

The Foreign Hypocrisy View

This view, widely held in Brazil, holds that it is presumptuous of Europeans and North Americans who have managed to desecrate their own landscapes with (so far, and depending heavily on tunnel vision) relative impunity to stand in the way of 'Amazonian progress'. This is a specious argument for the obvious reason that accusing a nation of hypocrisy isn't a good basis for following the destructive route taken by said nation in the first place. It is also doubly perplexing: first because the financiers and beneficiaries of the razing of Amazonia are themselves Europeans and North Americans; and second because those who spout this line generally seem to believe that there is a magical relationship between land-clearing and industrialization and that, as in Europe and North America, the one automatically follows the other.

It's hard to have too much sympathy for this line; and equally hard not to recognize that those nations most responsible for the high-trash-content lifestyle can hardly occupy the moral high ground. Being a gringo is no joke, as any safari-jacketed environmental consultant attempting to moderate gold-miners' use of mercury will tell you.

The Business Reality View

A second view is that Amazonia is a singularly rich repository of raw materials, extraction of which cannot be allowed to escape those redeeming 'market forces'. As commodity prices rise and/or become less predictable, it is hardly unusual that cheaper sources be sought. Given the failure to derive profit from Amazonia through agricultural or industrial means, it is necessary to resort to what is natural and appropriate: extraction of minerals (gold, iron ore, bauxite, manganese) and timber, and hydroelectric power. Fuller development of this argument can be found in (almost) any business magazine.

It is closely linked to the 'stupid *latino*' theory, which is particularly popular in government circles and among those who write for financial publications. The linked set of underlying assumptions (although frequently enough made explicit) is that Third Worlders are inherently incapable of managing their own affairs. If left to do so they will invariably fall asleep at the wheel, and will ultimately require First World expertise to save their collective asses. In the old version of this model (i.e. pre-Second World War, pre-World Bank) at the centre of things is the man in charge of a banana republic. That version held sway as the Cold War posture matured, and indeed may still be widely found. He has ecological fit.

In the new version there is an inept, corrupt, not infrequently coke-addicted bureaucrat who, in the words of the last of the great Texan *philosophes*, could fuck up a wet dream. Within this analysis, Amazonia is threatened not so much by being felled/mined/developed/poisoned as by having such acts performed without the benefit of imported management expertise of the Business/Executive Class variety (the field boffin in short-sleeved, white nylon shirt, plastic protector in pocket, follows in Economy Class).

The consequences of *latino* profligacy, according to this analysis, are that scarce and valuable resources will be wasted, and that the West will have to carry the can. The solution: professional consultants, responsible financial management, 'a realistic assessment of the situation', and 'it's all here in the report'.

In spite of basic differences, this shares at least one crucial perspective with the 'we are the environment' view, and this is that the pathology of eco-destruction is happening somewhere 'out there' in a world which doesn't know any better. Obviously the reasons offered for not knowing any better are different, but they achieve the same effect of eliding 'the problem' and the 'Third World'. They also share the patronizing attitude of the petty bourgeoisie offering the *noblesse oblige* of the technocratic age. In this case we have the unsolicited advice donor, the one who sees red when a Third Worlder points out that the impressive agricultural productivity of English feudalism was in no small part achieved at the expense of serious forest.

A recent article in *The Economist* (18 March 1989), basically a review of a World Bank discussion paper, illustrates very well how the two positions can be brought together. The article documents the way in which Brazil encourages deforestation through various legal and tax devices – making it possible, for example, to use land as a tax haven and encouraging a particularly predatory kind of smallholder resettlement – and by failing to enforce those sanctions available under the law. What the article says makes sense as far as it goes, but there is a lot left unsaid.

It claims, for example, that '[Brazil's] prodigal fiscal and monetary policies mean that inflation is high and unstable (last year prices rose 933%). No one saves money as cash and Brazilians find it safer to invest in land.' It notes that 'the government has virtually exempted agriculture from taxes', and that 'government agencies give tax credits for investors in the Amazon'.

Difficult not to observe that we are dealing here with elements of a classic stupid *latino* scenario with, as the article concludes, a dash of something green: '[A] proper economic analysis suggests that it is not even in Brazil's short-term interest to destroy the jungle . . . it should surely not be impossible for [Brazil] to benefit both itself and the rest of mankind by taking those tax breaks away.'

Brazil's prodigality is not, in spite of the imputation, a home-grown product. The structure of the national economy is inseparable from the US hemispheric policies in which Brazil has not only functioned as the gendarme of South America, but also as a major market – controlled between 1964 (when a US-backed coup delivered Brazil into the hands of a cabal of generals) and 1985 (when the generals slunk out of office) by a class which did a fantastic job of lining its pockets. The allegations of prodigality should be viewed in light of the fact that foreign banks have had Brazil in a full nelson for some time. According to Branford and Kucinski:

> Between the end of 1976 and the end of 1981, Brazil received $73.9 billion in foreign loans, but spent 75 per cent – $55.8 billion – on debt-servicing, and lost another $7.1 billion in

> capital flight. The country received a net transfer of just $5 billion during the five year period.

It is hard to see how Brazil could be said to have had any resources with which to be prodigal.

Given Brazil's heavy dependence on agriculture for foreign revenue, it is not surprising that the agricultural sector is so well treated by tax laws. The suggestion that this is merely blinkered perversion overlooks what Brazil's global role has been since Europeans drew it into the world economy: an alternative (i.e. cheap) source of tropical exotica and raw materials. So what's new about favouring export agriculture? That's what Brazil was designed for.

As for tax credits (needless to say, absolutely unheard of in Britain or the US), Brazil found itself in the mid-1970s between a rock and a hard place – or, in keeping with the tropical theme, up to its ass in alligators. Having allowed open access for foreign capital, the state was having a hard time delivering benefits to its own bourgeoisie, especially that fraction which in alliance with foreign capital was hysterically rolling in cash and looking for a place to invest it. With the national economy so extensively penetrated by foreign investors Amazonia was a good bet for absorbing some of that cash.

These are empirical matters. What is not is the rather sanctimonious suggestion that for the benefit of (1) itself and (2) the rest of mankind Brazil ought to bite the bullet, cease and desist, take a hike, pack up its tensions and steal away into the night, light a rag, take a powder – in short, do what it's told.

The Fateful View

A third view, and one increasingly held by environmentally concerned Amazonians unconvinced that the current development path can be resisted, is that desecration is inevitable, but may be mollified once the current political crisis is superseded. This is an almost millenarian belief, but perhaps one as realistic as any given the very low level of access to objective political resources by those who are the immediate victims.

On the Tapajós River, for example, whose flow from Mato Grosso to the Amazon is interrupted by gold-mining operations near Itaituba, the poisoning of fish – not to mention humans – as a result of mercury used in gold extraction has already provided a sound demonstration of the costs of unregulated extraction.[2] Ten years ago, for Santarenos,

Itaituba was a euphemism for possible good times. Men would check out from their families and join the rush to this equatorial Klondike. Local radio was as much a party line as a broadcast service: 'Manuel would like to let all his relatives know that he is well and is sorry that he can't return for the funeral. He'll be back next month, if God wills.' This time around, Itaituba is no longer the honey pot, the gold-buying establishments having pulled up the tent stakes and moved into Santarém to escape the high levels of social conflict which occur in the gold fields. The cutting edge of frontier capitalism has thus become just another pit-stop on the Transamazonica.

This is not an unusual development. On the Tocantins River, below the hydroelectric dam at Tucuruí, peasants' livelihoods, uncertain but viable in years past, have taken a turn for the worse because both *cacau* production (an important cash crop) and fish yields have fallen drastically as a result of the interrupted river flow. Cases like this are increasingly being taken up by the green lobby, but unfortunately their critique is not only a dollar short but a day late.

The relevant elements have already been assembled and taken through a rehearsal in Araguaia, in the gold fields at Serra Pelada. Most readers will know of Serra Pelada even if they don't recognize the name. It's the landscape which looks as though it was assembled by Geiger: masses of mud-coated and bag-laden couriers ascending near-vertical wooden ladders from a pit of rough-terraced excavations.[3] At first glance, it's from another world. Scenes like this haven't existed since, well, at least the building of the pyramids, but instead of whipmasters there are extras from a spaghetti western. This is what a labour camp looks like when capitalism is purified and all that fair day's work for a fair day's wage nonsense is done away with: labourers so coated in mud that the features of their faces have disappeared, drawing gold from the loose bowels of a felled Amazon. It's standard-issue Sunday supplement material, but also featured on pop culture artefacts such as Jerry Harrison's *Casual Gods* LP. For his fan-base Serra Pelada's image is perfect postmodern pastiche – bizarre enough to be an elaborate Hollywood set.[4]

When workers at Serra Pelada took action late in 1988, they got, as the sheriffs are contractually obliged to say, what was coming to them. To protest at conditions, miners (and women and children) blockaded the bridge which carries the road over the Tocantins River. There were approximately 1,500 people demonstrating, mainly people connected with the mines but also passengers from vehicles waiting to cross the river. Several hundred police approached the bridge from both ends shooting tear gas, blank charges and bullets. People panicked and some tried to escape by leaping off the bridge and plunging two hundred feet to the river. According to reports published in British newspapers, police were seen throwing the bodies of people with bullet wounds into the river, including those of a pregnant woman and a small boy.[5]

Events at Serra Pelada exposed the scaly underbelly of wealth accumulation in the forest: just go ahead and shoot the bastards. The green approach is once again tardy and inappropriate. The 'Be nice to nature and she'll be nice to you' line is not unappreciated among those who assembled at the bridge, but they do not choose how they make a living. 'Save a tree and save yourself' may make sense on a T-shirt, but it's hard to eat.

The 'We Are the Environment' View(s)

A view held by the majority of researchers not in the pay of commercial interests is that the desecration of Amazonia – a keystone of which is large-scale felling which has repercussions across a wide range of terrestrial and riverine life systems – is an assault against reason

comparable to the worst human desecrations of the landscape yet committed.

Among the points raised within this critique are: (1) the fact that Amazonian life systems are mutually interdependent in a manner far more complex than that of eco-systems within which speciation has been interrupted by Ice Age incursions;[6] that the great diversity but low concentration of Amazonian flora and fauna, as well as the high degree of specialization evident, attest to the long overall stability of the region (although the meaning of 'stability' has been modified by *refugia* theorists), and that apparently casual human intervention (the building of a road) can have dramatic consequences in terms of blocking the reproduction of dense networks of species; (2) that Amazonia contains crucial genetic stock not found elsewhere; (3) that a great number of plant and animal species in Amazonia have not even yet been identified – which exposes the claims for a 'resource management' approach put forward by current forest-levellers as manifestly empty of empirical content; (4) that development projects to date have a very poor track record in terms of environmental degradation and local economic benefit.[7] (The fragility of the tropical forest is not a new discovery. A major limiting feature of the forest – the short nutrient cycle – has been recognized at least since Richards' pioneering work in the 1950s.)

A problem with most we-are-the-environment views is that instead of providing the basis for a thorough analysis of the causes of wide-scale destruction, research insights tend to be employed in the service of 'environmental awareness' campaigns offering marketable wisdom in the form of short, snappy phrases, preferably with not too many words of more than two syllables. Laid out on the table, that means: Greenhouse Effect; How To Live With Melanoma; Melting Polar Ice Cap; Ozone Fear; Genetic Stock. The language of politics is the marketable phrase, not the convincing argument, and under present conditions bottle recycling is treated as just as weighty an 'environmental issue' as the recycling of nuclear waste.

What seems quite clear is that, regardless of how well the eco-critique is pitched (and the best pitch would show how the character of an eco-system is shaped by the social system which occupies it, not the other way around), by the time it finds its market it has usually been gutted of its crucial social content. For example, much of the criticism of large-scale development projects in Amazonia – mines, hydroelectric dams – has boiled down to damage limitation proposals. The assumption is that these projects are going to go ahead anyway, so the best that critics can do is try to mitigate some of the more odious ecological effects. That mines and dams should simply be driven off the agenda for social reasons is regarded as an unbalanced view.[8] You won't know the results, say the sage statesmen, unless you try.[9] The energy salesmen have thus managed to seize the initiative and present an argument in which it appears that the only choice is the *prix fixe* menu.

The ecology brigade, meanwhile, is flummoxed. Success, as measured by public consciousness, has been too great. Who can say no to an appeal to befriend a tree in the name of the earth's continued tolerance of human habitation? The greening of Thatcher and Co reveals some of the inadequacy of the ecological broad front appeal – its just too easy for them to pick up a trivial item on the agenda and have a gullible press applaud the emergence of a new green champion. Greenness has in many ways asked for it by allowing the notion of old-fashioned political solutions to cruise off, leaving New Age, Whole Earth style impulses to take centre stage.

The 'we are the environment' view is the reference point for a variety of otherwise quite different people, groups and movements in varying degrees disenchanted with capitalism's customer service division. (Actually, capitalism *per se* is rarely the cause of worry. Conventional wisdom has it that capitalism can be reformed, modified or fine-tuned – but remains the fundamentally 'natural' system, and as such isn't the sort of thing you should tamper with too much.) It includes those who have arrived at some version of greenness after working through other possibilities (Bookchin and Gorz are examples), those for whom greenness is both outside normal politics yet mobilized strictly in terms of it, those who are simply (if reasonably) pissed off (the late Edward Abbey), and those who feel that consumer pressure is a form of passive resistance which has – in the fullness of time – active consequences. The list goes on, but I shall not. If I have not made clear what I'm talking about by now, it's not going to happen. There are great differences represented in the groups lumped under this heading, but they share First Worldness (or, as in the case of some Brazilian greens, a European/North American orientation), pride in their consumer consciousness, a reforming sensibility, and a social democratic political disposition.

By far the most widely reported and popular – if not necessarily the best understood – critical position in the First World, this view tends to ignore the unevenness of development throughout the world, which is why the key words attempt to impose a unity on peoples who don't have that much to do with each other directly. Forest-felling consequences are generalized, producing a package of quality-of-life-inhibiting effects. The solutions are sought through educating consumers in the First World, lobbying investors and governmental agencies, modifying individual behaviour ('organic' food, bottle banks, unleaded petrol) and generally treating the future as though it were not in any way structured by the past.

Amazonia's role in all this is ambiguous. On one hand it is a symbol of the new paradise lost, a potentially major guilt item which is used to instil compassion and thoughtfulness in all good nature lovers. On the other hand, however, the actual transfer of Amazonian resources into the lives of First Worlders remains invisible. Does the aluminium in your compact discs have a country of origin mark on it? What was your hardwood toilet seat doing in its previous incarnation?

This discussion of the environmental critique has strayed (for more straying, see Chapter X), but I think that is inevitable given that the primary focus on 'nature' is itself problematic. To argue, as do many, that nature is a system with which humans interact is not to say very much. Nor is it saying much to argue that, given the interdependence of humans and nature, it is important that humans do not demand more than nature can endure. The flaw in this is that humans are always implicated in social systems, and it is these which interact with the environment rather than individuals. Social systems are dynamic

in a way denied 'nature', if only because they represent a species which is a lot smarter than trees. Their smartness may not get them to heaven or wherever they think they're headed, but they aren't going to have to wait around to be pollinated by a bumble bee either.

A lot of words to make a simple point, but it is one which escapes much green output, especially that in which a primary claim is made for the oneness of wo/man and her/his environment. That oneness is an argument that just doesn't move: if we were indeed 'one' with nature, we wouldn't have (or be able, in fact) to do anything except hang on and go with the flow – a mixture of Zen and free-market economics, not to put too fine a point on it.

This brief and limited survey of some of the published views on the wisdom of turning up the heat in Amazonia is intended to convey the complexity of the issues facing both those who live in Amazonia and those who see events in Amazonia as important in themselves and also as having some bearing on developments outside the region. For example, I would think that observing commodity markets is just as significant for an understanding of Amazonia as is an appreciation of short nutrient cycles, and I hope it is apparent that attempts to

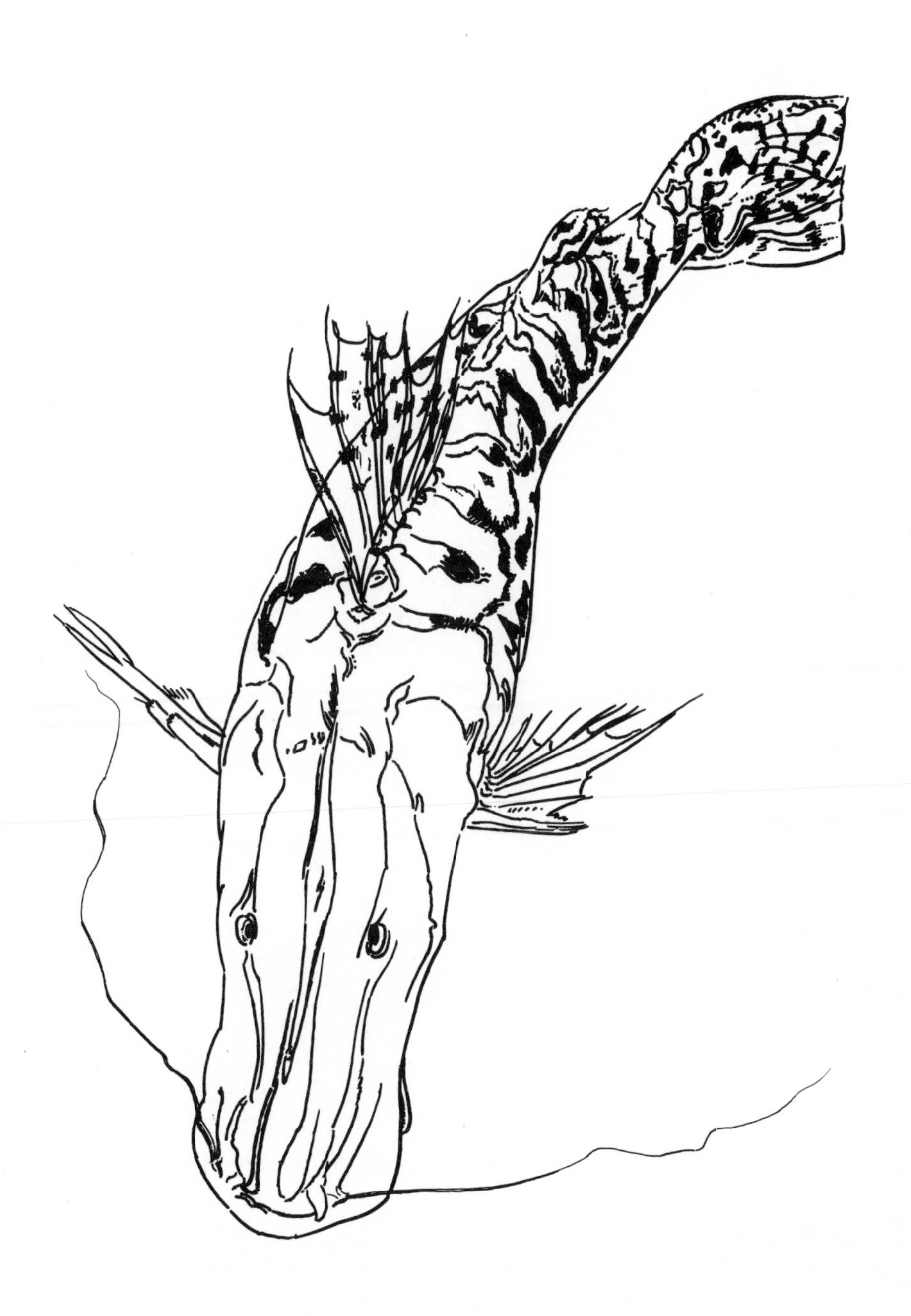

separate issues of ecology from issues of political economy hinder any understanding of the processes actually at work in the region. The critical remarks about environmentalists are not offered in a spirit of spitefulness as much as one of warning. The greening of Amazonia has already been hijacked by everyone from the Brazilian government to the major corporate offenders. The Nossa Natureza programme initiated early in 1989 is a federal smokescreen which is meant to convey to the world Brazil's deep sensitivity to environmental dangers in Amazonia. What it actually displays is Brazil's deep sensitivity to criticism of the complete absence of any concern about the long-term impact of current development proposals.[10] The programme has no funds to speak of, but it has the power to vet future research in Amazonia and make, as they say, the necessary adjustments. If the point still hasn't got through, take note of the fact that Nossa Natureza operates out of the Brazilian government's National Security offices.

In this climate, environmental groups are successful in annoying the powers that be, but as yet pose little threat. The rain forest which is the focus of so much well-intentioned attention remains a tiny element in a large and complicated social landscape. A perhaps apocryphal story popular in Brazil in the summer of 1989 and told with a knowing wink was that after Sting's widely publicized meeting with President Sarney, his *Excelentíssimo* retired to a meal of *tartaruga* (turtle), a threatened species protected by federal law.

For a more practical approach to the problem of what to do with Amazonia, it's worth looking at the activities of those who have been doing something with it for a lot longer than the developers. In historical accounts, the evolution of Amazonian *caboclo* society has had few chapters of note and no heroes or heroines to speak of. A widespread rebellion in the mid-nineteenth century, the *cabanagem*, suffices as recognition of their presence. Later, with the immigration of rubber-tappers and a usurious mercantile system, *caboclos* came to be depicted as sinister lumpens, characterized, for example by a representative of the British rubber industry, as 'international scum'. With the collapse of the rubber industry, as noted earlier, the term 'stagnant' came to be widely used to describe the Amazonian economy and those who sustained it. In recent times, the Amazonian *caboclos* have had their poor image maintained through unfavourable comparisons with the new breed of pioneer carving a swath through Acre and Rondônia.

The *várzeas* (flood plains), the traditional focus of high-yield agricultural activity in Amazonia, are the breeding grounds of phantom characters in Amazonian literature beginning from year dot. When Heriarte wrote in 1662 of a *várzea*-dwelling 'tribe' which could call upon 60,000 warriors (implying a population of 240,000), he documented an observation which has served as a point of ridicule to this day. The received wisdom in Brazil is that Amazonia could only support small bands of Hollywood-issue hunter-gatherer Indians, guys (and the odd Amazon of course) with low-tech blowpipes and a propensity to travel – driven, in the accounts of many, by a desire for protein which could not be satisfied by standing still. The problem with this dismissive line is that there is much evidence which suggests it is wrong.[11]

The degree to which contemporary Indian societies resemble those of their forebears is a matter of dispute, and may never be resolved given the paucity of archaeological work and the difficulty of reconstructing the sequence of decimation. But it is worth pointing out the advantage of maintaining the myth of the noble savage: some of the legitimacy for the current path of Amazonian development is based on the idea that in social terms Amazonia is a blank slate. The Amerindians who occupied Amazonia in pre-colonial times, this argument goes, failed to evolve, trapped as they were by the rigidities of the tropical forest eco-system. It is the white man's burden, somewhat relieved by hi-tech shoulder straps, to drag Amazonia out of the Stone Age.

In fact, the *várzea*-based *caboclo* societies of contemporary Amazonia already use the land about as sensibly as they can, even if they do so in a manner that remains mysterious. It can perhaps be explained by contrasting it with Old MacDonald's Farm, the fundamental Western agrarian archetype. On Old MacDonald's Farm continued production depends on being able to co-ordinate certain activities and natural processes on a fixed piece of land – rotating, fertilizing, adjusting to changes in weather, and so on. The *várzea* system, by contrast, depends on being able to control an unfixed piece of land: the nutrients which make possible high *várzea* yields come from outside Amazonia, delivered by the annual flood and therefore largely beyond the direct control of the cultivator. It is unknown how extensive the flood will be and it is by no means certain that a bit of land cultivated one year will still be there the next. Not only does this chronic uncertainty pose technical problems for the cultivators, but also it's really hard to get a bank loan using disappearing land as collateral.[12] The agricultural advantages of using *várzea* rather than upland plots outweigh the disadvantages, but successful utilization of *várzea* requires a co-ordination not only of agriculture *per se* (organizing a sufficient labour force to harvest crops before they are drowned, for example) but also of complementary processes, especially cattle-raising, and riverine and terrestrial extractive activities.

Várzea cattle, in addition to sharing with cattle around the world the ideal typification of the term 'dumb beast', are also lumbered on *várzeas* with physical demands for which they are comically unsuited, having to occupy an aquatic habitat for months of the year. As the waters encroach, farmers corral their beasts on tiny islands, building up the base to ensure that the beasts' noses stay above water. This cruel and unusual practice is hard on the herder as well, for instead of passively supervising grazing cattle, s/he has to get up in the morning, paddle off in a canoe, cut grass, and paddle it back to the cattle. Not exactly Marlboro Country.

It works, however, although cattle health is not the best and in years of extreme flood not a few beasts are lost, both to predators and by drowning. It's part of a system in which *caboclos* spread their time over a number of activities: *várzea* agriculture and pastoralism, upland cultivation, hunting, gathering and fishing, wage labour, craft production – in sum, coping with the vicissitudes of the environment by not specializing in one activity. The development lobby, needless to say, has a *várzea* attention span of about two seconds. Although there is no shortage of recommendations that the *várzeas* are where it's at agriculturally, they are entirely overlooked.

One of the reasons, mentioned earlier, is that the *várzeas* are weird property, a bit too ephemeral for the ledger books. Another reason is that the *várzeas* are of principal importance for food production and if there is one thing development money does not overly concern itself with it is investment in food production. Markets for food, yes, but actual provision, no. Third, development of an agricultural policy requires long-term planning, an affliction notably absent in a national economy orchestrated by foreign bankers for almost twenty-five years.

It seems obvious that the peasant lobby hasn't a lot going for it. The reasons for this are summed up by the banks' lending policy: food is for feeblies. What the banks are interested in is a good return. This seems so obvious that I am somewhat embarrassed to have to mention it, but in the face of a recurrent and apparently widespread belief that banks are philanthropic organizations I'll shake off any reservations. In *caboclo* terms, bank personnel are used-car salesmen of the worst

kind, white-shoe smoothies whose contribution to modern life is getting someone else to bite the bullet.

It is hard to get to grips with the fact that in Amazonia the trivial and the important to depend on each other in peculiar ways. For example, non-Amazonians' dismay at forest-felling is based on realistic self-preservation interests. However, what concerns them – and what they try to get genned up on – is totally irrelevant. When you cut the forest you do not in any simple sense destroy a crucial link in the oxygen–carbon dioxide exchange. In fact, you probably improve your terms, exposing all kinds of ambitious plants to new long- and short-term career possibilities. The problem is that by burning the trees you also release a lot more carbon into the atmosphere than it can take, hence contributing to the so-called greenhouse effect. Put another way, people's instincts vis-à-vis Amazonian forest-felling are right, but when it's time to deliver the reasons the trivia flies thick and fast.

A classic example of the double whammy built into Amazonian logic is provided by the humble cayman. A lot of Amazonian flora and fauna look like extremely specialized, minor cult items left over from that blank period linking dinosaurs with so-called higher forms. The mega-dillo looks like it wandered off the set of *The Lost World*. The albino cockroach is another vital missing link curiosity. Many of the animals now on the verge of dismissal lived quite happily well into the early modern period. The homely cayman was one of them.

In one of the more compelling studies of recent years, although it lacks the cinematic qualities essential to ensure a big audience, E.J. Fittkau (1973) illustrated how specialized are the links among various Amazonian life forms. After the Second World War, attempts to improve fish yields in Amazonia included the widespread decimation of caymans. One of the consequences was an unexpected decline in fish yields. Fittkau removed caymans and installed them in aquaria in the Max Planck Institute in Berlin for the express purpose of measuring the chemical content of their faeces. What he was attempting to discover was a kind of relationship which in Amazonia is quite normal: the high specificity of links between seemingly remote life forms. During the period of flood (when the river's margins are extended by thirty to sixty kilometres) the cayman's role in food chains alters. Withdrawn from this chain because of mass slaughter, the crocs' absence brings some things to a halt. What Fittkau discovered was that whether crocs are eating or not, they shit chemicals of consequence, completing food chains, bringing it all back home, parking brownies with a vengeance.

This kind of research suffers a number of defects. Probably the most important of these is the incredulity effect. 'So what else is new?' 'I don't want to hear about crocs, find me a scientist who can tune my satellite dish.' Another response is: 'We told you so. The only thing this place is good for is hardwoods, iron ore, bauxite, gold and manganese.'

What the account does provide, however, is an explanation for an observable phenomenon. Unfortunately this virtue is less recognized in these information-saturated times and the disappearing cayman explanation becomes just an amusing story. Also unfortunately for Amazonia, a lot of vital connections are similarly 'amusing'. The brazil nut *(castanha do pará)* is an important forest product (producing, for example, more protein per hectare than a cow) which has suffered from the expansion of cattle pastures in Pará. In some cases, the brazil nut trees have been left intact but, as in the case of the cayman, there is a missing link: brazil nut trees are pollinated by a bee (*euglossine*), but in order to stay in business, male bees require access to orchids because their scent attracts the females. The upshot is that without relatively intact forest around the brazil nut trees there is no way to keep them fruiting.

These are examples not only of Amazonian esoterica, but also of the fact that this kind of study is frequently prompted by crisis – as when the fish yields decline or the brazil nut trees stop producing. Only then – too late – does the significance of this or that relationship become apparent. To recapitulate an earlier point, the sensibility of the eco-domain is made apparent by the ways in which the social system acts upon it, and the way the social system is acting now ensures that many such links will be lost before they are discovered.

IX

VIEIRA

THE KING OF LAMBADA

Ocean's preparations for the trip to Amazonia had consisted mainly of perusing the sleeve photo of an LP I had given him. The books I'd offered were accepted, but returned unmarked by dog-ears, underlining, or any blemishes indicating major outlays of midnight oil.

In the LP photo in question, a boat is coasting along a vaguely tropical canal, but there is not a lot more information to go on. It could be an old example of a rock publicity photo, early 1970s, east LA perhaps, a *chicano* group hoping to make the leap from obscurity to cultural icon. Or it might be a gang of illegal workers snapped as the river patrol boat moved in to make the arrest. Nine dour countenances, wife-swapper moustaches, serious bellbottoms, white belts. It is Vieira and his combo.

Looking for our own little Amazonian window on the world of World Music, Vieira seems to fit the bill. Though he is (with sincere modesty) self-ordained King of Lambada,[1] his domain is less than regal, more a peripheral, subcultural fiefdom than a full-blown kingdom, and his residence would be too unsightly to feature even as a chicken coop in Graceland. Vieira is somewhere on the street end of the service sector – the other end being occupied by the managerial élite in service to foreign firms, those for whom the declaration 'Your wish is my command' has no ironic subtext. But service sector implies a smoothness of scaling that doesn't do justice to the fact that Vieira is down among those who really do serve.

In my neighbourhood, there is something exalted (slightly at least, but more often rather greater than that) about being a musician, but even First World metropolitans addicted to the music-biz hype which accompanies each small shift in the culture-industry growth charts become weary under the flood of monarchical or godly status claims. What Elvis was 'the King' of is obscure. What exactly is 'the Boss' boss of anyway? 'Greatest Hits' becomes a euphemism for relentless market torture routines and even surefire nostalgia fixes acquire a negotiable half-life. But in Belém we're in a different territory, one where all the space between musicianhood and celebrity is already occupied by imported froth and what's left to local talent is a semi-quaver.

Brazilian popular music is best known outside Brazil for its influence rather than directly for its artists. In spite of considerable musical talents, Brazil is lumbered in the international record market by two things: one is that there are enough Brazilians for a national artist to carry on singing in Portuguese and still make a living, hence less pressure for Berlitz-pop; second, Brazil still suffers under the weight of its Third World status when it comes to penetrating the global pop market. There's too much to be debunked before any serious product action.[3] First you have to shed carnival, then you have to give an account of Brazilian geography – already more than a major label product manager can cope with.

There are a couple of exceptions – Astrud Gilberto, Sergio Mendes – whose Brazilian-ness can stand up beside their middle-of-the-road associations (deserved or not), but generally speaking the identity of Brazilian artists is subsumed under style labels – 'samba', 'bossa nova', or even just 'Latin American'. In the late 1960s the Tropicalist movement associated with Caetano Veloso, Gilberto Gil, Chico Buarque and others threatened to carve out a bigger niche, but its politics ran afoul of the scenario then on the drawing-boards of National Security State apparatchiks and the 1970s saw the rise of Iglesias-style balladeers such as Morris Alpert and Roberto Carlos[4] – tight trousers and good dentists. Flora Purim and Airto get a large nod; Paulinho da Costa has a full-session credit CV; Nana Vasconcelos gets an occasional look-in; but Milton Nascimento is apparently too big for travel, and ECM artists don't count.

We were in search of authentically obscure game, someone who embodied a regional style which could still be encountered in pre-culture industry form. *Carimbó*, from which *lambada*, by some accounts, is more or less descended, had been associated with one name, Pinduca, and sounded something like a polka which had taken

a dodgy compass reading, hit the South Atlantic coast, fragmented, and emerged after extensive surgery as Tex-Mex with the wrong percussion instruments.

In London, I had come across a European release of a Vieira LP and visited the company which issued it. An unenthusiastic Dutchman ('Please, I am eating my lunch. Come back later.') informed me that he was responsible for licensing it, had never been to Belém, knew nothing about the artist, but thought it was a good idea to 'develop' these regional Brazilian styles which used Caribbean rhythms.

Joaquim de Lima Vieira, simply Vieira professionally, does represent a different kind of Brazilian music, one specific to Amazonia but influenced not only by Caribbean rhythms but also by styles from the north-east of Brazil (the major source of Amazonian immigrants) and a soupçon of what sounds like country and western filtered through The Ventures and The Shadows. Unlike most other musicians in Belém, the only big town near his base in Barcarena, Vieira makes his living performing – weekend dances with his nine-piece big band and weekday bar jobs with a four-piece. And unlike a number of other local musicians he has yet to move to São Paulo and try for a national audience. This is not through want of trying. He has recorded ten LPs

and has appeared on national TV, but he's no spring chicken and, much as remaining near Belém is a serious impediment to remunerative celebrity, the work is regular.

We tracked down the producer of the Vieira LP, Jesus, resting behind the regional desk of Continental Records. Jesus has the look of a proper culture-industry record producer, a smoothie – maybe a touch of Philadelphia – but a hard man with the sleepy malevolence of a prefight press conference, bandito moustache and shades with frames the colour of cheap silver nail-polish. Outside there should have been a BMW and he should have been wondering whether to step out for a toot or risk it in front of strangers. On the other hand, he also looks like the kind of guy who might stand between us and a replacement car radiator hunted down at great length. Make me an offer?

Outside Jesus' office, in place of the BMW, is a guy on a stool. He's selling combs made of buffalo horn. To get into the building you have to pass through a watch repair shop. The building directory lists mainly lawyers and gynaecologists. Two floors up there is a broad hallway decorated in Early Bureaucratic. Getting past reception means fighting through force six gusts emanating from a Mitsubishi floor

model fan. Once into Jesus' office it's air-conditioned, and he's suggesting we tape the interview for posterity. We talk about Paraense music for a while, then I tell Jesus that Vieira has got our attention. He gets his secretary to ring a number in Barcarena and leave a message. I explain that we'd be only too glad to travel to Vieira's place, but Jesus insists that it's no trouble for Vieira to catch a boat into town ('You have come from London; he can come from Barcarena') and we arrange to return the next day to meet the King.

At 2.30 the next day, Jesus' office is still closed for lunch. We rest our legs. A man climbs the steps slowly, passes us on the landing and returns after looking around the corner. He's probably not a gynaecological patient, but nor does he have the haunted look of a man seeking legal advice.

Neither of us recognizes him. I don't know Ocean's excuse, but mine is that of the nine people standing atop the river cruiser, I'd picked out the evil bastard at the front, the one with the Jim Thompson glint. Instead, we're presented with a cross between Burl Ives and Duke Ellington.

I suggest that since Jesus is not available we should retire elsewhere for the interview. Vieira demurs. Little though he regards Jesus as his minder, Jesus was the one who set up the interview, and we can't just skive off.

I tape the interview with Vieira while Ocean draws him. It is very strained, an interview with 'English journalists' overseen by a representative of the record company with whose assistance Vieira has not made a bean after ten LPs. Jesus interrupts frequently to set the record straight. For him, Vieira is a country-simple tunesmith, a regional artist pretty low on the priority list. We wrap things up and walk with Vieira down to the wharf, arranging to visit him at home the following weekend.

To get to Vieira's house, we have to catch a boat from one of the many small quays which line the Belém waterfront as it curves away from the Guajará Bay and becomes the north shore of the mouth of the Guamá River – a minor Amazonian tributary, but minor in the Amazonian scheme of things means it's kilometres wide. Barcarena, Vieira's hometown, is less noted for its musicians than for a now-defunct product – firewater – and a new one – aluminium.[5] It is, however, on the same stretch of water, Igarapé Miri, where Pinduca – Pará's most famous musical son – was born.

Looking forward, I see cool green islands, thirty-metre-high canopies, *furos* flooded at high tide. I also see, between hairline and T-shirt neck, three bands of scorched flesh representing three different neckline altitudes of exposure to that which mad dogs and Englishmen are alleged to covet as it skirts along, in this case just south of the equator, blocked only by the passing *urubú*. These bands of flesh, purple, magenta and medium rare – or *Mal passado?* in the garçon's query – belong to Ocean, by now adjusting nicely to his role as tapeworm host, the man who eats for millions.

Looking back, I see framed between palm-shielded islands, the skyline of Belém. From a distance it actually looks like a reasonable version of paradise. I'm forced to remind myself of the unlikely sight of Charlie Boorman scaling a Jungian, Belém skyscraper on behalf of *The Emerald Forest*. Rousseau, jungle pussy, moral aerobics. The Belém skyline disguises the ground zero action.

What was excluded from view in that film is also hidden beneath the modern skyline as one moves by river out of town: substantial remnants of colonial architecture and the sprawl of impoverishment, undeniably colourful but with the glow of fever victim rather than celebrant. Belém is not the Brazil of samba or *favelas* filled with Uzi-

toting crack czars, but it's not all bad news. It is still the Brazil of banama-creme polyester flares and floral-print shirts with collar points that dangle down to the pecs, and also the Brazil from which parrots, sloths, anteaters and other refugees from mega-death in the forest are salvaged and put on show in the market next to chilled Fanta, *agua mineral*, and – especially – Coke, frequently taken away in what look distressingly like colostomy bags.

We spend an hour on open water before creeping through rustic tropical islands to our port of call, then boarding a bus for Vieira's. From the bus stop we walk through the dust, asking at each cross-street how we are doing, and finally arrive at a run-down house. Out front, a girl is filling a pot at a standpipe. A puppy with the red, watery eyes of an eighty-year-old Piccadilly rent boy sniffs ankles and waits for someone to use a gun for something other than target practice.

In the front room there is a shrine: a row of water-stained LP sleeves crowning a TV set before which lie a crew of Lower Amazonian lager loutlets watching *Match of the Day*. Vieira emerges wiping sleep from his eyes, and sets about being the host.

Vieira was born near Barcarena. He spent his youth working on his father's plot, learning to play guitar early, but not deviating from local standard career pattern until his forties, when he jacked in the peasant profile and became a full-time musician. He has nine children – a couple of whom play in his band – by two wives. He broke up with the first for reasons he says he does not understand. Number two, he says, was a slim *morena* when they were courting, but has transmogrified into 'a nice little fatty'. I can't tell if he offers this comment by way of complaint or pride.

Ocean and I are clearly awkward visitors and, roused from his post-prandial Sunday snooze, Vieira is struggling to entertain us. Having spoken at length in Belém, he doesn't really have a lot more to say. In Jesus' office we talked about being a working musician, how Vieira fits into the regional scene, how popular music had changed over the past decade, basically confirming my misgivings about how little relevance my terms of reference had for local sensibility about what a musical style was. I wanted to know how musicians saw *carimbó* differing from *lambada*, where the overlap with *brega* began, and other headshakingly obtuse matters.

One of Vieira's older LPs, *Lambada*, is available on Stern's Diaspora label and although not his best effort it presents well the combination of rhythms and styles which sets Amazonian popular music apart from national and other regional forms. While the 'international' orientation of such major artists as Gil continues to provide the broad context for the assimilation of reggae and various disco and hard-rock sub-genres, Vieira is in a position analogous to that of such North American veterans as Flaco Jiminez, the foremost exponent of Tex-Mex border music, an artist whose 'authenticity' consigns him to a speciality market. I don't get it. The World Music I'm presented with in London is either stuff I've listened to all my life (never realizing, in mature but modest couch-potato mode, that I was ahead of the pack) or is late colonial retread. What 'World' means in London is 'Lost Empire', music from the continent they never cracked, Africa. The music of Vieira, or Jiminez for that matter, doesn't qualify as World Music because it too successfully resists appropriation by First World patrons. It falls just the wrong side of the folk art divide – uncoverable by First World artists, yet still not up for museum display.

At home, Vieira's musical identity takes a dive. In Barcarena he may be the King of Lambada, but all that means is that he works nights rather than days. As we walk down the road from Vieira's crib to the dock I'm stumped for gambits. From one vantage, he is one of the precious resources of a popular culture, a guy on the fringe who writes and performs music which, given lucky circumstances, may find an appreciative audience beyond the Amazonian interior. From another, however, he's just a guy who makes a living with a guitar rather than a machete. Certainly as an artist in Barcarena his standard of living is no better than that of his hard-labouring neighbours. His celebrity is like that of a priest, someone who's part of the local community but just happens not to have to work in the fields. It is hard to assess the exact cost of moving from shack-bound authenticity to making a decent living. I'm depressed. He wants to visit the local *acaí* house and talk about the postcards of the Tower of London I'm going to send. What he doesn't want to do is discuss being a musician in a small Amazonian town. I explain that I'm trying to find out how he places his music in relation to what he's heard from abroad, how he thinks Amazonian music fits into the bigger picture, but the problem is, what picture? All I've done is rouse him from his pre-gig nap. When that World Music audience rolls up, fine, but until then, can't he crawl back into his hammock?

This was not supposed to be relentless, humourless fieldwork interviewing, but it has that feel. Vieira is willing to talk about his music, but in fact we talk about anything but music and spend the time wandering around town looking at background. I want to talk to the artist, but he's gone all country on us. Check out the sound system at the town's premier club. Do I really want to look at a forty-kilowatt sound system which sits in the back room of a bakery?

The riverfront venue is bizarre. It looks like the art director indicated 'party set'. Through the narrow channel pass boats heading over a thousand miles upstream to Iquitos. Herzog missed his chance with *Fitzcarraldo*. He could have done a remake of *Beach Party Bingo* and sent Kinski back each evening to recover poolside at the Hilton.

Every aspect of the trip is depressing. Vieira is locked into a cycle of deep underdevelopment. His home turf is blemished by a bauxite processing and shipping plant. He lives in a place which is the bus/boat stop for urban merrymakers seeking that crucial beach experience before returning to the inflation-fuelled struggle downtown. They are herded on to cattle boats, fed junk (try an *egsburger*, become a vegan), and skate through it all with a good humour unmatched by the relentless Minogue/Jackson/Astley soundtrack.

We missed Vieira's evening gig to catch the boat back to Belém, but then lost track of a friend of a friend who owned both the bus and the boat and so ended up in a queue with a mass of returning holiday-makers. We squeezed on board the overloaded boat, and got back too late to secure that crucial evening meal of *frango na chapa* (chicken hit by a bus), rice, beans and *crème caramel.*

When Vieira says he is 'the King' all he means is that he's on the case in the *lambada* department, for what it's worth. Unfortunately, his prospects as a recording artist are undermined – if customer behaviour in Belém's record shops is any indication – by an attitude towards recorded artefacts which, although it has admirably modern nihilistic aspects, must be disheartening for the artist. In our attempts to procure a selection of Vieira records we spent time in a Belém record emporium where the standard routine is to take a selection of LPs and queue in front of a bank of headphone-equipped record decks which make a Dansette look like a DAT machine. In front of you is a potential customer who has a pile of a dozen records and is doing a thorough examination of each track. With a stylus fashioned from a fish hook and a cartridge attached with Sellotape, the deck keeps the customer happy until s/he has run through the pile, at which point s/he jams the records back into the sleeves, dumps them back on the racks and leaves.

At the end of the row of record decks is a deeply out-of-it fellow singing along to the headphone accompaniment with wild enthusiasm. He's so far gone that the staff are afraid to interrupt. The only time I saw them intervene in anything was when a fellow came in to sample records on offer from a street stall. This was going too far, but I can't see why they objected. No one seemed to buy records anyway, and the damage meted out to the wares was such that the shop might have been part of a *Which?* magazine survey investigating the durability of the modern LP. It's no wonder Vieira had such poor sales: the retail strategy involved the destruction of the records before they got out of the shop.

Ocean adopted the only appropriate alternative record-buying strategy. He chose records simply on the basis of artwork, content that even if the record inside was unplayable at least the visual pitch had something going for it. And that's where we started, looking at a record jacket and trying to read the story.

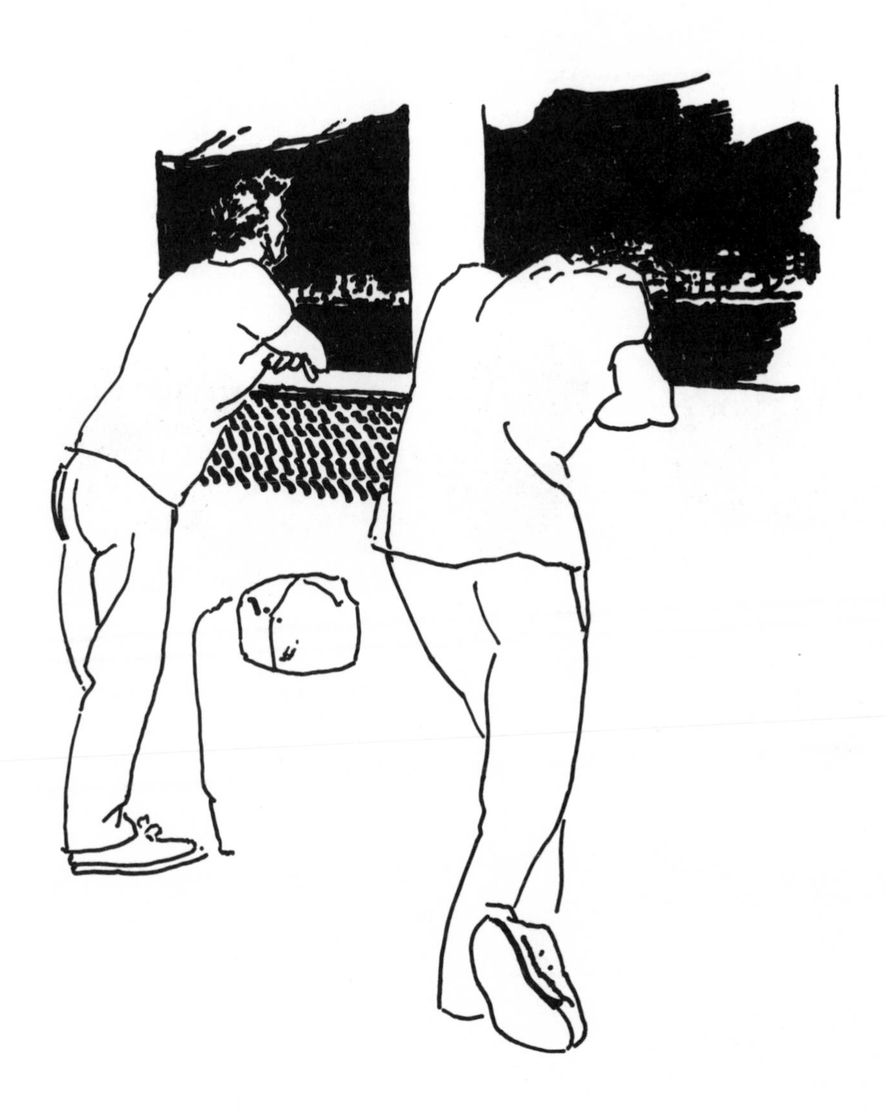

X

ECO-BABBLE
SHADES OF GREEN

Darwin's Lost Appendix – the Survival of the Brunch Bunch

A typical article on the state of eco-consciousness includes the following:

> Irreplaceable trees cut in the Brazilian rain forest resulted not only in desertification but in the loss of a unique resource to absorb industry-produced carbon dioxide and generate global oxygen, thus contributing to ozone depletion and global warming. The ensuing *Valdez* oil spill in Alaska didn't just despoil Prince William Sound, it ruined a pristine eco-system, resulting in the death of a wide variety of fish and game. Every chain of events led back to the same origins. Overpopulation. Ignorance. And greed. (from an article in *Vanity Fair* by Michael Shnayerson)

There is probably an increasing awareness of eco-issues (why else an article in that most unlikely of eco-organs, *Vanity Fair*?), but the corollary that holders of otherwise antagonistic political positions concede common ground on the subject is its own little eco-disaster. If ecology is a matter of agreement between people who fundamentally disagree on almost everything else, it must either be trivial or, as some greens argue, it must reflect a Spaceship Earth sensibility which cuts across political divides.

There is, unfortunately, no chance of getting Ambrose Bierce's views on the matter, but his *Devil's Dictionary* entry for politics makes a good start: 'A strife of interests masquerading as a contest of principles. The conduct of public affairs for private advantage.'[1]

There is nothing more political now than ecology, but what political means in this case is a non-partisan jousting contest. Eco-politics, it seems, is particularly worthy because it's not about divisiveness and privilege, but about oneness. It is easy to ridicule, as numerous dinosaur pundits selected for the task (perhaps their last) have revealed in their construction of the 'green backlash', but that's hardly the point. What is more important is the fact that a serious critique, one beginning with an examination of the preconditions for the eco-crisis – what is it, for example, about the way capitalism unfolds that demands the creation of an ecological crisis, little questions like that – has been put on a remote backburner. Instead, we have a lot of discussion of domestic management routines and smart consumer strategies. And, of course, exhortations from numerous fat cats who have 'seen the light'.

From another vantage point the subject matter of eco-concern is not so much ecology and the environment as the celebrity attached to promotion of such issues.[2] Ecology as a fixation of ordinary people is hardly newsworthy, but ecology as a pampered pet of media heavy-weights (check the list assembled in the *Vanity Fair* article) is another matter. It is important now, apparently, because a class of people who in fact epitomize the sort of conspicuous consumption which is far more environmentally threatening than anything an Amazonian peasant has ever done wish to be seen to have gone native. By all means, let them get on with it, but to cite their participation as an index of the eco-impact is rich.

If we look at the content of the Shnayerson article we may begin to see that the actual subject matter concerns the fact that it is now obligatory to be aware of the prominence of eco-babble. The fact that there is little of substance even in what seems to be a fairly uncontentious list of 'eco-disasters' (real or imminent) indicates the ascendancy of form over content. In the first sentence alone, there are several misleading references. It is wrong to refer to 'irreplaceable trees' – trees are replaceable, and in the right conditions even replace themselves. What isn't known is how long it takes to reconvene a complete (and, crucially, photographically viable) forest. 'Desertification' is an alarmist word in this context. There are lots of happy deserts which are ecologically sound. They may not be places where you would want to have a cocktail party , press conference or brunch, but they should be able to survive anyway. The word 'desertification' doesn't actually refer to deserts, but to denuded places such as garbage tips and patches of scorched earth. Cutting down trees doesn't necessarily produce either. Third comes the 'lungs of the earth' error, namely that the felling of forest will reduce the earth's capacity to absorb all that evil carbon dioxide. As mentioned earlier, felled native forest is soon replaced by (photographically unviable) secondary growth, which probably results in more carbon dioxide hungry biomass, a vigorous response to the release of all that material tied up in a mature forest. Yes, forest-burning does increase global warming, but compared to the contribution made by the apparatus of Western civilization, it is insignificant.

In the second sentence reference is made to a 'pristine eco-system'. By no normal meaning of the word has Prince William Sound been 'pristine' for a long time. What is meant, again, is photographically viable. The claim that 'Every chain of events led back to the same origins' is, like the rest of the factoids, simply wrong. Or am I not acknowledging poetic licence? In any case, in what (other than the most trivial) way does the *Valdez* disaster have anything to do with overpopulation? What does ignorance have to do with cutting down Amazonia? Amazonia is cut down by people who know exactly what they're doing. Greed? OK, but greed isn't exactly an ecological variable.

This pedantic exercise may be a futile gesture, but the meat of the matter is this: ecology makes such good copy that you can go almost anywhere with it. It can be scientific, dramatic, topical, political, personal, domestic and, perhaps most engagingly, lifestyle forming. In a run-down of dinner-party and fund-raising events, the *Vanity Fair* author notes, apropos a pair of the contributors to the new environmental consciousness,

> how rooted the Horns' environmentalism is in their life-styles. Forty-six year old Alan appears in jogging clothes, fiercely fit. Cindy, a former model, is at thirty-two not only strikingly beautiful but an almost blinding vision of health, with a radiant complexion and picture-perfect teeth. It's hardly sur-

> prising to learn that the Horns eat little but grains and speak seriously of not letting their baby outside for fear that the air may do it harm.

Leaving aside the fact that the article is engaged in a mild piss-take of the bandwagon jumpers, there are some things to be learned. The first is that little of consequence about the causes of Amazonian deforestation is common currency among those who write for what passes as the informed public, even after an unprecedented barrage of Amazonian news bulletins.[3] The second is that those of us who do not attend such gatherings may still have a chance if we get our diets sorted out.

Alan and Cindy's blinding, fierce, striking, picture-perfect, not to mention radiant attributes are, in fact, shared by others, some of whom actually live in Amazonia. How is this possible? I mean, is it conceivable that there are people not on any list anywhere who yet possess all these qualities (aside of course, from genderless children)? I'm not sure.

I do know, however, that there is one equation to which almost everyone involved in the eco-debate wants to lay claim, namely that 'the environmental' and 'the political' are one and the same. But what sort of politics is this? The equation has three mystifying aspects. The first is that in this context the term 'the environment' appears to refer to some imaginary eco-domain, beyond the fringes of the First World which has negligible social or human content. The second is that 'the political' refers to some assumed global policy in which the slogan 'One for all and all for one' is embossed on everyone's forehead. Third, the whole equation appears to be an argument for maintaining the status quo. This point was underlined by one of the most transparent greens, Margaret Thatcher, in an appeal for global co-operation 'to tackle environmental problems that know no frontiers'.[4] She stressed the widely reported 'polluters must pay' line (and we wait with bated breath to see how this is achieved in the Arcadia of non-regulation), but also stridently declared that 'those demanding a better environment must accept the costs involved', and that developing countries 'should not think that the problems – or the costs – belong in the advanced world'.

In Amazonian terms it is hard to imagine what this pay-to-play assertion could possibly mean. Much of the ecocide currently practised within the extractive industries in Amazonia already results from the demand that, regardless of long-term cost, Brazil repay its foreign debt forthwith. If sustained production of these exports is to carry on with appropriate environmental safeguards (assuming, just for the sake of fantasy, such a possibility), does this mean that foreign consumers will pay for the added costs? Just using a crude straw poll (the two cats and me): we don't think so. Such extractive industries are located in Amazonia precisely because they can produce the goods cheaply and without burdensome provisions designed to protect society and the environment.[5]

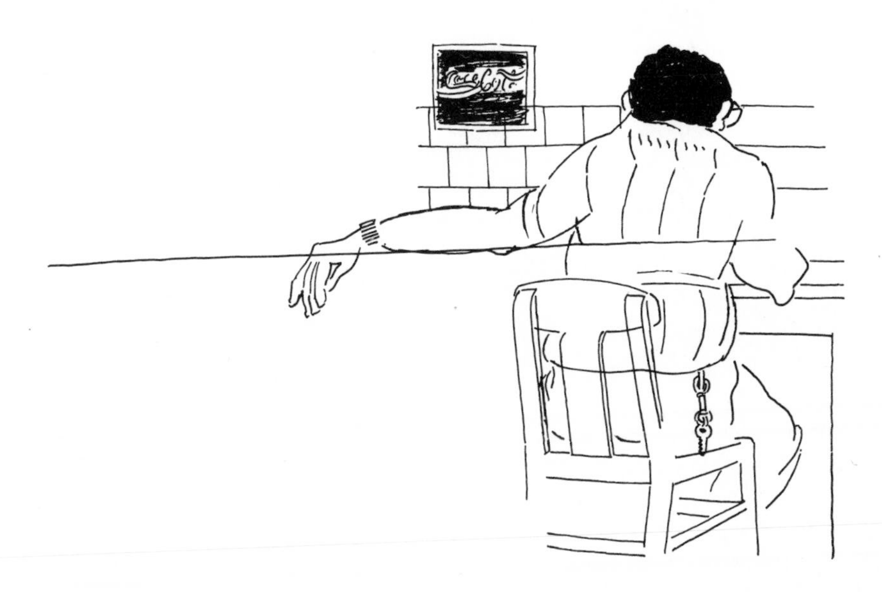

Thatcher's comments are unremarkable and represent the wisdom which would-be global managers such as the Club of Rome and numerous 'philanthropic' foundations have been touting for years. It is depressing that so much of the critical literature produced in response to the rise of such self-serving Global Village arguments has been consistently overlooked. Gore Vidal's[6] recent lashing out at the global management sub-text of much green posturing is in many respects a recapitulation of arguments available via Ridgeway and others almost twenty years ago. Vidal's version will probably be just as overlooked if the success of the kind of greenness now on offer is anything to go by.[7]

Since it looks like the current wave of green sensibility is going to flow around some crude cost–benefit analyses, it is salutary to look at a set of figures cited sixteen years ago in Enzensberger's prescient essay, 'A critique of political ecology'.[8] If, as Spaceship Earth ideologues argue, the earth's consumption of energy will have to be reduced if catastrophe is to be avoided (or merely postponed), at what level will consumption have to be pegged? If everyone in the world were to consume as much energy as the average US citizen, world production of energy would have to be increased sevenfold and the likelihood of getting around to finishing *A la Recherche du Temps Perdu* by electric light would not be very great. If per-capita consumption levels were stabilized at the current global average, there would need to be a slight rise in energy production, the Third World nations would see a threefold increase in their energy resources, and the Second World would have about the same. The historic energy gluttons (you, me), however, would have to suffer a period of contraction in energy consumption. When one reads, then, such claims as those of Mrs Thatcher who says that growth is 'not only environmentally compatible with environmental concern but necessary to pay for it', one is wasting valuable time that could otherwise be spent on Proust or, if Vidal is right, learning an Asian language.

Cold Sweat, Dead Trees and the Big Sting

I've been waking in a cold sweat lately, not – as you might innocently imagine – because of greenhouse-origin climatic shifts, nor indeed because of failure to engage fully in malaria prophylaxis. No, the cause of wee-hours distress is the announcement that the Amazonian rain forest is going to be saved by pop stars as well as the brunch bunch.

Why are they doing it? It is not normal behaviour. Do Metallica play save the whale benefits? Do ZZ Top play at the Chelsea Flower Show, or Dogs d'Amour promote unleaded petrol? Has Sir Cliff ever appeared at Greenham Common? The suggestion that ulterior motives are afoot would almost certainly be met with some tongue-clicking agreement, but not necessarily for very good reasons. The amount of flak that various participants in Live Aid projects received demonstrated that show-biz personalities' attempts to mobilize their celebrity in aid of something other than personal cash flow ran counter to a long list of cultural prescriptions, most of which were fatuous – leave aid to the experts; pop stars know nothing about the real world, unlike – say – frontbench MPs; welfare is an unnatural intervention in the normal state of affairs; and on and on. There was one criticism, however, which had and has a lot going for it, and this is that such forms of aid are at best palliatives and at worst allow those who should be doing something to abrogate responsibility for resolving the sorts of structural deformities which make crises inevitable. When raised in the context of Band Aid, this argument was generally rejected as irrelevant, given the immediacy of the problems. However, since the height of Band Aid it is hard to see what efforts are being made to forestall more such crises – overlooking, for the moment, that even that crisis is hardly resolved. The reaction next time around will almost certainly take the same form: bung in some warehoused wheat and let them get on with it.

The impending crisis of the Amazonian rain forests presents conditions for a kind of preview of reactions to come, and one of the more widely featured mobilizations is that associated with Sting and the plan to save the rain forests by establishing reserves. The 'Sting Solution', in spite of its apparent progressiveness, bears a striking resemblance to the major item in the First World's social engineering tool kit: privatization.

What little I know of the 'Sting Solution' is gleaned from the press, although I have to admit that by chance I saw it featured on 'Wogan' – a spectacle so unwholesome that one almost expected members of the audience to be invited on stage to touch the lip-plug worn by Raoni, the Indian brought along to lend colour to the proceedings. The Indian-rainforest reserves plan seems to consist of gathering funds from the Sting record purchasing catchment area and fan base, the money to be used to buy for the Indians what they already own. This is designer imperialism for the 1990s. Hobson, Lenin, Luxemburg, what did they know? They all failed to predict that once core countries had managed to shift their crises decisively to the Third World through the mechanism of 'aid' pegged to floating interest rates, the next stage would consist of getting selected regions of the Third World to start buying themselves. The various debt buy-back schemes widely mooted (a portion of debt is written off in exchange for environmental preservation orders) represent the kind of commercial resolution that would seem to be the blueprint for the immediate future.

Schemes intended to preserve the traditional territory of Amazonian Indians have an obvious public appeal, and they do seem to provide a mechanism for minimizing some of the more gross violations now occurring.[9] At the global level, however, such schemes are little more than the implementation of the policies of something which might be termed 'neo-ecology'.

Initially, ecology as formulated by Haeckel[10] was concerned with the ways in which a single animal species interacted with its organic and inorganic environment. This was a fairly restricted object of

analysis when compared with subsequent ecological research strategies which hoped to study the totality of relations between plant and animal species and their organic and inorganic environments. With the inclusion of the human species in this, things got completely out of hand, not only because of the frequently incompatible and mutually baffling methods and aims of the numerous sub-fields now implicated in the ecological or eco-system research, but also because no such thing as the human species is conceivable outside a thing called a social system. Social systems tend to have things like history and classes which are not so much part of a given eco-system as its creators. In short, once social systems are included as part of eco-systems, ecology no longer exists; rather, we have a social theory – neo-ecology – disguised (and, it appears, doing a very good job of it) as a complex and incomprehensible theory of natural systems.

Maybe such projects as the Sting plan will ensure that the felling of the forest will be impeded, and that Amazonians will be allowed to get on with their lives less encumbered by the predations of cost–benefit addicts. Or maybe, as that Portuguese nugget of wisdom has it, if shit turned to gold the poor would be born without assholes.

What the theme park plans will not do is affect the structures which virtually guarantee that the autonomy of Amazonians stays off the agenda. If such projects are implemented it will be because of the ascendancy of a new global management apparatus.[11] In fact, the only way that such projects could succeed would be under the auspices of management groups capable of mediating at the highest level among the various national governments (and regional bodies such as the EC and the OAS), banks and private enterprises.

There is no suggestion here that the undoubtedly sincere efforts of the preservationists are compromised, but that hardly ensures that the immediate ends of the projects are not co-optable. In fact, they cannot avoid being co-opted. Simply by proposing the reserves solution, such projects have abandoned larger questions about the rights of Amazonians as Amazonian residents and as Brazilian citizens. And they've done it not even in the (neo-ecological) name of the eco-system, but in the name of something which doesn't even exist – that is, a rain forest as pristine and primitive as the Garden of Eden.

The Sting plan just happens to be around promoting this particular greenish line. It certainly didn't invent it, nor is it responsible for it, and in a mature gesture I might even concede that the attention Sting's celebrity brings to the issues might have some benefits. The overriding problem, however, is that this particular rendition of the crisis of

Amazonia produces a completely mystifying discussion in which comforting but ineffective formulae are recited – save a tree and save the world, repeat after me, save a tree . . . – and people believe that somehow, magically, it will happen.[12] Regardless of the good intentions of the proponents, crises which are structural and not episodic cannot be solved by short bursts of rock-star publicity. In Amazonia at present, all you have to do is mentioned the phrase 'save the rain forest' and, like magic, you get a sardonic smile and the word 'Sting'.

Is it fair to pillory these honest if somewhat misguided gods, to hold them up as paragons of a kind of greenness which is characterized more by flag-waving fervour than analysis? Maybe not. I might have kept quiet, but I made the mistake of buying *Q* magazine. I am not touting a 'listen only to the experts' line, but there is something disagreeable about the fact that for an Indian genocide story to reach the cover of a popular magazine there has to be a good public relations hook. For the magazine, the story is Sting. For Sting, the story is the Indians. For the reader, there is an awkward grafting of the two – a serious topic mediated by a celebrity who might as well be talking about seal-culling.

About Amazonian Indians Sting says in *Q*: 'I think they hold clues as to who *we* are. I have a theory that we don't really understand the world, we think we do, but we don't. Like I don't know where my shoes came from, I don't know who made them or how they were made. I don't know where most of the things in this house came from.'

The crucial item here (aside from the shoe discussion, a long-neglected classic in the philosophical literature) is the italicized *we* – as is clear from a statement which occurs later in the same interview in answer to a question about the rapid turnover of charity fashions: 'I've got a feeling this is such a fundamental problem to all of us. Heroin is something where you can say, Well I'm not taking heroin and nobody in my family is, so I can push that away. The Ethiopian famine, you can say, It doesn't affect me. But the rainforest problem affects us all.'

The 'we' and 'us' in these phrases are not, in spite of appearances, quite as collectively referential as might be imagined. They obviously exclude heroin users (unquestionably, it goes without saying, bad) and Ethiopians (my stomach is not your stomach). In fact, they don't refer to 'us' in any normal sense. They refer to First Worlders who recognize that their high standards of living have had costs and consequences which are no longer as easily suppressible as they have been in the past. Once this is clear, the concern for the Indians becomes more explicable (and it needs explaining: after 450 years of persecution, this concern for their welfare is a volte-face of some size).

So, 'we' are saving 'ourselves'. This is hardly news. Eco-discourse has long embodied this ambivalence vis-à-vis the common good on one hand and individual advantage on the other, but it's an awkward argument which depends on some spurious notions about the character of society. Is there a common interest, a 'we-ness', for example, between members of different classes, different ethnic groups and different countries? What exactly does the 'we-ness' adduced by the reserves plan add up to? What is claimed as the bond between us and the Kayapó Indians is intended genuinely enough, I suppose, but is trivial inasmuch as it really amounts to little more than a common need for breathable atmosphere.

One point certainly missing from both text and photos in the *Q* feature is that the forest is part of a complicated social landscape, one in which for most actors the issues of forest preservation are vague distractions. It is the absence of this wider picture which leaves the Sting solution looking so pallid. How is his (or any other's) magic celebrity wand going to solve the problems engendered by the grotesque maldistribution of agricultural land, the absence of official commitment to existing legislation, the effects of unregulated extraction throughout the region? Not to mention that one-legged Amazonian street urchin wearing a Jeff Healey T-shirt. Well, it's not, and things aren't helped by pretending that it will.

On the other hand, it's probably not such a bad idea to keep an eye on what the celebrity ecos are looking at. They're in touch with the market – which is the whole wide world now that Baudrillard & Co have kitted us out ready to inhabit the postmodern semiosphere – and are capable of picking up on a wide range of these meta-cultural shifts. Right now they're saying get greenish. What is going on here is not, as unkind commentators might suggest, that this eco-pitch is simply part of a self-aggrandizement routine, but that they're mouthing and representing comforting wisdom. The whole delivery displays the charm and ease with which sensitive, thoughtful, concerned First Worlders would like to comport themselves. Let's listen to Sting describe his meeting with Brazil's president, Jose Sarney: 'How I managed this I don't know. But I arrived on the Saturday and on the Sunday morning I was walking into the Palace gates, in my fatigues, to meet the President of Brazil.'

Just like that. Upon first reading this I thought that his incredible casualness was very likely the result of having walked into the Palace gates rather than through them, but then I got a grip on myself. He simply wants us to savour the fact that he was wearing fatigues when he met the president. He wants us to get straight exactly who is *Excelentíssimo*. Now you know.

This kind of nonsense reveals an important conceit – an old one, but still active – which prevails in discussions of First World–Third World and North–South relations and is just as familiar in liberal eco-discourse as it is in Cold War Pangloss-speak: however bad things may look, they can be controlled; that stench can be engineered out of the way, that pile of crap can be disposed of, that one-armed thing on a home-made skateboard is just a temporary aberration; and once the market restabilizes, the Third World will get on up.

The Sting plan has visibility and importance not only because it is the *Sting* plan – and not, say, the Nugent–Ocean plan, the NO plan to insiders – but also because of its anodyne content and utter palatability for First Worlders: it keeps serious analysis at arm's length and it simplifies the issues. In an era in which the term 'consciousness raising' has become yet another cheap armament in the war chest of marketing, it may seem damning with faint praise to say so, but still, credit where credit's due: better that Amazonia be somewhere near the agenda. But the concrete results of this example of consciousness raising are likely to enhance the notion that the solution lies in the superior abilities of 'the civilized', who in no small way are responsible for the problem in the first place.

For the remote observer, perspectives on Amazonia, to the limited degree that they are available at all, are frequently combined in confusing ways. The gathering in Altamira in February 1989 in protest at the proposed Xingu hydroelectric project was a particularly good opportunity for many confusions and contradictions to rear their variously pleasing and ugly little heads.

Pope John Paul, for example, was reported in the *New York Times* (26 February 1989) to have 'sent a message of spiritual solidarity', especially bizarre and cynical given his notable lack of support for the numerous priests who have defended (not infrequently at the cost of their lives) the rights of the Indians and peasants at the receiving end of Amazonian progress. From another perspective we have, presenting a decidedly self-preservationist argument, the deputy prime minister of the Netherlands declaring that 'if the Amazon is lost, the resulting greenhouse effect would, among other things, flood Holland' (*Guardian Weekly*, 2 April 1989). British banks – Lloyds, NatWest and Midland – pencilled in for a tradition-shattering private bank participation with the World Bank in funding the hydroelectric scheme, were somewhat flummoxed by the extent of public dismay (*Guardian Weekly*, 12 March 1989).

Perhaps the most telling story, however, was that which revealed a significant confusion within the Brazilian Workers Party (PT), to which Chico Mendes, the murdered rubber-tapper organizer, belonged and which is now led by the internationally famous Lula, who was largely responsible for putting trade unionism back on the Brazilian map. The party 'had enthusiastic speakers at Altamira expressing solidarity with the Indians'. But, as one said: 'We need jobs, so we need factories, so we need power, so we need nuclear energy and/or large dams, and the best place for large dams is the underpopulated Amazon' (*Guardian Weekly*, 12 March 1989). With this kind of support you can see why Amazonians too are waking up in a cold sweat.

Elsewhere we have people like the anthropology lecturer on whose office door is a sign which reads: 'Defend the Indians: Our Jobs Depend on Them'. He's a card.

A clipping floating on my desk is headlined: 'Brazil Police Close in on Mendes Killer' (*Guardian*, 31 December 1988). Months later, there is little news on the hit-and-run murder front. The men widely reported (one of them, as I remember, confessed more than a year ago) to have killed Mendes are still being 'processed', but the Mendes story, as far as the press is concerned, is located elsewhere, namely Hollywood, where a Chico biopic is in production. The real fracas concerns who has the greatest moral right to 'tell Chico's story'. The clipping pile grows, but I don't know how to sort it out. Today's clipping is 'Rain Forest Campaign "Ignores Natives" ' (*Guardian*, 7 June 1989). Last week's goodie was 'Deformities of Lust in Amazonia' (*Guardian*, 2 June 1989 – a mercury story).

After the dust has settled we have the bleat of corporate reason, in the form of British Petroleum's Sir Peter Walters' reply to a critical article (*Sunday Times*, 25 June 1989) about BP's cassiterite operations in Amazonia. In the face of a claim (not refuted) that BP's operation has 'adversely affected as much as 250,000 acres' of Amazonia, Sir Peter answers that, 'You can be sure that BP's commitment to the "pursuit of excellence" remains as firm as ever throughout the company. That phrase means exactly what it says: striving to achieve excellence.' Gosh.

The Correct Explanation

Having discussed the range of attitudes to the course of Amazonian development (here and in Chapter VIII), I cannot shirk the business of presenting my own position. The Correct Explanation begins with the observation that the dilemmas of Amazonia are not exclusively located in Amazonia, are not particularly about green or biological phenomena, and are not obviously fixable. Too many of the solutions mooted in the First World are based on the egotistical assumption that 'We can handle it'. This view may be understandable after so many years of habit-forming rehearsal, but as the twentieth century draws to a close, the evidence is that the supervision of developments on the periphery, in the so-called Third World, has fallen beyond the reach of traditional control; and in spite of soaring confidence in the generic West, the transformation of the Third World is currently increasing the distance between core and periphery standards of living rather than reducing it. Genuinely charitable aid – i.e. aid given without any strings and which is at least ostensibly directed towards or shaped by a concept of autonomous development – represents a very small proportion of total 'aid', the gross misnomer which covers bilateral, multilateral, and private bank lending.[13] The dominance of such 'aid' ensures not only that good intentions are often ineffective, but also that even if for some reason the lenders and developers packed it in, the effects of half a millennium of development could hardly be reversed. In other words, however much enthusiasm might be drummed up by however many First Worlders sympathetic to the Third World, there is little evidence to suggest that cheerleading has any chance of mitigating the effects of development in the worst remunerated sectors in the global division of labour.[14]

The Correct Explanation differs from other theories about Amazonian development in that I cannot claim to be offering a simple prescription for a happy Amazonia, nor am I confident that such a thing can exist. Thus far the historical record is pretty empty of evidence that even if a solution existed it would be implemented; and there are developments in the Third World which suggest that confidence in the West's position behind the wheel of history is at a low ebb. Leaving aside the evidence that the action is moving from the West to the Pacific rim,[15] there is also trouble in the form of non-standard social movements.

The *Sendero Luminoso*, the Shining Path movement of Peru, may be a realistic prototype of near-future social movements in countries where

the developmentalist graft simply hasn't taken. The *Senderistas*, to the limited degree that they have been willing to make their intentions plain, are in a number of crucial respects different from other dissident or anti-systemic movements. They do not want their fair share, they do not want state power, they do not want allies. They want demolition of the system *tout court*. They may well exonerate Fanon's claims about the special revolutionary potential of those who have nothing left to lose. They have learned a lesson, or maybe just observed a lesson being learned by others: successful Third World movements have been presented with two versions of themselves – one which works internally, and one which is forced on them in order to meet the demands of larger powers. For instance, Zapata and Villa didn't want to displace capitalism and replace it with a socialist utopia, as the larger powers claimed, they wanted to get the landlords off their backs. Once that internal goal was achieved, they were gone. But that wasn't enough for the big powers, according to whom they had to be developed into superbad frito banditos. Fidel Castro would probably have liked one day to have had lunch with JFK at Four Seasons,[16] but no chance. He was given a leading role in the Evil Empire. Recognizing this (and having the example of Nicaragua to remind them as they go: Daniel Ortega could stand in front of the White House, eviscerate himself, and still be accused of 'grandstanding', 'duplicity', 'insincerity'), the *Senderistas* have done what every campus rebel who ever delivered a missive claimed to have done: presented a set of non-negotiable demands. They are non-negotiable in part because the *Senderistas* refuse to talk to their enemies, but they are also non-negotiable because there is not, apparently, anything to negotiate. They aren't asking for a larger slice of the pie; they aren't even asking for the whole pie. They just aren't talking about it.

Not a very good prognosis, especially when the prime example is something as obscure (and romanticizable) as *Senderista*, but the drift is this: belief in a shining future is alive and well, and it's not, as once, extraordinary or supernatural. Looting of supermarkets, as in Brazil over the past few years (or Venezuela, or Argentina), is separated in the popular consciousness from, say, demonstrations of Islamic tarantism; but the difference is only that in the latter case a tradition is (distant observers assure us) being revived, while in the former case – and as with the *Senderistas* – the movement is in the first throes of creating a tradition, declaring objectives quite different from those the First World would like to see achieved. Here again the *Senderistas* provide a salutary hint of the elaborate possibilities to come, combining as they do a fundamentalist Maoism, nativistic/First People/ Quechua rootsiness, urban terrorist routines (random explosions meant to create panic in the populace and undermine the credibility of both civilian and military claims to control) and rural direct challenges to the state (frightening or assassinating local office-holders or, as recently reported, Europeans on walking holidays). To cap it all, the *Senderistas* seem to have come to local agreements with the narco-capitalists who share an interest in minimizing the state's ability to function in the interior and whose success in forging alliances with local growers has been a spur to the US Drug Enforcement Agency operatives clamouring for action.

As it happens, police raids on drug gangs in Rio's Rocinha (a prominent *favela*) have already laid out the basics for the Brazilian version of this secular millenarianism. Hollywood is no doubt agog, but the problem for film-makers is that the journalistic reality is going to inure the public before the big-screen version is ready. Just as the Hollywood western's lifespan was shortened by television coverage of the real thing (US soldiers murdering South-East Asian Indians), cinematic portrayals of urban violence will have to compete with reality, a tough act to follow.

I have strayed, but for good reason. Part of the Correct Explanation should be some concrete advice on what to do. It simply isn't fair to knock the other – putative – solutions and then not offer a viable alternative: 'If you can't say something nice, don't say anything at all.'

I'm not too sure about this prescription. What if there isn't anything to be recommended? What if, after careful perusal of every corner of the heart of hearts, there simply isn't a good word to be said? Is there still a case for making an effort, showing willing, not letting the side down? Maybe, but it seems kind of desperate, like shining your shoes just before you go in to have your legs amputated. What if, in a domain ruled by demagogues, narco-capitalists, thugs, experts and quislings of every description, there simply isn't a better programme on another channel? What if, option-wise, the *Senderistas* are where it's at? Or what if, in fact, the *Senderistas* are just sandbox stuff and around the corner are the serious grown-up ones, the ones who don't even believe in a utopia because their experience has given them nothing from which to construct one? What if the future anti-systemics, in fact, actually match the horror of those who have for so long been running the show?[17] What if you buy a book on dog training and it turns out you don't have a dog at all but an HIV-positive *latino* Jaws clone with extreme prejudice, one with mercury limbs and a complete indifference to the space programme and the Pepsi/Coca Cola war? That may be the conclusion, but there are things leading up to it which suggest some mollifying variations.

One of the premises of this book is that Amazonia is, in South American terms, a special case, a place which is undeniably part of the broad sweep of Iberian, luso-tropical colonial society, but which has for various reasons maintained a separate identity. One aspect of this identity is that it has – until recently – failed to impress itself upon the outside world except in terms of a number of stereotypes – from blowpipe to *boto,* lip-plug to *puta,* piranha to padre – which are not fabrications, but which are hardly representative either. A simple question follows from this: if lived-in Amazonia isn't the same as Amazonia consumed from a distance, why the discrepancy?

The answer which immediately presents itself is that the maintenance of the fake Amazonia, or the falsely perceived Amazonia, serves someone's interests; and one of the reasons why it is difficult to see these interests is because they're devoid of any throbbing tropical

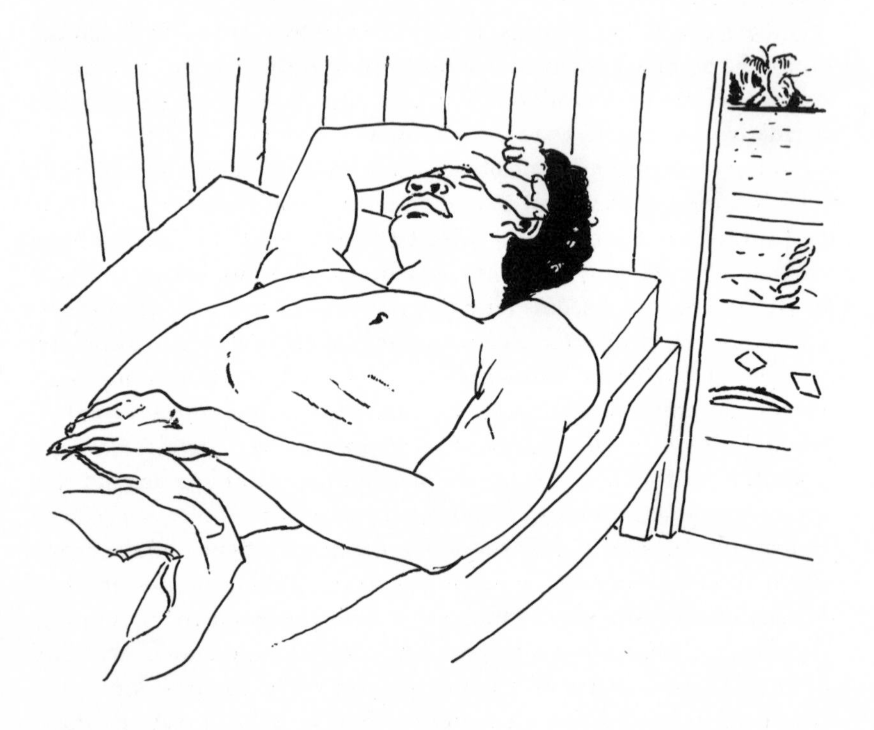

vibe, any exoticism, any difference. They're mundane, normal, relaxed to the point of narcolepsy, a bunch of statistics on import/export ratios and debt-repayment boondoggles and capital-flight scams and tied loans. Crucially, as far as critical perceptions of Amazonia go, they are largely external to Amazonia and Brazil, and they have a dramatic ability to transform what they touch regardless of what Amazonians themselves are up to or interested in. In the very grossest terms, there is demand for various raw materials: gold, iron ore, bauxite, manganese, cassiterite, timber, and perhaps some (or a fair amount of) *coca*. First Worlders and allies are intensely interested in these raw materials. Japan is keen to build a road into Amazonia from Bolivia so that it can have more direct access to cheap timber (Japan, virtually covered in forest, would prefer to use others' first). The EC is one of the major backers of the iron-ore mining operations in Serra do Carajás, a project which has stimulated the mass felling of forest to be used in pig-iron smelting. In relation to all these forms of extraction for export, Amazonia is, as noted before, raw materials. From this perspective the local Amazonian social landscape, for reasons examined earlier, is simply irrelevant. Forget the imaginative possibility of the rain forest *flâneur*,[18] let's talk preferred shares.

From the viewpoint of the state, too, Amazonia is pretty much a social dead zone. Geopolitically, Amazonia is seen as a massive buffer between Brazil and its northern and western neighbours and in the pronouncements of national politicians Amazonia is a military domain still depicted as a prize yet to be secured.[19] The region has been treated as the social equivalent of a landfill, an overspill zone to which have been directed resourceless labourers from the north-east (and in recent years, a slightly better-off petty entrepreneurial cohort from the south). Given the focus of commercial agriculture in the more temperate regions of Brazil on export crops, the opening of Amazonian territory to a smallholder peasantry has made possible the cheap production of staple foodstuffs without distracting capitalist agriculture from its more important task of securing foreign exchange.

In relation to these two perspectives then – that is, Amazonia as a gross resource domain for Brazilian speculators as well as foreign investors, and as an abused child of the state – it's hard to see how any seriously upbeat message might emerge. For one thing, the eco-despoliation of Amazonia is not happening because those responsible (or in a position to affect things) don't know any better, but rather because they are at best indifferent (I'm thinking particularly of those subscribers to the stupid *latino* theory (see Chapter VIII) who are quite happy to shrug their shoulders and say, 'You know what it's like down here in *mañana*-land . . . ' and turn purple at the thought that the Sandinistas should not be subjected to deeply corrective treatment). For another thing, despoliation is not taking place because things are unsupervised. Quite the opposite, they are planned and administered although it is difficult to disentangle rationale from consequence. For example, the annual burning of rain forest is illegal (as are, for that matter, invasion of Indian land in search of gold or timber, as well as a variety of lower-ranking felonies), yet the prosecution of malfeasants is as rare as the discovery of hens' teeth. For some observers, that laws are unenforced or unenforceable is simply a fact of life which should come as a surprise only to the hopelessly naive. For others, however, this apparent slippage between intention and reality is a structured relationship and one which is, to say the least, highly profitable.

The failure to distinguish between intended and unintended effects crops up in many critiques of Amazonian development policy. As far as I can tell, most researchers in Amazonia have given the benefit of the doubt to the planners, administrators and corporate investors who have created the mess. The line which researchers are almost compelled to take is that more research is needed in order for the same mistakes not to be repeated. This was OK for a couple of years, the time, say, it took for the original goals of Transamazonica – establishment of a state-planned smallholder peasantry – to be abandoned (about four years, starting with the construction of the road begun in 1970); but after that it was craven to pretend that larger scams were not afoot.

The most widely articulated view on Transamazonica is that it was a mistake. It was poorly planned, it was too ambitious, it was ill-informed, it was – in short – a typically cack-handed exercise along the lines prescribed by the stupid *latino* theory. I think there is something to be said for that explanation; not a lot, but something. What about the widely cited connection between the families of certain generals and certain road-building contractors? What about the very short period of time between announcement of plans for the highway and commencement of its construction? What about the failure to settle more than 4 per cent of the projected number of colonist families in the official projects? What about the obvious fiscal advantages to clearing forest regardless of whether the resulting production is profitable or not? Lots of mistakes were made which needn't have been made.

Far more importantly, hand-wringing and finger-pointing over Transamazonica disguises its very notable and destructive successes:

the mere presence on this scale of the state in Amazonia legitimized its obliteration of local government (much of this being done via various National Security imperatives); and the continued presence of the World Bank conferred an ultra-pukkaness which has yet to be successfully challenged; a country with one of the most decadent agrarian structures in the world was able to offer cheap land (however minimal its agricultural utility) to a land-poor rural mass and claim a still barely diminished ideological victory (*Integrar Para Não Entregar* – Integrate in order not to lose it to foreigners, or in sloganese, 'Use It or Lose It'). The building of the road also enhanced the possibility and profitability of economies of scale, giving extended life to larger investors as well as introducing into Amazonia, on an unprecedented scale, people who could not possibly survive without cutting down the forest. The latter are far from responsible for the large-scale felling which has occurred, but their presence in such numbers is symptomatic of the degree to which Amazonian development politics has changed. You may feel strongly about the hunter/fisherman/farmer who knocks off a monkey/manatee/brazil nut tree, but s/he is nothing compared to the person who knocked off thousands of the same for no reason grander than the fact that it was cheaper to do so in Amazonia than in the Philippines, the Congo, Indonesia or Malaysia.

By this analysis, unfortunately, Amazonia is far from being a failure. It is a great success story, and this is the main problem for the green critique as well, I think, as for the 'it was all a big mistake' theorists. The obvious question here is: who benefits? Well, not Amazonians by and large; and it is a self-fulfilling prophecy that this will continue to be the case because Amazonians are going to be disciplined into submission as the 'Amazonia is a disaster' routine is played out.

The big-time exploitation of Amazonia (i.e. the dams, iron-ore extraction, timber-felling) is dependent on foreign investment, and the nature of foreign investment is that the immediate benefits are realized in the investing countries. For example, the long-term strategy of Carajás investors may well be to procure assured, cheap supplies of iron ore, but if for some reason cheaper sources appear elsewhere, such investors will already have recouped a lot of their development costs, inasmuch as they will already have been paid for many of the capital inputs. Sure, they'll be unhappy at having to pack up and move, but it's hardly the end of the line. They've done it before after all (remember the 'rubber boom'?). What will remain is the 'Amazing Amazon', that 'challenge of the tropics', that 'big frontier'. Next time around, of course, tropicality may well have given way to something

more akin to a New World Sahel. But hey, what's life without a challenge?

If you really want to do something useful in Amazonia, thinking greenish thoughts or trying to get offending Amazonians to think greenish thoughts is inconsequential. Given the party political configuration in Britain, most concerned citizens devote themselves to consumer issues which, if they don't have any effect on despoliation, at least begin to educate those for whom mahogany toilet seats are simply made in factories. A number of research programmes have now adopted a kind of 'enlightened management' position: if Amazonia is being destroyed by greed merchants, show them that they can make as much or more money by exploiting a managed forest rather than a cleared one. (For instance, Friends of the Earth have organized a conference on the subject in London in May 1990.) Debt buy-back schemes, if they ever get beyond the theme park stage, may help as well.

In general, though, it's hard to see how a situation which results from the asymmetry of Amazonia's relations with the First World is going to be positively transformed without without a modification of that asymmetry. The 'wise management' of Amazonia is still the 'management' of Amazonia, and management is just a euphemism for the historical antecedents: subjugation, genocide, colonial exploitation, and 'trading partnership'. A positive outcome of the impending crisis, unless it is directed from within Amazonia and Brazil by those whose lives and livelihoods are immediately affected, is hard to formulate.

I can't claim that this is a widely held view. In fact it is an unpopular and dismissed one, and for two understandable – but unsound – reasons. For those who live in Amazonia, the idea that things are not suddenly going to get better is unpalatable, and even more so coming from a supposedly sympathetic First Worlder. For many First Worlders, especially Americans, optimism – by some Mendelian quirk of nature – is an unshakeable part of their genetic make-up and they are constitutionally incapable of conceiving of impossibility. The idea that solutions might not be found is the monster from the swamp of the near future.

Out of this, something positive is concoctable, says the reluctant chef. But if it's upbeat, it's also restrained.

The quick rendition is this: there are two main Amazonian antagonists, those who use raw materials and those who make possible the extraction of raw materials. The former are global consumers who could not care less whether their plywood comes from the Philippines or Amazonia. The latter are epitomized by those who have already made their money before anything is produced. If, for instance, you make tree-felling tractors or hydroelectric turbines or barges and big diesel engines, it really doesn't matter whether your equipment actually does what is outlined in the long-term brief. As long as it has already been incorporated (i.e. paid for) in the development scheme/scam, things are cool. As noted earlier, if the iron ore in Serra do Carajás becomes too expensive in the near future, those left holding the bag will find themselves in a familiar role – Third Worlders who have just demonstrated again why they are unqualified to join the First World: they're too easy to rip off.

But the interesting developments will take place among those left (again) high and dry, 'the dregs', and while not wishing to romanticize the prospects of the *caboclos*, it's hard to avoid the historical antecedents.

The version of Amazonia which survives the attentions of Europe and North America seems pretty hopeless. It's very hard, for example, to find a lot in the specialist literature which suggests that *caboclos* have much going for them. If you read the non-specialist literature you'd be lucky to recognize that *caboclos* are much more than transitory blushes. We're talking trees as the big actors here. Nevertheless, one of the few historical constants in Amazonia is riverine society. It was there before the colonial sword and flag showed up, and it has remained in spite of post-Columbian attempts to do things differently.

The Amazonia that has so far proved durable lies beyond the lust for large-scale extraction of terrestrial commodities. Put another way, if Amazonians had depended on terrestrial resources there would be no Amazonians, and those Amazonians who have survived without the assistance of developers have found that a riverine focus is far more life-enhancing. This is not to say that the forest *per se* is or has been a null set in survival terms, but only that for these people the river has proved a vastly more important resource than the forest. This is true not only in terms of the agricultural advantages of *várzea* soils, but also in terms of fishing over hunting. There is hardly anyone who has studied modern Amazonian societies or mapped Amazonian food resources who has not argued that the *várzeas* make a lot more sense than any other eco-zones. Comprising only 2 per cent of the land available in Amazonia, the *várzeas* are disproportionately fecund. But it is no surprise that they are overlooked in the big plans offered by the professional advisers. Food is not where it's at, and certainly not food grown and consumed by the same people. That's absurd. If you're modern you buy your food.

The current emphasis on terrestrial resources is an import, and it reflects the priority placed on production whose value can be realized outside Brazil and Amazonia. For the moment these industries sustain a short-term and incohesive neo-Amazonia which is detached from its past because it has had no say in the way this development fantasy was thrust upon it. Fortunately there is still another Amazonia which remains invisible. It is invisible both because it has been excluded (most new investment in Amazonia displaces peasants and doesn't reabsorb their labour – they are casual background), and invisible because it still has to make a living and does so where the short-term future can't afford to operate. The highly criticized low-tech Amazonian, getting by on fish, *açai* and a bowl of *farinha*, is going to be there long after the monuments to development are enveloped by the dust kicked up by the heels of the retiring managers and consultants, and the rise of rural labour organizations is a testimony to the resistance which Amazonians themselves can muster.

XI

ADVANCED TOURISM

HAPPY TRAILS, FORESTS AND FOREIGNERS

'Eco-babble' is a cheap shot, but not quite cheap enough. The outcome of externally-organized development in Amazonia is almost certain to pale into insignificance as 'environmental concern' increasingly comes to be a euphemism for an extensive range of global interventions under the guise of 'wise management'.

What is put forward in various global management schemes is the following argument: the future of the planet is too important to be placed in the hands of the unqualified (i.e. non-First Worlders, NGOs and environmental lobbyists). William C. Clark, for example, in a programmatic discussion of what is to be done, notes that:

> Pluralism has much to recommend it. But are we not nearing a point of diminishing returns where too many meetings, too many declarations and too many visiting experts leave too few people with too few resources and too little time to actually do anything? The immediate need at the international level is for a forum in which ministerial-level co-ordination of environmental-management activities can be regularly discussed and implemented, much as is already done for international economic policy.

The amount of pent-up enthusiasm shown by those whose economies are already administered via centralized international economic policy forums can only be guessed at.

Beyond the impression of a schoolmaster who has lost control, there is the strong whiff of a system running away with itself, and the voices making the loudest demands (remember, pluralism is no longer affordable) are those who already have privileged managerial access to the podium. For those without such access it may be difficult to appreciate the difference between the status quo and the proposed globalist agenda.

The problem has been raised in previous chapters, where some effort has been made to puncture the green life-raft – not in the name of vandalism, but in the name of a kind of realism which seems to have vanished from the social landscape. Amazonia belongs to Amazonians. Useful though others' efforts might be, they should probably know some of the basics before they presume to pitch in. The Amazonia portrayed in most tree-hugging accounts is fictional. If you are interested, there is a real one out there.

That must be the introduction to the conclusion, the measured lead-in to a wisdom-saturated summing up. Wise counsel informs me that there is an obligation to provide not just the Correct Explanation, but also the Correct Solution. But much as I recognize the sincerity of such an appeal, each time I open a newspaper I'm confronted with evidence which leaves me feeling not up to the task. On the 'wild frontier' front there is an account of Roraima gold miners killing Yanomami. On the 'stupid *latino*' front there is coverage of a Varig airline pilot said to have been so concerned with the outcome of a Brazil–Chile football match that he lost track of where he was and crashed the jet in the middle of the forest, hundreds of miles off course.

For a quick reality check it is worth looking at two articles which appeared on the same day (5 November 1989) in the same newspaper (*Sunday Correspondent*). In one, a prominent green spokeswoman discusses how she came to get involved in the Green Party and makes the sort of point which dramatically reveals the distance between the lifestyle imperatives of inhabitants of the First and Third Worlds.

> Women in the Third World put pots on their heads and walk 20 miles to get water from the river. We get in our cars and

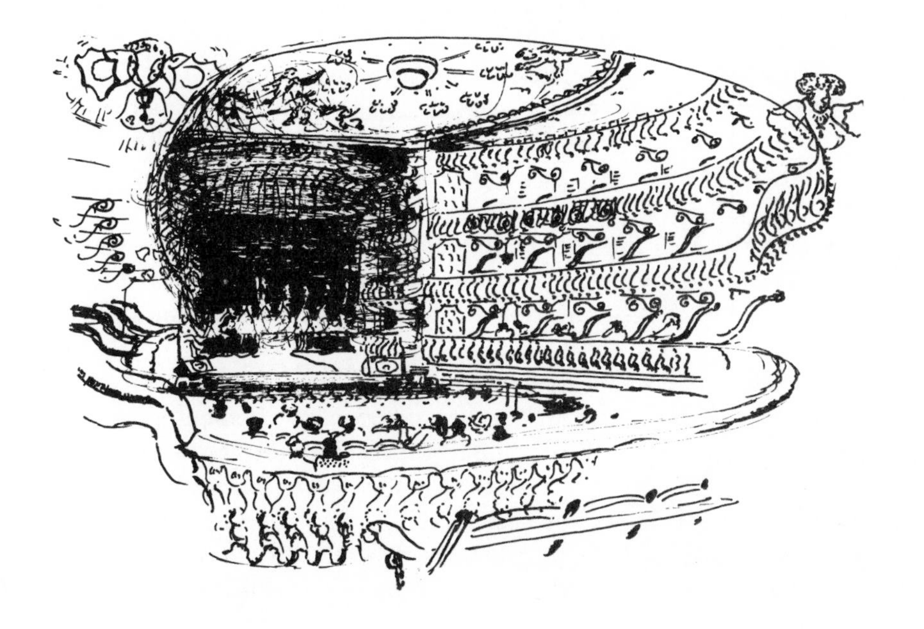

> drive 20 miles to buy it in plastic bottles in the supermarket. So what is progress, what is civilization?

It's a good contrast, but how real is it? It underlines the absurdity of a system in which privilege is reflected in being able to drive (unleaded, we hope) to the deli to get a bottle of Perrier, but is the twenty-mile hike typical of Third World societies? A lot of people in the Third World would not recognize themselves in such accounts. Leaving aside these small details, we move on to the statement that:

> Businessmen may actually be the last to become green, but they will eventually have to because we have no choice. We're all going to have to green our lifestyles in order to survive. It is going to be forced on us by external, maybe unpleasant circumstances, or are we going to do it in an orderly way, by choice? That is the question of the Nineties.

This view of the world simply does not take advantage of the information currently available. In fact, the imperious pride taken in its correctness is inversely proportional to its grasp of the most basic questions. Who is this 'we'? It is clearly not the 'businessmen', who will only be dragged along later. What are these 'external circumstances'? Are they extra-terrestrial? Are they properties of social systems, those things with features such as class, property, privilege – all that stuff that 'oneness' no longer recognizes?

The other story concerns a new Brazilian presidential candidate, Silvio Santos, host – according to the *Sunday Correspondent*'s correspondent – of 'one of the world's most vulgar variety shows'. That this should be regarded as a defect, or even noteworthy following eight years of Ronald Raygun's careering around the wheelhouse of the ship of state may come as something of a surprise to those still awake, but such is the mystery of life. Still, the message is that Brazil is in danger of having its democratic process subverted by an unqualified clown.

These two stories represent well the difficulty of the task outlined in the Correct Explanation. In one, the complexity of others' (and our own) lives is reduced to a comparison of lifestyles. Such a process reflects virtually nothing of what is actually known about others' lives, only a cartoon version. The second article is an uncritical replay of a standard routine – the irresponsibility of a so-called 'fledgling democracy', and reflects the resilience of non-biodegradable cultural stereotypes even in the age of 'increasing global awareness'.

Beyond these two stories lies another, one in which 'the Amazon speaks', to cite a convenient subtitle. This other story is fighting against the odds. On one flank is a view of the Third World in which the heterogeneity of other peoples is downplayed in the face of crisis management imperatives. Within the new global management view, Amazonia, Bangladesh, Gabon are interchangeable. What they have in common derives from their being positioned by social landscape architects whose cartographic skills are, unsurprisingly, honed by self-interest. On the other flank is a reformulation of views (including, prominently, anthropological ones) which has a similarly reductive effect – the transformation of other people's worlds into a palatable form.

Rediscovering Amazonia

The rediscovery of Amazonia via both the cynical and sincere promotion of green issues – as well as viewed through the gauze of the new anthropology-as-literature – has stabilized the image of the nature ideal, and has laid the groundwork for new conceptions of Amazonia which are clearly revealed in two realms: advanced tourism and 'management studies'. These two realms also impinge on the contradictory role of anthropology when it is obliged to explain itself in public. On the one hand, anthropology's claims to expertise are based on a more thorough knowledge of the other than is available to the 'mere tourist'. On the other hand, when anthropology is pressed to justify its existence, one of the pat answers is that a thorough appreciation of the lives of others permits a more sympathetic understanding of what has been demanded by expansionary social systems and provides a basis for useful commentary.[1]

In historical terms, the concern of anthropology has been to analyse not only how various systems work and their underlying characteristics, but also the way such an understanding comes to be widely appreciated or systematically misrepresented. For instance, Columbus didn't discover America – America was created by being incorporated into various competing imperial systems. The Third World is not those bits of the globe which are not First or Second – the 'Third World' is a

fictional social space where the contradictory character of capital accumulation is most graphically revealed. Culture (difference) is not irrevocably fixed, but is an arena of negotiation. Those kinds of critical observation which used to inform some anthropology are perceived to be falling by the wayside in the face of the allegedly bigger issues represented by various 'Spaceship Earth' perspectives as well as 'the World Is a Shopping Mall' view. That Spaceship and that Mall, though, regardless of the perspicacity of some of its navigators/customers are, in global terms, parochial: white, middle-class, consumer-fixated, and effectively insulated even from what their class allies elsewhere in the world are doing (water-skiing on the Amazon).

Those who try to mediate between 'back home' and 'out there' have a revealingly hard role to play. T.E. Lawrence expresses the unresolved contradiction partially fulfilled in the quest for a uniting vision. Bob Geldof, the post-imperial model, embodies the contradiction suspended by an unlikely alliance of music and famine. In both cases, the Third World becomes a foil for a filtered, self-conscious awareness of the 'dilemmas of development', but an awareness which does little to alter the character of the dilemmas. Africa is unignorable, but forced to acknowledge it, it's not surprising that most people would prefer to get to grips with the sounds of Soweto than the deadly silences of Soweto.

In Amazonia, one of the big rediscoveries has been that the more publicity given the imminent demise of the rain forest, the greater the tourist demand. An article in the *New York Times* (8 August 1989), for example, quotes the co-ordinator of the Ecotourism and Resource Conservation Project: 'Ecotourism is protecting the natural resources by stressing the tourism value of those resources over their exploitation or other development.' The idea here is that as long as an alternative, profitable use can be made of the forest its viability is secured.[2] And the place of Amazonians in this scheme? 'Priority for employment should be given to local inhabitants, especially for training as guides.'

This is an ideal arrangement, a spin-off of the Good Neighbour Policy: not only can you get cheap domestic labour via the Central American Refugee Creation Programme, but when you go on your Amazonian holiday there will be someone there to show you around the rain forest. The proposal underlines the durability of the image of Amazonia as a nature reserve – its value revealed in serving the leisure demands of the privileged.

The acceptable face of eco-tourism promoted in articles such as this feeds a delusion which points the finger at the usual suspects. The *bête noire* cited in the article is a familiar character, the dumb peasant with a chainsaw (*o caboclo com motoserra*), a felon whose reputation is now so well established that he even features in *caboclos'*[3] own accounts of the evils of Amazonian development. The article also reports that the governor of the state of Amazonas has resumed the controversial policy of distributing free chainsaws to 'jungle settlers'. It's those damned peasants again, aided and abetted by your standard issue, corrupt politico.

This bogeyman in the forest story is a lie, and a useful one: in the face of these chainsaw psychos the advanced tourist use of the forest is proposed. But back home, the advanced tourists and the *actual* felons occupy the same social space.[4] Those wielding the chainsaws may be *caboclos com motoserras*, but they are hardly the *reason* for the felling. The advanced tourism line on the forest is necessarily oblivious to such considerations. What is of interest is not how the system functions, but how the tourist potential can be maintained.

From the 'management studies' side, it is noteworthy that much of the (justified) attention paid to recent work on long-term viability of traditional modes of forest extraction rarely acknowledges the very similar arguments which have been common currency within anthropological discourse for decades.[5] A recent example from outside anthropology is the highly-regarded work of Chris Uhl,[6] in which the deforestation of southern Pará is transformed into impressive and comestible numbers: each hamburger produced requires half a ton of cut wood or 6.25 square metres of forest transformed into pasture. In the municipalities he studied, each hectare of cleared forest could support only 0.73 head of cattle and the annual ratio of meat per hectare was twenty-two kilos. On the same amount of land could be produced (in money terms) seventy times as much *farinha*, twenty times as much maize or beans, or thirty kilos of brazil nuts (with a nutritional content superior to twenty-two kilos of burger beef). Uhl's work, like that of a number of other researchers, draws attention to what seems to be a major oversight on the part of the greed merchants: if you want to make money out of Amazonia, there are better ways of doing it than by cutting down forest.

This is news, but it's not new. Long before Yankee/Euro-style decimation hit its stride, lowland forest was being 'managed', that is, exploited without the kind of degradation obvious in modern Amazonia. According to Irvine, for instance, to cite an anthropological study informed by the new management perspective, 'swidden agriculture has represented a significant disturbance in lowland tropical forests for at least 2000 years' – a disturbance not in the sense that the 'natural' unfolding of the forest's career has been seriously disabled by human intervention, but in the sense that it has been a long time since the 'primordial forest' was primordial. The difference between archaic and modern forms of disturbance is that with the former the forest soldiers on while with the latter it tends to disappear. The work of Peters *et al*, Anderson, Hecht and May, Uhl, and others demonstrates that the rationale for extensive clearing doesn't make even the kind of economic sense promoted by Amazonia's big players. The point is that this particular line on Amazonia, present for years in another literature, now makes more sense when cast in terms of market metaphors. However, given that two important underlying reasons for extensive deforestation in Amazonia have been the tax incentives offered by the state to investors and the rising value of land in a highly inflationary economy, the issue is not so much how Amazonia can be exploited more profitably, but how it can be exploited at all.[7]

This rediscovery of that which was never lost, at least to Amazonians, is now presented as a new solution. It is actually a device which may be used to ensure that Amazonians will be integrated into larger systems under the supervision of experts. Regardless of their sympathies for Amazonians, such experts will be agents of the kind of highly acquisitive forces to which this sustainable profit solution is most likely to appeal. In an earlier era, the news that primitives or peasants or plain others actually knew what they were doing was, at best, inserted into a culturally relativistic outlook in which it was acknowledged that society assumed lots of different interesting forms; and at worst was assimilated into a number of ranking schemes in which material plenty was typically measured in terms of double-knit leisure suits and physical attributes unfailingly based on arbitrary and irrelevant criteria such as skin colour, nose shape, calf girth, and so on. The new forest management line is in danger of subverting one of its purposes (the demonstration that Amazonian modes of livelihood are entirely reasonable) by entering this approach as a profitable, wildly crowd-pleasing candidate in the Miss Global Development Competition.

The ascendent anthropological line on all this is represented in the literary-turn (see among many others, works by Clifford and Marcus, Clifford, and Marcus and Fischer), which has entailed a condemnation of explanation as a major goal of anthropological research. Some adherents seem to feel that an anthropology devoid of the tumour of science is a more humanist anthropology, one which is not a branch of the social sciences but a species of literary endeavour. A central claim is that the proper focus of anthropology is the act of writing as an expressive rather than explanatory gesture.

It would be fine if the lines were as clearly drawn as some protagonists present them – if, for example, the contrast between science and art were capable of bearing that much scrutiny. One particularly denunciatory voice committed to the 'science is bad, playful irrationality is good' view of the world is that of Stephen Tyler who, while

adopting a more extreme view than some of his allies, is symptomatic of a general tendency. For Tyler, the social scientific commitment to explanation is misguided not only because it is mere fantasy, the reductionist playing out of what he refers to as the 'exhausted master narratives of the 19th century – the fairy tales of Darwin, Marx, Freud, and Einstein', but also because it pretends to have real effects in the real world. 'Who,' he asks,

> now believes that politics or science works any positive transformation? Anthropology, modern science, and history have all conspired to teach us to disavow this hubris of the modern age, and now we know that change is only change, and its teleology only entropy, an ever-retreating horizon dissolving with us.

For Tyler, there is nothing to be argued because argument *per se* is merely emblematic of affliction. Where Marx said that religion is the sigh of the afflicted creature, Tyler would presumably substitute science.

One of the many paradoxes of the anthro-literary tendency (of which arch postmodernism is only one wing) is that in turning its back on what it sees to be the inauthenticity of conventional ethnography it champions (by implication) the superior artefacts of its own culture: the mannered essay, the fruit of individual genius, the anthropologist as tenured feature writer. The anthropologist is now engaged in self-consciously shrugging off of the viability of human agency and becoming a New Man[8] – open, concerned, and endlessly relativizing. In the face of the insuperable difficulties of conversing with the other, this style of anthropology has opted for talking to itself, reflecting on its own place in the world. In exchange for this new auto-therapeutic writing, of course, others' worlds are reassigned to the periphery of our concerns.

The reason for introducing what for most readers will be esoteric and irrelevant issues of anthropological disagreement is to underline the difficulties of the Correct Explanation. One of the points made in that discussion was that it was hard to conceive the Correct Explanation without a grasp of certain facts. An anthropological discourse which rejects, for example, the validity of distinctions between the trivial and the significant, and even denies that explanation is a possible or worthwhile aim, isn't going to help very much.[9]

The Correct Explanation embodies not only a disenchantment which is hard to displace, but also a prescription for sacrifice – a notoriously hard row to hoe unless the row happens to be elsewhere. It also implies a humility on the part of First Worlders for which there is little precedent, a recognition that the world does not rotate around that most decorous of the world's navels, mine own. It also implies that people must face the unthinkable: that things might, and almost certainly will, get worse.

The Correct Explanation founders on ignorance. Much of *Big Mouth*, for example, has been devoted to an Amazonia occupied by real people who work for a living as opposed to an Amazonia which is a nature and resource preserve. Any attempt to launch a solution depends on an appreciation of the fact that much of what is recognized as distinctively Amazonian is fundamentally misconceived, and in order to show that, it's necessary to resort to remedial education. Before the green critique, for example, can make any sense there must be something of which sense can be made. The rain forest is not such a something. The rain forest is an evocative image which makes it possible for First Worlders to allocate a certain amount of space to 'environmental issues' and then let business get on with the business of business.

On the ground in Amazonia the forces of ignorance are working even harder than usual. If there is an Amazonian at all known outside the region it is Chico Mendes, the Rubber Tappers' Union leader assassinated in December 1988. As the Hollywood version of Mendes' life is prepared, the significance of his work – putting Amazonia on the map as a site of social conflict as well as of a conflict between trees and men – recedes from public consciousness. In a *New York Times* article (12 April 1989), for instance, the caption for the photo of the widow Mendes, Ilzamar, achieves the required effect of naturalizing Mendes' death. Instead of being murdered by landowners, Mendes 'was killed three months ago by a shotgun blast and has become a symbol of the effort to slow the destruction of Brazil's rain forest'. In other words, his death was effected not by a social agent, but – in passive mood – by a machine, and Mendes is a mere sign. Those shotgun blasts are something else, like lightning and floods, or earthquakes and taxes for that matter, kind of inexorable and omnipresent.

Mendes was aware of the tension between the narrow ecological critique of Amazonian development and the political critique originating in the livelihoods of those who, like himself, were concerned about their environment but not much bothered about labels. For the rubber tappers and many other Amazonians, the issue of deforestation has an

immediacy that trivializes the preposterous claims of Europeans and North Americans 'concerned' about the greenhouse effect. (Only 5 per cent of all carbon dioxide emissions originate in the developing world – excluding China. 75 per cent are released from Europe, North America and the Pacific.)[10]

Among the numerous vile ironies thrown up in modern Amazonia is the inclusion of Mendes in Amazonia's export profile: the Dream Factory's clamour for film rights is eagerly reported in the Brazilian press[11] and one of the issues is whether Brazil is going to benefit from the film – that is, will the production include a significant Brazilian component?

This is wholly in keeping with the highly structured relationship between the destruction of Amazonia and Brazil's foreign debt. What is vital in Brazilian terms is how Amazonia can be employed in the great national adventure of keeping the bankers at bay. Pará, for example, whose southern and eastern portions are among the basin's most deforested regions, exported in 1988 490,598 cubic metres of timber.[12] Most exported timber is hardwood such as mahogany and the 1988 price of mahogany at port of export was $500 per cubic metre. The felling of 10,000 mahogany trees (estimating five cubic metres per tree) on Kayapó land in 1984 (in exchange for the timber company's construction of a seventy-kilometre road) produced timber worth $25 million.[13] Timber is only one export product, moreover, and in looking at a table of Pará's major export products[14] it is difficult not to anticipate a worsening of the predatory 'development' of the region in the name of debt repayment. As with felled mahogany trees, Mendes dead becomes a potential 'national asset'.

It used to be a commonplace to hang any discussion of modern Brazil on its similarities with the US. The bases of comparison were varied (geographical size, New World settler colony levered into the twentieth century on the fulcrum of slavery, ethnic diversity, resource potential, and so on) and not inappropriate. Until the 'economic miracle' of the early seventies ran out of oil, Brazil seemed to be on the verge of being promoted into the lower reaches of the first division, Western group, when a terrible thing happened: Brazil's client-state relationship was soured by its inability to pay its overseas bills. Since then, discussion of Brazil has invariably been prefaced by the phrase, 'largest Third World debtor nation'. Needless to say the mantle of guilt has been worn by the profligate, hedonistic, south-of-the-border types. This debtor label is deserved, but the prominence of its usage helps to disguise the fact that Brazil is actually the client state of a nation with an equally dramatic foreign debt, First, Second and Third World divisions. In other words, maybe the now-overlooked special relationship between the US and Brazil demands more, not less, attention – especially because of the increasing demands placed on Brazil to alter its environmental policies.

There are lots of grounds upon which to reconstruct the now forgotten marriage documents, but three are of particular interest: the aforementioned economic links; the National Security State model so successfully exported to Brazil (and from there to other sub-systems, Chile for example); and environmental politics.

The literature on the economic relations between Brazil and the US is vast. A general point, however, and one which has direct bearing on Amazonia's role in all this, is the fact that Brazil is still dependent on the export of what used to be called in the golden days of colonial history 'raw materials'. Brazil may be the world's eighth largest national economy, it may produce hi-tech goods of all descriptions (and have a lively weapons export division), but in the final analysis, when push comes to shove, we're talking coffee, minerals, timber, soya and various food products.

For a discussion of the National Security State, E.S. Herman's *The*

Real Terror Network provides a succinct analysis of the rationale behind the numerous sub-texts of the Alliance for Progress and related foreign policy programmes. Shoup and Minter's *Imperial Brain Trust,* another unjustly overlooked volume, provides a general background to the construction of a client–patron relationship at the highest corporate and governmental levels. Jan Kippers Black's *United States Penetration of Brazil* is another ignored account. None of these volumes (and they represent only a fraction of relevant critical works) is likely to be cited in a discussion of Amazonia. There is a good reason for this, and a poor one. The good reason is that there is nothing particularly unusual about US relations with Brazil (or the Amazonian sub-region) or with its other client states (see, for instance, Chomsky and Herman on the subject). The poor reason leads to the third-mentioned of the grounds for re-examining the close relationship between the US and Brazil – namely, environmental politics.

As there is little evidence that what is going on now in Amazonia is environmentally sound, we have to ask why it carries on. To recap: no serious evidence exists which shows that the slovenly peasant is responsible; a lot of evidence exists to show that the destruction of Amazonia is largely the responsibility of non-Amazonian Brazilian forces and international ones. Given that Brazilian development has largely been orchestrated by external power brokers, a first approximation of a solution might begin with the observation that it is in the nature of Brazil's relationship with the global economy that one might locate the actual destructive forces. Is this line of enquiry being seriously pursued within so-called mainstream debate? No, because Brazil cannot afford not to do what it is doing in Amazonia because it is compelled to produce foreign exchange earnings regardless of the long-term cost.

The local (i.e. Brazilian, since Amazonian political force is enigmatic at best) solution would be to desist, a shift for which there is no evidence of will. The external solution would be to find alternative sources of those products which now find such a willing market, a shift which in the deregulated world of collapsed (British) and collapsing (American) empires (to name but two of the West's Darkening Stars) is not only unvoiceable, but virtually unthinkable. I mean, who wants to become a peasant?

In this context, the West's incipient green consciousness appears to be an appeal to former colonials to pitch in for the 'greater good'. Such a request is all the more unseemly when one takes account of the fact that the speed of deforestation in Amazonia is an outcome of a fully

administered 'development' policy conceived, among other sites, in the dining rooms of the nicer parts of Washington DC and Manhattan.

Thus, when we begin to look at the most visible link between Amazonia and North America, we find that the environmentalist priority hardly represents a novel intervention. In fact, the environmentalist priority reflects the traditional asymmetry of First World–Third World relations. The underlying argument is that you all down there are important when what happens in your neck of the woods starts to impinge on the 'historic', 'traditional', or (especially in Amazonia's case) 'natural' relations between us.

There are several obstacles to viewing Amazonian development as something other than a tragedy in someone else's territory. One of these, perhaps so pursued that dragging it around the arena again is merely asking for trouble, is that of naturalism: Amazonia is conjured up as the mirror image of the wilderness squandered north of the border.

The second is that Amazonia seems custom-made to play the role of mythic little brother to the US: echoing the California Gold Rush there is Rondonia and Serra Pelada; in the axe-swinging, Paul Bunyan department we have the *caboclo com motoserra*; for the Hoover and other dams we have Tucuruí, Balbina and in the near future the Xingu complex; for the Lewis and Clark trail there is the Transamazonica; and as though one bout of Indian-killing frontierism wasn't enough to fuel the engines of manifest destiny, Amazonia functions as a living reminder of older horrors along the same lines.

The third is the feeble claim that, confronted with a disaster, accumulated expertise coupled with sanctimonious goodwill is going to have some positive effects.

The simple point that the *noblesse oblige* of environmentally concerned First Worlders – whether of the left or right, the issue magically unites them – differs very little from that of their immediate imperial ancestors is difficult to put across. Claims that colonial and imperial policies were for the general good are precisely mirrored in the current debate about Amazonian development via the 'we are the environment' arguments discussed earlier; but they also find more coded expression via the depictions by First Worlders of what is happening on the ground. In an exchange in *The Nation* of 18 September 1989, one pair of environmental spokespersons (Stephan Schwartzman and Bruce Rich of the Environmental Defense Fund) criticize the writings of another pair of commentators, geographer Susanna Hecht and political commentator Alexander Cockburn, whose article 'Lands, trees and justice' has irritated a number of Amazonianists (not me). In their reply to criticism, Hecht and Cockburn make the point that environmental lobbying does not go hand in hand with Amazonian progress. Lobbyists in the US, for instance, are compelled to negotiate their way through the political system by way of patronage, networking and stroking. Those upon whose behalf they are lobbying constitute a remote constituency and one which, crucially, has to be represented in a way which does not produce ideological knee-jerk reactions in the corridors of power. In the case of the Rubber Tappers' Union, this means representing them as a green caucus, not a trade union; it means representing Chico Mendes as a charismatic leader, not as a man whose political education took place under the tutelage of Euclides Fernandes Távora, a former army officer who participated in the revolutionary movement headed by Carlos Prestes, leader of the Brazilian Communist Party.[15] For the lobby lobby, the character of Amazonian opposition to developmental policy gets lost in the 'larger purpose' of environmentalism. At this point, the contradictions start sprouting – it appears that environmentalism isn't quite as broad church as it likes to pretend. It certainly doesn't want any horny-handed son of the soil tarnishing the apolitical purity of its 'larger vision'.

The two main consequences of the environmental *realpolitik* line are that the political agenda is set by, who else, those already empowered, and that Amazonian society is again demoted to the status of a mere aspect of the eco-system. That international awareness of the pathology of Amazonian development is important is an unobjectionable and indeed potentially positive claim. But it remains likely that the current development trajectory will be altered – if at all – regardless of Amazonians' own views on the matter. At best, the organization of Amazonians in a manner derived from the efforts of groups such as the Rubber Tappers' Union and others will result in recognition that Amazonia is an integral social space and not just a mismanaged theme park. At worst, however, Amazonians will still carry on doing what they have done for years: accommodating the vicissitudes of a rigid environment and subverting as best they can the encroachments of those for whom Amazonia is a mere object of greed and speculation.

I have gone into town to work in the statistics office. Afterwards I have a late lunch in a sandwich bar while waiting to catch a bus home. An air guitarist standing at the counter is playing along to *Sultans of Swing*. Albertus – half-man half-pavement – is up the road, clubs held high. A

young girl walks up to two European men at the counter and comes on by tugging coquettishly at their beards. They retire to a table in the back room for a chat-up session. When she comes out twenty minutes later she stops at my table and talks about going out to do something. I tell her I don't understand. She tweaks my nose. I know it's large, but a sex object? She strokes my knee and moves on.

Enter the family of a jungle-Gothic artesan. An eight-year-old girl is carrying a two-year-old. Father is dressed in a camouflage outfit, Adidas high-tops, hair down to the base of his shoulderblades. He's trying to barter a tropical-Gothic object for food and drink. It's a brandy bottle coated with epoxy, decorated with the large teeth of a herbivore, the jaws of a small mammal, fur and feathers. It's ugly as sin and exotic as hell. He's pulled it out of an incongruous blue-checked shoulder bag, the sort of thing which Shirley Temple might have used to carry her My Little Ponies off to camp. He buys five Cokes, four slices of cake and a bottle of beer. The kids drink and eat, then leave and cross the street to take food and drink to their mother, who's parked on a bench.

Jorge is a Chileno who has been on the road for eleven years. He is in Belém now because his pregnant wife wants to be near her parents for the birth. He shows me his documents (in every gringo lurks a bureaucrat): an alien registration card, renewable every two years, his merchant marine card, and photos from pre-peripatetic states – short-back-and-sides schoolboy, holiday snaps. He's been to Liverpool in the merchant marine and speaks fondly of its women. Next week he's off to the beach at Salinas to pick up on the tail-end of the holiday market, then (by bus, family in tow) to Fortaleza, Recife, Salvador, Porto Alegre, then over to Chile where the November elections, he thinks, will make living there tolerable.

Jorge is an invisible person who passes in and out of the invisible system. What *Big Mouth* has tried to do is present Jorge's Amazonia, and show that what it is threatened by is an apprehendable set of social forces, not simply a set of vague evils – greed, deception, corruption. By divorcing Amazonia from its historical and social framework, you make a spectacle of the place which evokes only an image of mysterious nature, and so underwrites the invisibility of its people.

The return flight from Belém is divided into two very different stretches: to Recife on the milk run, then from Recife to Paris and London. On the former we get to see for the first time the expanse of coastline and interior which separates the north from the rest. It is vast and takes half a day to cross. I keep wondering where all the *nordestinos* live. All I see is shorebreak and scrub. We stop at São Luis, João Pessoa, Fortaleza and Natal, with a meal for each leg. Ocean eats everything set before him – clean-plate policy with a vengeance, still eating for millions.

In Recife, finally sated and on the ground, Ocean finds himself set upon by Isabella, a mature street urchin from Bolivia. Isabella has come to the airport in the hope of getting free passage on a Brazilian Air Force plane bound for Rio, a service long offered in more remote regions. She is twentyish, rail thin, dressed in a purple chiffon dress and a folk-art necklace. Heavy eyeshadow, backwoods bridgework, and faded tattoos on her biceps complete the look. She also seems quite mad, as anyone would be who had slept in Recife's airport for two weeks.

She is an example of the subaltern cultural mandarin who subjects everything to her own routines. 'From England? You know the Queen? Is very cold there? What is the money, is it dollars? I have money from all over the world, you want to see? I have gold dollar from England, it is worth very much?' A motormouth, and Anglophile to boot. Ocean has usually been spared much effort in these encounters. Not speaking Portuguese he has been able to coast through the most tedious hands across the ocean exchanges with an affable shrug and grin. Not so with Isabella. She speaks good comic

English and is, in any case, very taken with Ocean, whose resemblance to Arnold Schwarzenegger – long overlooked by Hollywood, and indeed his friends – is wildly appreciated by our Andean friend. I pad off to search out a hotel and return in a quarter of an hour to find the normally equable Ocean pretending that English has been added to the list of languages in which he feels incapable of expressing himself. He is getting close to autism in fact. I have come back too soon. A few minutes more and his dark side might have come out.

Isabella, whose knowledge of Europe and North America seems, quite reasonably, to have been drawn almost entirely from movie mags and *fotonovelas*, is running through a list of famous dead people, squealing in glee as she remembers another one. Jimi Hendrix, then Richard Burton, then Romy Schneider . . . She grimaces and draws her hand dramatically across her throat after each name. Dead, dead, dead. Dream of a lifetime? To meet the Italian Stallion. Second prize? He's standing right here: Humphrey Schwarzenegger.

I'm talking with Vieira, the King of Lambada, in Jesus' office. Vieira is very patiently but unenthusiastically enduring the questions. It's more like interrogation than conversation.

'What have you done besides music?'

'I am only a musician.'

'What did you do before?'

'I was a technician, I was a mechanic, I was a peasant. I worked a plot of land, for twenty years. After that I decided I wanted a better life, life in the city. Now I am a musician, only that.'

'How often do you perform?'

'I have a nine-piece group. We play every weekend.'

'Where do you perform?'

'In Pará, only in this region, because after all, it's big. Pará is big. Tonight we will play in this *município*, next Saturday in another place. I spend my life like that.'

'Who plays in your band?'

'There are nine people in the band.'

'Any relations?'

'I have sons, two sons who play, one on drums, the other on guitar. I play guitar, I am the composer.'

'You write the music?'

'Only I.'

'The lyrics?'

'Only I. I prepare everything. The arrangements, everything . . .'

'You are Paraense. . .'

'I am Paraense.'

'Are there any other influences in your music, other writers, other styles?'

'We play everything. My group is the following: we play regional music and we play every style of music, we go as far as international.'

A peasant, a musician, an Amazonian: international.

NOTES

Chapter I

1. Chico Mendes is the most celebrated victim, but the Hall of Fame is not short of nominees.

2. From numerous accounts it would appear that 'kidnapping' and slave-raiding were well-established means of recruiting new members to a society. The 'theft-of-property' connotation of modern kidnapping doesn't necessarily work cross-culturally.

3. Except as the icon repository/last frontier, a foil – especially on the part of the military – macho flexing.

4. They have already gone beyond shaky. Some recipients, for example, according to a report in the *Guardian* (23 August 1989) are less than impressed with the aflatoxin levels in US maize exports.

Chapter II

1. The 'parallel' black market and official rates have now been joined by a 'tourist' rate (slightly less than the parallel) and all rates are published in the daily press. In a bizarre attempt to undermine the non-standard markets, the government will reward the happy saver (to the tune of 40 per cent interest/month) if s/he saves money in a

cruzado account. How this generosity can be sustained – short of keeping the printing presses working overtime – is a mystery.

Chapter III

1. In a number of tourist guides, Ver-O-Peso (watch the weight) is given a sinister reading: there are cheats about. The name more likely derives from the site's role as the home of the tax inspector, i.e. it's where the Portuguese registered exports and extracted their cut.

Chapter IV

1. See B. Meggers (1971) *Amazonia : Man and Culture in a Counterfeit Paradise*; D. Lathrap (1970) *The Upper Amazon* and A. Roosevelt (1980; 1987).

2. H. Palmatary (1960) 'The archaeology of the lower Tapajos Valley, Brazil', includes a number of impressive plates. Pyramids they did not make, but hunter/gatherism this is not.

3. The Belém estuary's main riverine/marine exports are catfish and shrimp.

Chapter V

1. Charges against Posey, Payakan and Kube-i were dropped after it became apparent that the Xingu dam project whose dangers they were publicizing would have to be postponed. Out of the frying pan and into the fire, Posey's story is being packaged by Hollywood with Jon Voight playing the lead.

2. Stephen Baines is a recent victim of manipulation effected under the new Constitution. Baines, a British anthropologist, has been working since 1982 with the Waimiri-Atroari, an Indian group on whose land there are significant deposits of cassiterite. Under the old Constitution, private mining companies were forbidden access to Indian lands. A campaign to alter the rules was begun in the pages of the newspaper *Estado de São Paulo* in August 1987. The charge made was that of a conspiracy between the National Council of Brazilian Bishops and CIMI (Indigenists Missionary Council) to maintain the control of minerals by foreign firms. Among the other ludicrous charges was that in which Baines was accused of being in the pay of the 'Tin Brothers of

South East Asia'. Under the new Constitution, private mining companies can enter Indian lands if they have the permission (1) of the Indians and (2) of Congress. Some of the false charges are based on a forged document alleged to have been produced by CEDI (Ecumenical Centre for Documentation and Information), a document which, curiously, contains the same mis-spelling of Baines' name (Baynes) as appeared in the *Estado de São Paulo* stories. When Baines arrived at the Waimiri-Atroari village this summer, he was met by a delegation composed of Waimiri-Atroari and FUNAI officials (the State Indian Bureau) and was informed that the Indians no longer wanted him there, that they wanted to strike a deal with the mining company Paranapanema. It would appear that under the careful coaching of FUNAI officials and mining company representatives, the Waimiri-Atroari have fallen into step. Baines' research is effectively at an end and, as a foreign scholar at the centre of such a dispute, his chances of justice are slim.

3. Access to Indian resources is somewhat more complicated not to say Byzantine (see Note 2) than some 'save the rain forest' cheerleaders let on. A central problem is that the conditions do not exist for enforcing laws prohibiting the felling of trees on protected land. Recognizing this, some Indian groups – or rather, representatives of groups, 'chiefs' who tend to be found partying down on the proceeds – have figured that the choice is between standing by while lumbermen pillage, or striking deals with them. Some of the more celebrated Indian figureheads in the fight to save the rain forest have been implicated in what can only be described as kick-back scams. See L. Greenbaum (1989) 'Plundering the timber on Brazilian Indian reservations', for discussion. She cites, among other examples, 'the death on 29 June 1988 of two young Cinta Larga men in a traffic accident while driving drunk with two white women – car, liquor and women paid for with lumber money' (1989:26). She also notes, significantly, that 'much of the lumbering on Indian lands is in areas of projects sponsored by the World Bank, which have provisions for the protection of indigenous groups and the environment. It will be instructive to see if any effective action is taken against lumbering by those in charge of monitoring implementation of loan provisions' (1989:26).

4. One of the earliest and most astute analyses of the expanding food frontier in Amazonia is Otavio Velho (1972) *Frentes de Expansão e Estrutura Agrária*. Also see J. Foweraker (1981) *The Struggle for Land : A Political Economy of the Pioneer Frontier in Brazil, 1930 to the Present* and

S. Branford and O. Glock (1985) *The Last Frontier: Fighting Over Land in the Amazon.*

5. Data from a Friends of the Earth briefing paper, November 1988, 'Hydroelectric dams & rainforest destruction in the Amazon Basin: Kayapó Indians' appeal mission to Europe & North America'.

Other reports in the daily press have claimed flooded areas three times the size of the UK and equivalent to 10 per cent of Brazilian national territory. The actual size of the proposed flooding is significant enough. The exaggerated figures reflect a tendency in well-meaning environmentalist accounts which is ultimately counterproductive. By promoting for dramatic effects such claims as 'Amazon forest, lungs of the world', proponents are easily discredited by those who are perpetrating the destruction – a green version of the Boy Who Cried Wolf.

6. The contract guarantees 'the provision of 13.6 million tons per year over a period of fifteen years, totally a value of US$270 million at 1982 prices' (Treece 1987:21).

7. I don't know what proportion of Brazil's borrowing directly affects Amazonia. The point of these numbers is to illustrate the character of clientage and the scale of dependency.

8. See K. Taylor (1988).

9. The Third World model impinges: in 1979, British building societies reported 2,530 house repossessions; in 1987 they reported 22,630. These figures do not include repossessions by new entrants to the housing market, high-street and foreign banks (*Guardian* 29 October 1988). Reports in mid-1989 suggest that repossessions are in the order of 40,000.

10. See Nigel Smith (1982) *Rainforest Corridors : The Transamazon Colonization Scheme* 14–15.

11. S. Davis (1977) *Victims of the Miracle.*

12. See T. Hayter and C. Watson (1985) *Aid : Rhetoric and Reality*; N. Chomsky and E.S. Herman (1979) *The Washington Connection and Third World Fascism : The Political Economy of Human Rights*, Vols I and II; E.S. Herman (1982) *The Real Terror Network.*

13. Quoted in Fred Pearce (1989a:42). Pearce reviews the debate between the *Ecologist* group associated with Teddy Goldsmith and the

World Bank/International Union for the Conservation of Nature and Natural Resources.

14. See discussion in Pearce (1989a:41), in which 'The bank admits to many past sins.' What, we would like to know, about future ones?

15. According to Bruce Rich (1983:12), 'of the Bank's approximately 5,250 employees, the Office of Environmental Affairs employs only 3 full-time professionals to review the approximately 325 new projects that are approved each year'.

Chapter VI

1. The widest-ranging discussion of the rubber boom is Barbara Weinstein's *The Amazon Rubber Boom, 1850–1920* (1983). More recent, and focussing more on Ford's plantation efforts, is Warren Dean's droll *Brazil and the Struggle for Rubber: a Study in Environmental History* (1987).

2. Another way of viewing this is that a valued species was transplanted from one colony to another, in this case into one under British control. The anti-malarial plant cinchona followed a similar path.

3. Dean (1987) is the source of much of this discussion.

4. If all claims of Indian attacks in Amazonia in the last twenty years were true, the neo-Amazonian population would be a lot lower. Correct response to storyteller: 'If I had a nickel for . . . '

5. Jan Rocha (*Guardian*, 21 September 1989) reports that of the 82 million potential voters in the forthcoming presidential elections (November 1989), two-thirds are illiterate or semi-literate and earn less than £125 a month.

6. But see A. Dorfman and A. Mattelart (1975) *How to Read Donald Duck : Imperialist Ideology in the Disney Comic*, and A. Dorfman (1983) *The Empire's Old Clothes : What the Lone Ranger, Babar, and Other Innocent Heroes Do to Our Minds*.

7. One of the reasons for this is that the West doesn't really distinguish very much between one Other and another. The Bororo in a cowboy hat is functionally/aesthetically equivalent to an Inuit with a Walkman, a Kung! in sunglasses, a Yekuanan in stilettos. What is constant is the Coke can; the drinker is interchangeable.

8. Although it's clear that 'ethnicity' is inadequate prophylaxis against high-art celebration/appropriation. See for example H. Foster (1985) *Recodings: Art, Spectacle, Cultural Politics*, especially 'The "primitive" unconscious or modern art, or white skin black masks.'

Chapter VII

1. The prohibitions attached to eating them are similar to those sanctions applied to the mistreatment of dogs in England. One television ad, no longer screened, may have run foul of the fact that canine deification in Albion is too sacred for satire. The ad in question – for 'Odour-Eaters' – was based on a post-prandial sitting-room scenario. Father, settling into easy chair after a dinner of faggots and cauliflower cheese, followed by gooseberry crumble with custard, kicks off his slippers and Fido keels over, a victim of pedal mustard gas.

2. The most recent big audience version of voodoo as the downside of cultural pluralism is Wes 'Nightmare' Craven's film of Wade Davis' *The Serpent and the Rainbow*.

3. A term also used to describe one of the torture routines for which Brazilian security forces were infamous.

Chapter VIII

1. In spite of numerous references to the Amazonian origins of many McDonalds, Whataburgers, Wendy's, Burger Kings, etc, exportable beef is simply not the profit inspiration for forest-felling. Amazonian beef production is highly unprofitable, in fact, each hectare of cleared forest producing only 22kg of meat. The value of such land from the 'cattle-ranchers'' point of view is that it holds its value well in inflationary times.

2. There are as yet few empirical studies of mercury poisoning in Amazonia. Once recent one is by Carmina, Rosa de Sena Couto *et al* (1988) 'Intoxicação mercurial : resultados preliminares em duas áreas garimperiras no Estado do Pará'. In this study, the researchers found significant levels of mercury in the hair of gold-miners and others working in the vicinity of mercury use and in the hair of Indians and others using water downstream from gold-mines.

3. According to Schmink (1988:172), Serra Pelada is now a hole 270 feet deep and 3,000 feet in diameter.

4. The standard reference here is Jameson (1983) 'Postmodernism and consumer society'. See also Pfeil's insightful commentary, 1985, ' "Makin' flippy-floppy" : postmodernism and the baby-boom PMC'.

5. See, for example, Jan Rocha's report in the Manchester *Guardian* Weekly, 24 January 1988.

6. A comprehensive overview is found in R.J.A. Goodland and H.S. Irwin (1975) *Amazon Jungle: Green Hell to Red Desert*?

7. See for discussion, P. Fearnside (1983) 'Development alternatives in the Brazilian Amazon : an ecological evaluation'.

8. A classic example of this commitment to balance was presented during the latter stages of the construction of the Tucuruí hydroelectric dam on the Tocantins River. The contract for felling the imminently flooded forest had not been honoured, and the prospect was that the newly formed lake, inundating mega-quantities of organic material, would become an aquatic compost heap (see Caufield, 1986, for discussion). One of the last-ditch proposals was to use Agent Orange-type herbicides to scorch the offending forest into submission. When there were outcries at the possibly deleterious effects of this 'better living through chemistry' solution, the bureaucrat responsible for supervising defoliation announced that it was 'unscientific' not to try it out. A 'balance' argument. This is like describing Russian roulette as a scientific experiment.

9. Speculating about the not-too-distant future, it's entirely possible that Amazonia the resource domain will have both felled/flooded forests and nuclear reactors, the ideal balance of old and new.

10. The successful halting of the Xingu hydroelectric scheme and the gathering of eco-forces at Altamira in February 1989 raised the international profile of Amazonia to a considerable degree. Only the pathologically optimistic think that the complex Xingu hydroelectric project will not go ahead.

11. Among the best recent articles which review the revisionist arguments and present new evidence is A. Roosevelt (1987) 'Chiefdoms in the Amazon and the Orinoco'. Also see her 1980 volume, *Parmana : Prehistoric Maize and Manioc Subsistence Along the Amazon and Orinoco*.

12. See, for example, discussion by W. Denevan (1984) 'Agriculture in the Amazon floodplain'. For a discussion of *várzea* types, see G.T.

Prance (1979) 'Notes on the vegetation of Amazonia III : the terminology of Amazon forest types subject to inundation'.

Chapter IX

1. I hope I haven't caught the last wave *lambada*-wise. A radio report from Paris tells us that *lambada* is the latest thing. This may be a case of Gallic overdetermination in that *lambada* appears from the report to refer to the group, the song, the genre. From the snatches allowed to penetrate the aggressive reporting, the *lambada* driving the French wild bears about the same relation to Vieira as Guy Mitchell bears to Buddy Holly.

2. Leaving town, however, is a smart adaptation move. Amongst recent evacuees who've found brass rings in southern latitudes are Beto Barbosa.

3. Unlike, apparently, musics from Africa which are casually lumped together, 'African music'. Tell it to the Moroccans.

4. That may be harsh re Carlos, who has worked in many areas with great panache.

5.The former was actually produced there and shipped inland; the latter is merely processed there and prepared for export.

Chapter X

1. First published in 1906 as *The Cynic's Word Book*.

2. In fact, that is part of the subject matter of the *Vanity Fair* article. Ecology is now more noteworthy because of the 'A' list status of supporters.

3. See, for example, the comment on p. 192 of Shnayerson (1989) where the author observes that 'The root problem is overpopulation: too many people farming too little land.' A good example of recycled Malthusian oversimplification and obviously comforting to those not dependent on their children's labour to keep body and soul together. In academic jargon, this is what is known as crap. It is, of course, a central tenet of the Stupid Latino thesis (see p.144).

4. This and the following quotations are from an article in the *Guardian*, 7 September 1989.

5. Some costs to First World consumers are more difficult to displace than others. The nuclear power industry in the US has seized the ideological global greenhouse possibilities with more boldness than others, proposing after a ten-year moratorium to revive nuclear power and sell it as an antidote to 'global warming'. Even sectors of the environmental lobby have fallen in line, the Audubon Society, for example, 'cautiously recommending "continued basic research directed toward the development of advanced, inherently safe nuclear reactors" ' (*Guardian*, 7 September 1989).

6. Channel 4, 25 August 1989. Later published in revised form in the *Observer*.

7. Particularly memorable was the Green Party spokeswoman's announcement after the recent Green gains in the European Parliamentary elections that their success showed that people were no longer interested in questions of left or right. 'We' are 'one'.

8. In *Dreamers of the Absolute* (1988). Enzensberger is worth quoting at some length. Writing in 1973, he says that the ecological crisis is a generalized crisis, it's not about 'resources', it's about the character of capital: 'That is why moral appeals to the people of the "rich" lands to lower their standard of living are totally absurd. They are not only useless but cynical. To ask the individual wage-earner to differentiate between his "real" and his "artificial" needs is to mistake his real situation. . . . We must reckon with the likelihood that bourgeois policy will systematically exploit the resulting mystifications – increasingly so, as the ecological crisis takes on more threatening forms. To achieve this, it only needs demagogically to take up the proposals of the ecologists and give them political circulation' (1988:293).

9. For a depressing account of the extent of timber extraction already taking place on Indian reserves, see Linda Greenbaum's 'Plundering the timber on Brazilian Indian reservations' (1989).

A number of Indian leaders who have recently received international attention as environmentalist point-men are said to live quite well on the proceeds. Scotch, white women and convertibles figure in their reported consumer profiles and even those – anthropologists, for example, who have worked with these groups for years – who are harshly critical of this particular manifestation of culture contact concede that the choice between (a) having the timber stolen and (b) selling the timber and getting laid and drunk doesn't leave a lot of room for manoeuvre.

10. Ernst Haeckel (1868) *Natural History of Creation*. For discussion see Enzensberger's 'Critique of political ecology' in his *Dreamers of the Absolute*, from which I have drawn much.

11. The best-named one to appear is Resources for the Future Inc., a Washington DC-based consultancy group. The World Bank with its reorganized internal structure (30 June 1987) provides one dominant model. See 'Appendix 3B: Officers and Departmental Directors of the World Bank after Reorganization', *The World Bank Annual Report* (1987).

12. Much as pundits have, quite rightly, ridiculed Thatcher's 'bag it, bin it, then we'll win it' homily; the difference between its logic and that of many more respectably green maxims is undetectable.

13. Teresa Hayter and Catharine Watson's *Aid: Rhetoric and Reality* (1985) presents a detailed breakdown of the structure of aid finance. Branford and Kucinski's *The Debt Squads* provides a similar account, but is confined to South/Latin American materials. For a concise analysis of the relationship between aid and national security see Frances Moore Lappé, Rachel Schurman and Kevin Danaher (1987) *Betraying the National Interest*.

14. One of the most sobering analyses of recent years is Geoffrey Kay's *Development and Underdevelopment* (1975) which in spite of the pleasing number of reprintings it has undergone is an unjustifiably under-cited work. The unpalatable course of his argument, it seems, is this: those structures and processes which have ensured a split between the trajectories of First and Third Worlds have not only impoverished the Third World in a relative sense, but in an absolute sense as well (grotesque demographic shifts, environmental degradation, social destabilization) thus minimizing the prospects for recovery even if, for some reason, the immediate causes of underdevelopment were to be called off.

15. See, for example, the very different but complementary discussions by Wallerstein (*The Capitalist World-Economy*) and Mike Davis.

16. According to Carlos Franqui (1980:84) though, on his second visit to NY in 1960, what Castro really wanted to do was hang his hammock in the UN gardens.

17. D'Aubuisson, for example.

18. Although see Taussig (1987) for an alternative account.

19. Absurd as the prospect of invasion/subversion by Venezuela, Bolivia, Peru, Colombia, Guyana, Surinam or French Guiana sounds, this geopolitical rationale is regularly trotted out as a major explanation for Brazil's pathological concern for the intactness of the virgin Amazon.

Chapter XI

1. Talal Asad's (ed. 1973) *Anthropology and the Colonial Encounter* discusses the ways in which the practice of anthropology is implicated in the administration of the objects of anthropological scrutiny. It was (and continues to be) a blow for some sections of the field to be reminded that the practice of anthropology is not benign and has strong affinities with the 'management' approach.

2. A lower profile scheme hatched under the same lightbulb concerns freshwater dolphins, the idea here being that more money can be generated through dolphin-focussed tourism than through the various activities which, inadvertently, destroy dolphins.

3. A standard joke on themselves among *riberinhos*.

Rising to the challenge, Juarez Cristiano de Jesus Gomez, a former gold-miner, has invented an amphibious chainsaw in order to harvest the timber resources flooded for the Tucuruí hydroelectric dam. As of August 1989, he had already logged 12 thousand m^3 of mahogany, ceder and ipê, as well as 36 thousand m^3 of firewood.

4. The felling of forest is large scale, capital intensive, organized, and mainly directed towards the export market (i.e. not peasant mode), and the privileged tourists are class allies of the loggers. From the mid-1960s, for fifteen years, Brazil approved more than $1 billion of financial support for Amazonian cattle ranching, an exercise which was never profitable in terms of producing beef, but which was enormously profitable in terms of evaluating public lands and laying the basis for subsequent sub-soil mineral claims (Schmink, 1988: 168-9). The Carajás iron-ore project (which a number of researchers commend for its relatively superior 'environmental impact' provisions) produces demand for 4 million tons of charcoal per year, derived from 20 million tons of wood (*IstoE-Senhor* 29/389).

5. The crucial difference, of course, is that for Amerindian and neo-Amazonian forest-users the 'management' of resources was struc-

tured by local demand for use-values as much if not more than production for sale.

6. *O Liberal*, 16 July 1989; Uhl, C. and Jordan, C.F. (1984) 'Succession and nutrient dynamics following forest cutting and burning in Amazonia', *Ecology* 63:1476–90. Also see the earlier work of Susanna Hecht.

7. For a review of various Amazonian development issues see Barbira-Scazzochio (ed., 1980).

8. A number of women have observed how anthropology in crisis insists on trying to keep surfing on the board of phallocentrism, marginalizing feminist critiques as though the latter are mere beach bunnies, standing on the beach along with other 'sub-fields', cf. Henrietta Moore (1988).

9. The affinity of empiricism and certain postmodern tendencies is not often acknowledged. The former declares that things are as they are because there is no reason to believe that they are anything else; the latter asserts that things are as they are because anything can be anything. Aside from the fact that the latter arrived at this position after various intermediate stops (e.g. post-structuralism), there is little to distinguish between them in the cake-tasting department.

10. See Tony Gross's introduction to *Fight for the Forest : Chico Mendes in His Own Words* (1989). But see also figures in Hecht/NLR, and Fred Pearce, 'Felled trees deal double blow to global warming', *New Scientist* 16 September 1989, for a discussion which suggests that CO_2 from forest burning is particularly destructive. For another estimate, see Ruckelshaus (1989), 118.

11. Among the reported competitors (summer 1989) are David Tottman (associated with Warner Bros), Robert Redford, Sonia Braga, Elliot Lewit (associated with Ted Turner's CNN); Costa-Gavras; Peter Guber (producer of *Rainman, Gorillas in the Mist*, and *Midnight Express*), *O Liberal* (Belém) 4 July 1989. Brazilian reporters are far removed from the action as reported by Alex Shoumatoff in *Vanity Fair*, April 1989.

12. Uhl, C. (1989) *'Comer um hamburger pode ser um rerforço para a devastação'*, *O Liberal* (Belém), 16 July 1989.

13. These figures are from an article written by an anthropologist who, wishing to carry on working in Brazil, writes under an assumed name, Linda Greenbaum (1989) 'Plundering the Timber on Brazilian Indian Reservations', *Cultural Survival Quarterly* 13(1), 1989. Little of this

money finds its way back to the reservations. Greenbaum reports that a 1987 contract between Indians in the Indigenous Area Rio Branco and a timber company stipulated a payment of only $25 per m^3 (for 5,000 m^3 of mahogany) delivered in the form of a 15-kilometre road, a Toyota, various hardware and consumer items, a pharmacy building plus supplies and some livestock: 'Certainly within three years very little will be left of these things. In general, nobody on Indian reserves is trained to fix such items.'

14. Jan/Nov 1988:

Product	Value in US$1000
Iron ore	389,798
Aluminium	366,566
Timber	131,175
Bauxite	116,492
Wood pulp	79,864
Black pepper	43,144
Frozen shrimp	38,890
Kaolin	29,380
Manganese	11,994
Pig iron	1,031

Source: Min., da Fazenda (Exchequer)

cited in: Bacury, S.R. de Lima (1989) 'A nova constituação federal e sua repurcussão na economia paraense', *Amazonia Hoje* No. 7, July.

15. See Chico Mendes (1989) *Fight for the Forest*. See also Ronald Chilcote (1974) *The Brazilian Communist Party : Conflict and Consensus, 1922-1970*.

LIST OF DRAWINGS

BIBLIOGRAPHY

Amnesty International (1988) *Brazil Briefing*. London: Amnesty International Publications.

Anderson, Anthony, Hecht, Susanna and May, Peter (1988) 'The subsidy from nature: shifting cultivation, successional palm forests, and rural development', *Human Organization* 17(1):25–35.

Anderson, Anthony and Ioris, Edviges Marta (1989) 'The logic of extraction: resource management and income generation by extractive producers in the Amazon estuary', paper presented at the International Workshop, 'Traditional Resource Use in Neotropical Forests', The Center for Latin American Studies, University of Florida, Gainesville.

Asad, Talal (ed.) (1973) *Anthropology and the Colonial Encounter*. London: Ithaca Press.

Bacury, S.R. de Lima (1989) 'A nova constituação federal e sua repurcussão na economia paraense', *Amazonia Hoje* 7 (July).

Barbira-Scazzocchio, Francoise (ed.) (1980) *Land, People and Planning in contemporary Amazonia*. Cambridge: Cambridge University Press.

Bates, Henry W. (1964) *The Naturalist on the River Amazon*. London: John Murray (first published 1864).

Bernal, Martin (1987) *Black Athena*. London: Free Association Books.

Bierce, Ambrose (1978) *The Devil's Dictionary*. Owings Mills, MD: Stemmer House (first published 1906).

Black, Jan Kippers (1977) *United States Penetration of Brazil*. Philadelphia, PA: University of Pennsylvania Press.

Bodard, Lucien (1971) *Massacre on the Amazon*. London: Tom Stacey.

Boorman, John (1985) *Money Into Light, the Emerald Forest: A Diary*. London: Faber & Faber.

Bourne, Richard (1978) *Assualt on the Amazon*. London: Gollancz.

Branford, Sue and Glock, Oriana (1985) *The Last Frontier: Fighting Over Land in the Amazon*. London: Zed Press.

Branford, Sue and Kucinski, Bernardo (1988) *The Debt Squads: the US, the Banks, and Latin America*. London: Zed Press.
Carmina, Rosa de Sena Couto *et al* (1988) 'Intoxicação mercurial: resultados preliminares em duas áreas garimpeiras no Estado do Pará', *Pará Desinvolvimentio* 23. Belém: IDESP.
Caufield, Catherine (1986) *In the Rainforest*. London: Picador.
Chilcote, Ronald (1974) *The Brazilian Communist Party: Conflict and Consensus 1922-70*. New York: Oxford University Press.
Chomsky, Noam and Herman, Edward S. (1979) *The Political Economy of Human Rights, Volume I: The Washington Connection and Third World Fascism*. Nottingham: Spokesman.
Clark, William C. (1989) 'Managing Planet Earth', *Scientific American*, 261:3:18–26.
Clifford, James (1988) *The Predicament of Culture: Twentieth-Century Ethnography, Literature, and Art*. Cambridge, MA and London: Harvard University Press.
Clifford, James and Marcus, George (eds) (1986) *Writing Culture: The Poetics and Politics of Ethnography*. Berkeley, CA: University of California Press.
Cousteau, Jacques-Yves and Richards, Mose (n.d.) *Jacques Cousteau's Amazon Journey*. New York: Harry N. Abrams.
Crowther, P. (ed.) (1987) *Don't Tread on Me: The Selected Letters of S.J. Perelman*. New York: Viking.
Crowther, Prudence (ed.) *Don't Tread On Me: The Selected Letters of S.J. Perelman*. New York: Viking.
Davis, Mike (1987) '*Chinatown*, Part Two? The 'Internationalization' of Downtown Los Angeles', *New Left Review* 164: 65–86.
Davis, Shelton (1977) *Victims of the Miracle*. New York: Cambridge University Press.
Davis, Wade (1986) *The Serpent and the Rainbow*. London: Collins Willow.
Dean, Warren (1987) *Brazil and the Struggle for Rubber: a Study in Environmental History*. Cambridge: Cambridge University Press.
Denevan, William (1984) 'Agriculture in the Amazon floodplain', in M. Schmink and C. Wood (eds) *Frontier Expansion in Amazonia*.
Denslow, Julie and Padoch, Christine (eds) (1988) *People of the Rain Forest*. Berkeley, LA and London: University of California Press.
Dorfman, Ariel (1983) *The Empire's Old Clothes: What the Lone Ranger, Babar, and Other Innocent Heroes Do to Our Minds*. New York: Pantheon.
Dorfman, Ariel and Mattelart, Armand (1975) *How to Read Donald Duck: Imperialist Ideology in the Disney Comic*. London: International General.
Douglas, Mary (1966) *Purity and Danger*. London: Routledge & Kegan Paul.
Enzensberger, Hans Magnus (1988) *Dreamers of the Absolute*. London: Radius.
Evans, Peter (1979) *Dependent Development, The Alliance of Multinational, State, and Local Capital in Brazil*. Princeton, NJ: Princeton University Press.
Fearnside, Phillip (1983) 'Development alternatives in the Brazilian Amazon: an ecological evaluation'. *Interciencia* 8(2):65–78.
Fittkau, E.J. (1973) 'Crocodiles and the nutrient metabolism of the Amazon', *Amazoniana: Limnologia et Oecologia Regionalis Systemae Fluminis Amazonas* 4:103–33.
Fleming, Peter (1933) *Brazilian Adventure*. London: Jonathan Cape.
Foster, Hal (ed.) (1983) *The Anti-Aesthetic: Essays on Postmodern Culture*. Port Townsend, WA: Bay Press.
Foster, Hal (1985) *Recodings: Art, Spectacle, Cultural Politics*. Port Townsend, WA: Bay Press.

Foweraker, Joe (1981) *The Struggle for Land: A Political Economy of the Pioneer Frontier in Brazil, 1930 to the Present*. London: Cambridge University Press.
Franqui, Carlos (1980) *Family Portrait with Fidel*. London: Jonathan Cape.
Friends of the Earth (1988) 'Hydroelectric dams & rainforest destruction in the Amazon Basin: Kayapó Indians' appeal mission to Europe & North America,' briefing paper. /November.
George, Susan (1988) *A Fate Worse than Debt*. Harmondsworth, Middx: Penguin Books.
Goodland, Robert J.A. and Irwin, Howard S. (1975) *Amazon Jungle: Green Hell to Red Desert?* New York: Elsevier Scientific Publishing.
Greenbaum, Linda (1989) 'Plundering the timber on Brazilian Indian reservations', *Cultural Survival Quarterly* 13(1).
Hayter, Teresa and Watson, Catharine (1985) *Aid: Rhetoric and Reality*. London: Pluto Press.
Hecht, Susanna (1989) 'Chico Mendes: chronicle of a death foretold', *New Left Review* 173:47–55.
Hecht, Susanna and Cockburn, Alexander (1989a) 'Lands, trees and justice: defenders of the Amazon', *The Nation* 22 May:695–702.
Hecht, Susanna and Cockburn, Alexander (1989b) 'Rain forest politics' (reply to Stephan Schwartzman and Bruce Rich, same issue), *The Nation*, 18 September: 2.
Hemming, John (1987) *Amazon Frontier: the Defeat of the Brazilian Indians*. London: Macmillan.
Herman, Edward S. (1982) *The Real Terror Network*. Boston: South End Press.
Household, Geoffrey (1980) *Dance of the Dwarves*. Harmondsworth Middx: Penguin Books.
Irvine, Dominique (1985) 'Succession management and rainforest distribution in an Amazonian rainforest', in Darrell A. Posey and William Balée (eds) *Natural Resource Management by Indigenous and Folk Societies in Amazonia*. New York : New York Botanical Garden (in press).
Jacoby, Russell (1987) *The Last Intellectuals: American Culture in the Age of Academe*. New York: Basic Books.
Jameson, Fredric (1983) 'Postmodernism and consumer society', in Hal Foster (ed.) *The Anti-Aesthetic: Essays on Postmodern Culture*. Port Townsend, WA: Bay Press.
Kay, Geoffrey (1975) *Development and Underdevelopment: a Marxist Analysis*. London: Macmillan.
Lapham, Lewis H. (1989) *Money and Class in America: Notes on the Civil Religion*. London: Picador.
Lappé, Frances Moore, Schurman, Rachel and Danaher, Kevin (1987) *Betraying the National Interest*. New York: Grove Press.
Lathrap, Donald (1970) *The Upper Amazon*. London: Thames & Hudson.
Lazere, Donald (ed.) (1987) *American Media and Mass Culture: Left Perspectives*. Berkeley, LA and London: University of California Press.
Marcus, George and Fischer, Michael (1986) *Anthropology as Cultural Critique*. Chicago and London: University of Chicago Press.
Meggers, Betty (1971) *Amazonia: Man and Culture in a Counterfeit Paradise*. Chicago: Aldine.
Mendes, Chico (1989) *Fight for the Forest: Chico Mendes in his Own Words*. London: Latin American Bureau.
Moore, Henrietta (1988) *Anthropology and Feminism*. London: Polity Press.
Noyer, Adrian Du (1989) 'White Man's Burden', *Q*, 32: 40–46.
O'Hanlon, Redmond (1986) 'Amazon adventure', *Granta* 20: 15 – 54.

O'Hanlon, Redmond (1988) *In Trouble Again*. London: Hamish Hamilton.
Palmatary, Helen (1960) 'The archaeology of the Lower Tapajós Valley, Brazil', *Transactions of the American Philosophical Society* n.s. 39(3).
Pearce, Fred (1989a) 'Kill or cure? Remedies for the rainforest', *New Scientist*, 16 September.
Pearce, Fred (1989b) 'Felled trees deal double blow to global warming', *New Scientist*, 16 September.
Peters, Charles *et al* (1989) 'Valuation of an Amazonian forest', *Nature* 339:655–6.
Pfeil, Fred (1985) ' ''Making' flippy-floppy'': postmodernism and the baby-boom PMC', in Mike Davis, Michael Sprinker and Fred Pfeil (eds) *The Year Left*. London: Verso.
Phelps, Gilbert (1964) *Green Horizon: Travels in Brazil*. New York: Simon & Schuster.
Porter, Henry (1989) 'Bonfire on the Amazon', *Independent Magazine*, 15 February.
Prance, G.T. (1977) 'Notes on the vegetation of Amazonia III: the terminology of Amazon forest types subject to inundation', *Brittonia* 31:26–38.
Pratt, Mary Louise (1986) 'Fieldwork in common places', in James Clifford and George Marcus (eds) *Writing Culture*.
Price, Willard (1954) *The Amazing Amazon*. London: Vanguard.
Rich, Bruce (1983) 'The challenge of sustainable development', *The Global Reporter* 1(3):9–12.
Richards, P.W. (1952) *The Tropical Forest: An Ecological Study*, Cambridge: Cambridge University Press.
Ridgeway, James (1970) *The Politics of Ecology*. New York: E.P. Dutton.
Roosevelt, Anna (1980) *Parmana: Prehistoric Maize and Manioc Subsistence Along the Amazon and Orinoco*. New York and London: Academic Press.
Roosevelt, Anna (1987) 'Chiefdoms in the Amazon and Orinoco', in R.D. Drennan and C.A. Uribe (eds) *Chiefdoms in the Americas*. Lanham, New York and London: University Press of America.
Ruckelshaus, William D. (1989) 'Toward a Sustainable World', *Scientific American*, 261: 3: 114–120.
Said, Edward (1978) *Orientalism*. New York: Pantheon Books.
Schmink, Marianne (1988) 'Big business in the Amazon', in Julie Denslow and Christine Padoch (eds) *People of the Tropical Rain Forest*.
Schmink, Marianne and Wood, Charles (eds) (1984) *Frontier Expansion in Amazonia*. Gainesville, FL: University of Florida Press.
Schwartzman, Stephan (1986) 'Seringueiros defend the rainforest in Amazonia', *Cultural Survival Quarterly* 10(2):41–2.
Shnayerson, Michael (1989) 'The hot issue', *Vanity Fair*, September.
Shoup, Laurence H. and Minter, William (1977) *Imperial Brain Trust: The Council on Foreign Relations and United States Foreign Policy*. New York and London: Monthly Review Press.
Smith, Nigel J.H. (1982) *Rainforest Corridors: The Transamazon Colonization Scheme*. Berkeley, LA and London: University of California Press.
Stone, Roger (1986) *Dreams of Amazonia*. Harmondsworth, Middx: Penguin Books.
Taussig, Michael (1987) *Shamanism, Colonialism, and the Wildman: A Study in Terror and Healing*. Chicago: University of Chicago Press.
Taylor, Kenneth (1988) 'Indian rights in Amazonia', in Julie Denslow and Christine Padoch (eds) *People of the Tropical Rain Forest*.
Treece, David (1987) *Bound in Misery and Iron*. London: Survival International.

Tyler, Stephen (1987) 'Still RAYTING', *Critique of Anthropology* 7:1:49–51.
Uhl, Christopher (1989) 'Comer um hamburger pode ser um reforço para a devastação', *O Liberal*, 16 July.
Uhl, Christopher and Buschbacher, R. (1985) 'A disturbing synergism between cattle ranching, burning practices and selective tree harvesting in the Eastern Amazon'. *Biotropica* 17(4):265–8.
Uhl, Christopher and Jordan, C.F. (1984) 'Succession and nutrient dynamics following forest cutting and burning in Amazonia', *Ecology* 63:1476–90.
Velho, Otavio (1972) *Frentes de Expansão e Estrutura Agrária*. Rio: Zahar.
Vidal, Gore (1989) 'Gods and greens', *The Observer*, 27 August.
Wallace, Alfred J.R. (1972) *A Narrative of Travels on the Amazon and Rio Negro*. London: Ward, Lock (first published 1889).
Wallerstein, Immanuel (1979) *The Capitalist World-Economy*. Cambridge: Cambridge University Press.
Weaver, Ken (1984) *Texas Crude*. New York: E.P. Dutton.
Weinstein, Barbara (1983) *The Amazon Rubber Boom. 1850–1920*. Stanford, CA: Stanford University Press.
Wolf, Eric (1982) *Europe and the People Without History*. Berkeley, LA and London: University of California Press.
World Bank (1971) *World Bank and IDA: Questions and Answers*. Washington DC: World Bank.
World Bank (1987) *The World Bank Annual Report 1987*. Washington DC: The World Bank.

INDEX